# The Impact of the Economic Crisis on East Asia

# The Impact of the Economic Crisis on East Asia

Policy Responses from Four Economies

*Edited by*

Daigee Shaw

*President, Chung-Hua Institution for Economic Research, Taiwan*

Bih Jane Liu

*Vice President, Chung-Hua Institution for Economic Research, Taiwan*

IN ASSOCIATION WITH THE CHUNG-HUA INSTITUTION FOR ECONOMIC RESEARCH

**Edward Elgar**
Cheltenham, UK • Northampton, MA, USA

Published by
Edward Elgar Publishing Limited
The Lypiatts
15 Lansdown Road
Cheltenham
Glos GL50 2JA
UK

Edward Elgar Publishing, Inc.
William Pratt House
9 Dewey Court
Northampton
Massachusetts 01060
USA

A catalogue record for this book
is available from the British Library

Library of Congress Control Number: 2011924311

ISBN 978 0 85793 169 6

Typeset by Servis Filmsetting Ltd, Stockport, Cheshire
Printed and bound by MPG Books Group, UK

# Contents

## PART III   POLICY CONSTRAINTS

# Contributors

**Pi Chen**   Assistant Research Fellow, CIER, Taipei, Taiwan.

**Un Chan Chung**   Former Prime Minister of South Korea, Professor of Economics and Former President of Seoul National University, South Korea.

**Chih-Chin Ho**   Dean, College of Social Sciences, National Cheng Kung University, Taiwan.

**Yu-Shan Hsu**   Assistant Professor, Department of Economics, National Chung-Cheng University, Taiwan.

**Sheng-Cheng Hu**   Academician, Academia Sinica, Taiwan.

**Masahiro Kawai**   Dean, Asian Development Bank Institute, Tokyo, Japan.

**Chia-Hui Lin**   Analyst, CIER, Taipei, Taiwan.

**Chih-Yung Lin**   Department of Finance, National Taiwan University, Taiwan.

**Bih Jane Liu**   Vice President, CIER, and Professor, Department of Economics, National Taiwan University, Taiwan.

**Ching-Shin Mao**   Associate Professor, Department of Economics, National Taiwan University, Taiwan.

**Daigee Shaw**   President of CIER, Taipei, Taiwan.

**Chung-Hua Shen**   Professor, Department of Finance, National Taiwan University, Taiwan.

**Shinji Takagi**   Professor, Graduate School of Economics, Osaka University, Osaka, Japan.

**Jiann-Chyuan Wang**   Vice President, CIER, Taipei, Taiwan.

**Lee-Rong Wang**   Director, Center for Economic Forecasting, CIER, Taipei, Taiwan.

**Yongding Yu**   Director, Chinese Academy of Social Sciences, Institute of World Economics and Politics, Beijing, China.

# Preface

This book is for anyone who is interested in the economic conditions and policy response of four major East Asian economies in the wake of the 2008 global economic crisis. It is a compilation of ten academic theses written by a distinguished group of Asian social scientists from the region's top national universities, state research institutes, regional economic institutions and think tanks.

Largely a scholarly work of normative analysis, this synthesis study summarizes the economic impacts of the crisis on individual countries and their policy responses over the past years, with particular emphasis on carefully scrutinizing the immediate and remote causes of the crisis. It not only offers assessments of the impacts and identifies measures that can be undertaken in specific countries to stabilize the situation, but also looks at the crisis from three important disciplines of economies: a healthy fiscal system, international trade and the energy market. It offers reasons for the strategic programs needed for recovery and for promoting sustained economic growth. Although none of the authors provides a complete answer to all the problems, all the authors provide useful information and new ideas to fashion a workable program.

It will be apparent that we have addressed a wide range of economic issues in this volume. Yet, the ten theses are grouped into three parts based on common themes they share with one another. Each part offers treatment of a distinct area of study of economics, appropriately positioned in the context of economic crisis. Chapters 1 to 3, constituting the first part of the volume, examine various aspects of financial systems, since this economic crisis began with a financial crisis. In Chapter 1, orienting us with a detailed account of how the crisis first originated and then affected Taiwan, Hu offers a close examination of the recent US financial regulatory reforms in the aftermath of the crisis and presents us with a succinct evaluation of both the US and the Taiwanese banking systems. In Chapter 2, drawing lessons from the experiences of the pound sterling in the 1920s after World War I and the circumstances surrounding the British abandonment of the gold standard in 1931, Wang offers us her study of the possible demise of the dollar standard system after the recent crisis and the rise of the Chinese yuan as the world's primary reserve asset. Shen and Lin then present us in Chapter 3 with an analytic framework, based on multiple case studies, that suggests that the underperformance of government-owned banks commonly observed in developing countries during economic crises may be contingent on bad mergers with troubled private banks.

Chapters 4 to 8 are concerned with the impacts, consequences and policy responses of the crisis in several economies, particularly those in East Asia such as Taiwan, Korea, Japan and China. The focus of Part II is to present the reader with key findings on how the economic crisis affected trade, investment and growth in the four economies and the implications for crisis policymaking and management in East Asia. In Chapter 4, Liu gives an empirical account of the linkage between economic crisis and export performance, providing evidence that exports both in Asian and in advanced economies experienced an excessive fall and overshot their long-run equilibrium values during the 2008 and 2001 recessions. She makes some important preliminary clarifications concerning the occurrence of the so-called 'export overshoot' phenomenon and in this context examines factors and conditions that render Taiwanese exports susceptible to crisis. In Chapter 5, Wang and Lin identify Taiwan's most pressing development challenges in the further instability threatened by the recent crisis. They provide details of the nation's action plans for tackling these challenges, whose success is anchored heavily on the signing of the ECFA with China and the development of the six 'flagship' strategic industries in creating new drivers of growth. In Chapter 6, Chung presents a succinct account of how the Korean economy suffers from 'super capitalism' and an internal imbalance of investment and savings similar to the one seen in the US, and how the country is being held hostage by the complications of the deregulation policies applied in opening its burgeoning financial sector. In Chapter 7, Kawai and Takagi offer an empirical examination of the structural changes in trade and industrial structure that have taken place during Japan's lost decade, and how, based on their estimation, those changes have made the Japanese economy less resilient to adverse external shocks. In Chapter 8, Yu discusses China's overcapacity problem resulting from its investment-driven and export-led growth and the implications for Chinese output of the fall in global demand. He offers reasons why China could use a sizable economic stimulus package to boost its internal demand as the country has faced a sudden collapse in global demand and has found itself in the 'dollar trap'.

Finally, Chapters 9 and 10 make up the last part of the book and analyze the crisis from two broader perspectives, that is, fiscal discipline and energy crisis. In Chapter 9, Ho, Hsu and Mao develop a dynamic general equilibrium model under uncertainty that captures the debt-smoothing mechanism of the economy. They give a robust theoretical exercise on formulating exit strategy for different fiscally disciplined regimes, as they warn governments not to spend their way out of recession by piling up debts with expansionary fiscal policies. In Chapter 10, Shaw and Chen show that the energy crisis was one of the causes of the economic meltdown that predated the bursting of the financial bubble, by describing the interplays between the energy and economic crises. They call it the dual crisis of energy and economy, and offer solutions to the challenge of finding a balance between the rising demand for fossil fuel energy and economic growth in the face of climate change; they show that the role of government may have upset the delicate balance of achieving sustainable development.

At the core of our endeavor, albeit one with many limitations, to compile a book about policy responses to the economic crisis is our firm belief that we can contribute in some way to a good contextual understanding of the individual economies from the region as the world slowly emerges from the Great Recession of 2008. For policymakers prioritizing resources to address the impact of the crisis, we believe that the key findings and policy recommendations of the study will serve as a useful source of information and ideas. For economists keen on keeping abreast of important economic issues of these East Asian economies immediately following the crisis, this book will give a good overview.

# Acknowledgments

This book emanated from an international conference held at the Chung-Hua Institution for Economic Research in Taipei in July 2009, where calls for papers in macroeconomics, finance, banking, international trade, industrial policy, natural resources and conservation were submitted as a series of Dr Sam-Chung Hsieh Memorial Conference Papers.

Dr Sam-Chung Hsieh (1919–2004) was a former Governor of the Central Bank of China and the founding Director of the Asian Development Bank. As Secretary-General of the Joint Commission on Rural Reconstruction and later as Chairman of Taiwan's National Development Bank, he played a leading role in efforts which sparked the 'Taiwan Miracle'. He also served as Chairman of the Chung-Hua Institution for Economic Research, of the China Trust Bank and of the Industrial Bank of Taiwan. He was a professor at National Taiwan University and a visiting professor at the Cornell University–University of the Philippines joint programs.

# Abbreviations

| | |
|---|---|
| ADB | Asian Development Bank |
| ADBI | Asian Development Bank Institute |
| AIC | Akaike information criterion |
| AIG | American International Group |
| AS | Akciová Společnost (Czech: Joint Stock Company) |
| ASEAN | Association of Southeast Asian Nations |
| BIS | Bank for International Settlements |
| BRIC | Brazil, Russia, India and China |
| BVC | Biotechnology Venture Capital |
| CAM | Crédit Agricole de Maroc |
| CBC | Central Bank, ROC |
| CBO | Congressional Budget Office (US) |
| CDO | collateralized debt obligation |
| CERA | Cambridge Energy Research Associates |
| CIER | Chung-Hua Institution for Economic Research (ROC) |
| CPI | consumer price index |
| DGBAS | Directorate-General of Budget, Accounting and Statistics (ROC) |
| DRAM | dynamic random access memory |
| EASE | East Asia Seminar on Economics |
| ECFA | economic cooperation framework agreement |
| EIA | Energy Information Administration (US) |
| FAI | fixed asset investment |
| FDI | foreign direct investment |
| FPI | foreign portfolio investment |
| FSC | Financial Supervisory Commission (ROC) |
| FTA | free trade area |
| GCC | Gulf Cooperation Council |
| GDP | gross domestic product |
| GNP | gross national product |
| GOB | government-owned bank |
| HSBC | Hong Kong Shanghai Banking Corporation |
| ICT | information and communications technologies |
| IEA | International Energy Agency |
| IMF | International Monetary Fund |

| | |
|---|---|
| IP | Intellectual Property |
| IPB | Investični a Poštovni Banka |
| KDI | Korea Development Institute |
| KIEP | Korea Institute of International Economic Policy |
| KPI | key performance indicator |
| LDC | less-developed country |
| LED | light-emitting diode |
| MA | moving average |
| MOEA | Ministry of Economic Affairs (ROC) |
| MUFJ | Mitsubishi UFJ Financial Group |
| NBER | National Bureau of Economic Research (US) |
| NDRC | National Development and Reform Commission (PRC) |
| NIEs | newly industrializing economy |
| NT | New Taiwan |
| ODM | original design manufacturing |
| OEM | original equipment manufacturing |
| OTC | over-the-counter |
| PBOC | People's Bank of China (PRC) |
| PPP | purchasing power parity |
| ppt | presentation (PowerPoint) file extension |
| PRC | People's Republic of China (Mainland China) |
| RMB | renminbi |
| ROC | Republic of China (Taiwan) |
| RT | Részvénytársaság (Hungarian: Public Limited Company) |
| SA | Société Anonyme (French: Limited Company) |
| SDR | special drawing rights |
| SIC | Supra Information Center |
| SMEs | small and medium enterprises |
| STB | Société Tunisienne de Banque |
| STEP | Senter for Innovasjonsforskning (Norwegian: Center for Innovation Research) |
| TFDA | Taiwan Food and Drug Administration |
| VAR | vector autoregression |
| WSJ | *Wall Street Journal* |

# PART I

# Financial system and financial crisis

# 1. The global financial crisis: lessons for Taiwan

**Sheng-Cheng Hu**

## 1.1 INTRODUCTION

The US subprime mortgage problem became an apparent crisis in summer 2007 and soon escalated into the worst global financial crisis and economic downturn in 60 years.

In the global financial crisis, the five largest investment banks in the US became history and would either disappear or no longer exist in their current forms.[1] The government-sponsored agencies such as Fannie Mae and Freddie Mac also had to seek assistance from the US government. The US Federal Reserve System (the Fed) had to come to the rescue of non-banking financial institutions such as Bear Stearns, Merrill Lynch and AIG, while allowing to fail some others (such as Lehman Brothers) that had looked too big to fail.[2] The UK experienced its first bank run (Northern Rock) of any macroeconomic significance since 1866 (Miline and Wood, 2008). The three largest banks in Iceland, accounting for about 85 per cent of its banking sector, collapsed within a span of slightly more than a week, and the country avoided bankruptcy only with emergency assistance from the IMF in November 2008.

The IMF (2009a) estimated global bank write-downs for 2007–10 to be US$2.81 trillion. According to a study commissioned by the Asian Development Bank (Loser, 2009), capital losses in financial assets world-wide (including stock market valuations, private and public debt, and bank assets) in 2008 amounted to US$50 trillion, while those for developing Asia were US$9.6 trillion, or just over one year's worth of its gross domestic product (GDP). The losses caused a bank liquidity crisis, as well as a decline in domestic demand.

The US and other governments responded to the current global financial crisis by collectively undertaking drastic expansionary monetary and fiscal policy measures. They first tried to stabilize financial markets by providing liquidity and by repeatedly lowering interest rates to historically low levels. They then stimulated their economies by cutting taxes,

*3*

raising subsidies to the poor or to the affected industries, and increasing public infrastructure expenditures. According to the IMF (2009b) estimates, fiscal balances (in percentage of GDP adjusted for purchasing power parity (PPP)) worldwide would rise from −0.5 per cent for 2007 (the pre-crisis year) to −6.7 per cent for 2009 and −5.6 per cent for 2010. The situation was worse for advanced G20 countries. Their fiscal balances rose from −1.9 per cent for 2007 to −9.7 per cent for 2009 and −8.7 per cent for 2010. And their general government debt (gross) would rise from 78.2 per cent for 2007 to 98.9 per cent in 2009, then to 106.7 per cent in 2010 and further to 118.4 per cent in 2014. Although these concerted stimulus measures have helped stabilize the world economy and speed up its recovery, the resulting increases in government debt have already caused Greece and Ireland to request rescue efforts by the IMF and European Union. They can carry further danger if other countries give a perception of a lack of fiscal discipline, and if this perception is realized. (Freedman et al., 2009.)

The global financial crisis has drawn attention to regulatory weaknesses, and there have been calls for re-examining their design (Blanchard, 2008). The Obama administration has already released a plan to overhaul the US financial supervision and regulation (US Department of the Treasury, 2009).[3] The Obama financial reform plan calls for robust supervision and regulation of financial firms, comprehensive supervision of financial markets, improved protection of consumers and investors from financial abuse, provision to the relevant government agencies of the tools to manage a crisis, and upgrading of international regulatory standards and improvement of international cooperation.

As the global financial crisis began to unfold, Taiwan's financial sector was relatively healthy. However, as a mid-sized, export-oriented open economy, Taiwan could not be immune from the crisis. The Taiwan economy suffered the contagion of the crisis through three channels. First, the crisis resulted in losses in the market value of Taiwanese stocks and overseas assets held by Taiwanese investors, including mortgage-based securities and other toxic assets. These losses in turn depressed domestic demand. Second, the crisis caused a greater volatility in Taiwan's financial markets, although this was relatively mild. Third, and most importantly, the crisis brought about a deep slowdown in the global economy and thereby Taiwan's exports. The decline in exports and domestic demand in turn caused the worst economic slowdown in Taiwan since World War II.

The financial crisis can be studied from a number of directions. First, in view of the deep economic downturn brought about by the crisis, what should be Taiwan's policy response to a financial crisis like this one? Second, what would be the possible structural changes in the global economy in the aftermath of the crisis, and how should Taiwan react? Third, what are the regulatory weaknesses revealed by this crisis, and how should Taiwan take the lessons into account in its own financial reform? This chapter takes the last direction. It first reviews briefly the causes of the crisis, then considers its impacts on the Taiwan economy, and finally discusses the regulatory implications.

## 1.2 IMPACTS ON THE TAIWAN ECONOMY

When the global financial crisis began to unfold, Taiwan's financial system was relatively healthy and was more globalized than before. At that time it was considered one of the least vulnerable to a financial crisis among emerging market economies.[4] Most importantly, Taiwan had just cleaned up nonperforming loans, improved capital adequacy, and disposed of zombie banks. The nonperforming loan ratio for domestic banks fell from the peak of 11.27 per cent in April 2001 to 1.84 per cent in December 2007. The Bank for International Settlements (BIS) capital adequacy ratio rose from 10.4 per cent in 2001 to 11.72 per cent in 2007. All zombie banks but one had been disposed of by the Financial Supervisory Commission (FSC), Executive Yuan, ROC. Some other financially troubled banks had either been acquired by other banks or found new capital injection. In taking over the zombie banks, the FSC in conjunction with the Central Bank and the Ministry of Finance had developed expertise in crisis management.

In addition, Taiwan not only has very little foreign debt but also has built up a substantial foreign exchange reserve, which stood at US$266 billion at the outset of the crisis (June 2007) and at US$355 billion in March 2010, the third largest in the world, to cushion against any possible external shocks to the economy and financial markets (Figure 1.1).

In recent years, Taiwan has vigorously expanded globalization of its financial sector and encouraged foreign entry into the markets in an effort to develop a regional hub for fundraising and asset management. International banks such as Standard Chartered, Citibank, HSBC and Royal Bank of Scotland have all entered the market by acquiring local banks. The market share of branches and subsidiaries of foreign banks increased from 7.2 per cent in 2004 to 15.8 per cent in 2007. As a result of capital inflows into Taiwan's stock markets, the share of foreign ownership of stocks listed on the Taiwan Stock Exchange rose from 19.8 per cent in 2001 to 32.9 per cent in 2007. Foreign direct and portfolio investments concentrated heavily in the ICT and financial sectors, accounting for more than 50 per cent of shares in some of the largest firms in the two sectors.

Overall, as a result of the relaxation of restrictions on capital flows,

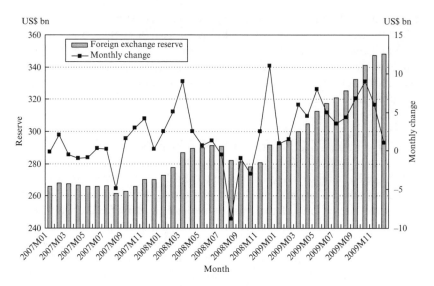

*Source:* Data from Central Bank, ROC.

*Figure 1.1    Taiwan's foreign exchange reserve.*

the stock of foreign direct and portfolio investment in Taiwan rose from US$84.9 billion in 2000 to US$388.5 billion in 2007, but declined to US$301.1 billion in 2008, while the stock of outward foreign direct and portfolio investment rose from US$274.1 billion to US$867.5 billion in 2007, and further to US$877.8 billion in 2008. The net cumulated outflow of capital, which was US$189.1 billion in 2000 but rose to US$576.7 billion in 2008, helped solve Taiwan's 'saving glut' (which was 11.45 per cent of GNP in 2009) and helped diversify the risks to the economy due to concentration of production and trade in the ICT sector.

The first impact of the global financial crisis on Taiwan was the direct loss in the value of its overseas assets. Taiwan held a total of US$137 billion of US financial assets. According to the FSC, Taiwan's direct losses due to toxic assets, including subprime mortgages, Lehman Brothers' structured products and others, were US$5.25 billion or 3.1 per cent of Taiwan's asset-holding in the US, or 1.4 per cent of Taiwan's GDP of US$366.7 billion (in 2008). These toxic assets were bought not only by institutions but also by a lot of individual investors.

The losses to individual investors imposed a huge social cost. In particular, around 50 per cent of Lehman Brothers' structured notes sold in Taiwan were purchased by a total of some 51 000 individual investors. When Lehman Brothers filed for bankruptcy, disputes erupted between

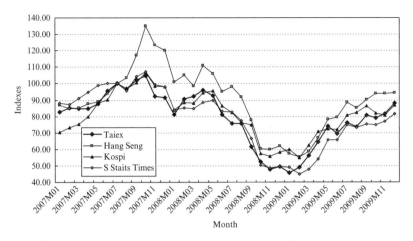

*Source:* Directorate-General of Budget, Accounting and Statistics, Executive Yuan, ROC (Data Bank).

*Figure 1.2* *Stock exchange indexes: Taiwan, Hong Kong, Korea and Singapore (2007M07 = 100).*

these individual investors and financial institutions that distributed the products regarding the latter's marketing and sales practices. The disputes brought the attention of the public, the legislature and the regulatory agencies to the fact that financial stability is important not only for financial development but also for the economic security of its citizens. The regulators have been under pressure to tighten the regulation of securitizations to improve on risk management and investor protection.

Taiwan's stock markets, like those in other countries, were hurt badly by the crisis. In 2008, the Taiwan Stock Exchange (Taiex) index declined by 46.0 per cent, compared with a fall of 40.7 per cent in South Korea (Kospi), 48.3 per cent in Hong Kong (Hang Seng) and 49.4 per cent in Singapore (Straits Times). However, much of the losses was recovered in 2009: the Taiex index jumped up by 78.3 per cent, compared with 49.7 per cent in South Korea, 52.0 per cent in Hong Kong and 64.5 per cent in Singapore (Figure 1.2). The P/E ratio for Taiwan stocks declined by 36 per cent from 15.3x to 9.8x, compared with a decline of 46.6 per cent from 16.8x to 9.0x for Korea, a decline of 67.7 per cent from 22.5x to 7.3x for Hong Kong, and a decline of 53.3 per cent from 14.7x to 6x for Singapore (Figure 1.3). Despite the losses in 2008 from foreign portfolio investment incurred by financial institutions, the financial Taiex fell by only 36.5 per cent, less than the fall in the overall Taiex index of 46.0 per cent.

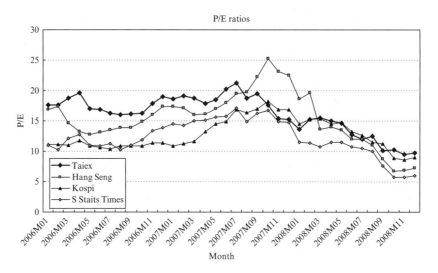

*Source:*  Directorate-General of Budget, Accounting and Statistics, Executive Yuan, ROC
(Data Bank).

*Figure 1.3    P/E ratios: Taiwan, Hong Kong, Korea and Singapore.*

These numbers seem to suggest that the decline in the Taiwan stock index
reflects changes in the fundamentals as much as changes in the conditions
in financial markets.

During the global financial crisis, there were greater fluctuations
in capital flows in and out of Taiwan as the parent companies of
foreign financial institutions needed capital injection and as hot money
looked for arbitrage opportunities. According to the Central Bank, the
stock of inward foreign (direct and portfolio) investment declined by
US$87.4 billion between 2007 and 2008 (year end). Although the value
of the Taiwan dollar per US dollar was more volatile during the crisis, it
remained relatively stable compared with those of neighboring countries
(Figure 1.4). The ratio of the standard deviation of the value of the NT
dollar rose from 0.86 per cent in 2007 to 3.47 per cent in 2008, compared
with a rise from 0.92 per cent to 15.21 per cent for the Korean won, and
from 2.21 per cent to 3.57 per cent for the Singapore dollar (Table 1.1).

Despite the fluctuations in capital flows, Taiwan's financial sector did
not have a liquidity problem. However, banks did become more cau-
tious in their lending practices, causing the Executive Yuan (Cabinet) to
engage in moral suasion by announcing in October 2008 a 'Three Supports
Policy' initiative. The government pledged itself to support banks, but

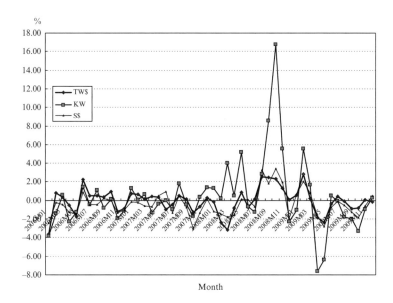

*Source:* Directorate-General of Budget, Accounting and Statistics, Executive Yuan, ROC (Data Bank).

*Figure 1.4 Monthly changes in exchange rates: Taiwan, Korea and Singapore.*

*Table 1.1 Fluctuations in exchange rates (per cent)*

|  | Taiwan $ | Korean Won | Singapore $ |
|---|---|---|---|
| 2006 | 1.18 | 1.73 | 1.77 |
| 2007 | 0.86 | 0.92 | 2.21 |
| 2008 | 3.47 | 15.21 | 3.57 |
| 2009 | 2.16 | 7.70 | 3.30 |

*Note:* Table shows the ratio of standard deviation of monthly exchange rates to the annual mean exchange rate.

*Source:* DGBAS Data Bank (monthly data).

urged banks to support businesses (by not tightening credit), and businesses to support workers (by not laying them off). The implementation of the policy initiative depended primarily on government-controlled banks, as the overall loans-to-deposits ratio has continued to decline since the announcement of the policy initiative (Figure 1.5). The interest-rate

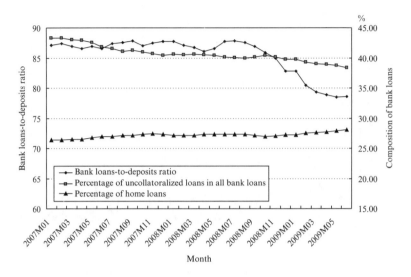

*Source:*   Directorate-General of Budget, Accounting and Statistics, Executive Yuan, ROC
(Data Bank).

*Figure 1.5    Bank loans-to-deposits ratio.*

differential with respect to the CBC deposit rate rose to its peak at end of
2008 (Figure 1.6).

Taiwan's banking sector is dominated by government-controlled banks
(including government-owned banks and those in which the government
is a major shareholder), which turned out to be a stabilizing factor during
the global financial crisis. Government-controlled banks account for eight
of the ten largest banks in Taiwan, and hold a market share of more than
40 per cent. During the global financial crisis, these government-controlled
banks became a safe haven for depositors who were worried about the
financial health of private banks (particularly those known to have a low
capital-adequacy ratio) and for investors who were afraid of investing in
stocks or other financial products. The government-controlled banks were
also the ones to implement the Three Supports Policy.

During the crisis, there were no bank runs, although there was evidence of increasing flows of deposits from financially weak private banks
to government-controlled banks. In response to such a situation, the
Executive Yuan announced in October 2008 a policy to guarantee all
deposits in full amount, until the end of 2009, rather than the normal limit
of NT$1.5 million (or around US$46 150) per account. Since the lifting of
the deposit insurance limit, deposits in private banks have been stabilized.

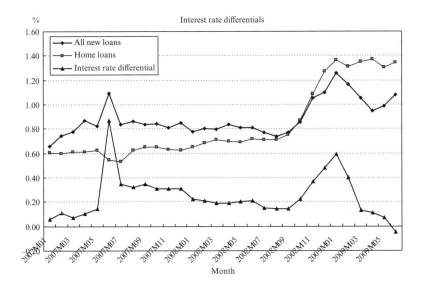

*Source:* Directorate-General of Budget, Accounting and Statistics, Executive Yuan, ROC (Data Bank).

*Figure 1.6    Deposits and loan interest rates.*

After a one-year extension, the full deposit-insurance policy exited at the end of 2010, but the government raised the insurance limit from NT$1.5 million to NT$3.0 million.

Although Taiwan's financial sector remained relatively stable and the fluctuations in the stock prices were consistent with those in neighboring countries, Taiwan and other economies such as Japan and Korea with a large share in GDP of advanced manufacturing such as ICT products and autos experienced sharper output declines than their peers during the crisis (Sommer, 2009; *Economist*, 2009a).

According to the Directorate-General of Budget, Accounting and Statistics, Executive Yuan (DGBAS, February 2010), the Taiwan economy suffered a decline in exports by 24.7 per cent in 2008Q4, 36.3 per cent in 2009Q1 and 30.6 per cent in 2009Q2 (year-on-year), the worst in 55 years. With the sharp decline in exports, Taiwan's economic growth rate for 2009 was −1.87 per cent, 6.95 percentage points below DGBAS's original forecast of +5.08 per cent in August 2008. The unemployment rate rose rapidly from 3.95 per cent in June 2008 to the peak of 6.13 per cent in August 2009 before declining back to 5.74 per cent at the end of 2009. The government had to take extraordinary expansionary fiscal policy steps (costing 5.8 per

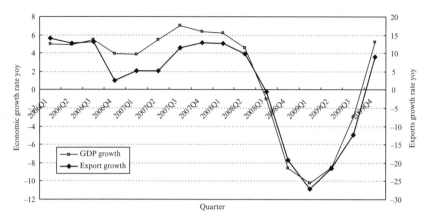

*Source:*   The Directorate-General of Budget, Accounting and Statistics, Executive Yuan, ROC (Data Bank).

*Figure 1.7    Exports and economic growth: the Taiwan case.*

cent of GDP) to counter the sharp downturn in the economy at the possible expense of fiscal stability, and the Central Bank reduced the discount rate six times from 3.625 per cent to 1.5 per cent between September 2008 and June 2009.

The deep economic slowdown in Taiwan was due in part to the fall in asset value, which depressed domestic demand, but more importantly to the sharp decline in exports, which accounts for more than 60 per cent of Taiwan's economic growth (Figure 1.7).

Taiwan's exports concentrate heavily on the Chinese and the US markets. Exports to these two markets accounted for 39 per cent and 12 per cent, respectively, of Taiwan's total exports in 2008. For the first half of 2009, Taiwan's exports to China fell by 37.5 per cent, while its exports to the US fell by 48.1 per cent year-on-year. The deeper-than-expected decline in the real growth rate also reflects the fact that Taiwan's industrial production concentrates heavily on the ICT sector, as electronic, optical and IC products account for 34.5 per cent of Taiwan's total exports (2008 statistics), and they suffered deeper export declines than other products in this crisis.

## 1.3   CAUSES OF THE GLOBAL FINANCIAL CRISIS

The global financial crisis appears to have been triggered by the subprime mortgage problem brought about by the US housing bubble in 2007

(Mizen, 2008). There has been the view that the housing bubble would not have taken place without the easy-credit policy of the Fed under the chairmanship of Alan Greenspan (Taylor, 2009). Greenspan (2009, 2010) in his own defense argues that in the early 2000s, there was a decoupling between monetary policy and mortgage rates, and it was the global saving glut, not easy monetary policy, that caused the fall in the mortgage rates and the housing bubble. Thus, (easy-credit) monetary policy could not be held responsible for the housing bubble.

The 'global saving glut' refers particularly to a situation where the Asian and other emerging economies have too much saving relative to investment opportunities in their home countries (Cooper, 2007). The saving glut in these countries manifests in the chronic current-account surpluses with respect to the US. Coulibaly and Millar (2008) find empirical evidence that in the aftermath of the Asian financial crisis, corporate investment expenditures were cut across a wide spectrum of countries, industries and firms in Asia, which exacerbated the saving–investment gap and hence the saving glut outside the US.[5] Taylor (2009), on the other hand, disputes the global-saving-glut argument. He argues that although there was a saving glut outside the US, it was balanced by an equal-sized saving shortage in the US, thus there was no global saving glut, or global saving–investment imbalance.

Regardless of whether or not it was caused by the Fed's policy, the housing bubble was presumably not much worse than the bubble in the 1980s that caused the S&L debacle, and subprime mortgages comprised only a small portion of all US mortgages.[6] Why, then, did the housing bubble and the subprime mortgage problem escalate into the worst global financial crisis in decades so quickly? The answer to this question provides insight into how financial regulations should be reformed. A possible explanation lies in the recent rapid expansion of mortgage-based securitization, which, according to the Securities Industry and Financial Markets Association, now stands at US$6.38 trillion or 54 per cent of all US mortgages outstanding (Goswami et al., 2009).

Securitization is an innovation that changes mortgage lending from the 'originate and hold' model to the 'originate and distribute' model. The new lending model allows financial institutions to shift their mortgage risks to other institutions that are more able to bear the risks by packaging mortgages into such securitized assets as mortgage-based securities (MBSs), collateralized mortgage securities (CMSs) and collateralized debt obligations (CDOs). As such, it helps improve not only capital allocation but also risk management. By turning illiquid mortgages into tradable securities, securitization also creates liquidity and thus improves diversification and resilience of financial markets (Caprio et al., 2008).

However, as financial institutions tried to squeeze more profits out of securitization, they made securitized assets more exotic, complex and opaque. Because of the complexity and opacity, when some subprime mortgages became delinquent, all assets containing mortgages and their derivatives, whether in default or not, became toxic '*ex ante*' and suffered Akerlof's (1970) 'market for lemons' phenomenon. In other words, their value was quickly depressed as if they were all toxic. The free fall in the value of securitized assets in turn paralysed financial markets and weakened financial institutions, leading to the financial crisis.

Free and rapid cross-border capital flow further sped up the contagion worldwide. Many of the mortgage-based securities and other securitized assets are sold overseas. According to a press release from the US Treasury Department on 17 February 2009, at the end of the first half of 2008 foreigners held a total of US$10.3 trillion of US financial assets, of which US$137 billion was held by Taiwan. It is not surprising that the losses in asset values spilled quickly over to other countries and the US housing bubble became a worldwide financial crisis. No country from Iceland to Argentina could escape it.

Of course, securitized assets are rated by credit-rating agencies. Unfortunately, the credit-rating agencies assess only the default risks, but their ratings are frequently interpreted as indicators not only of default risks but also of market and liquidity risks. That the credit-rating agencies are hired by the originators or issuers of the securities rather than by the buyers also invites suspicion of possible moral hazard. This is compounded by the fact that there is little accountability on the part of credit-rating agencies, as they claim to be expressing a mere opinion, which thus should not be taken as an investment advice (Mizen, 2008; Caprio et al., 2008). In fact, the credit-rating agencies have been accused of systemically issuing 'wildly inaccurate and unreasonably high ratings'.[7] It is thus not surprising that there have been calls to regulate credit-rating agencies.

The incentive scheme underlying 'originate and distribute' securitized products encourages imprudence (Mizen, 2008; Caprio et al., 2008). Under the 'originate and hold' model, the originator must bear the entire risk to the extent that it holds the mortgage until maturity; while under the 'originate and distribute' model, the originator's risk is limited to the period before the asset is distributed. The opacity of assets also makes it difficult to pinpoint the ultimate 'beneficiary' (risk-bearer) who would price the risk.

More broadly, the executive compensation scheme that emphasizes short-term profits encourages excessive risk-taking on the part of the financial industry at the expense of their firms and the entire economy. It is thus not surprising that reform of executive compensation became a key component of the Obama administration's plan.

The 'mark-to-market' accounting rule further exacerbated the crisis. The accounting rule improves over the 'mark to historic cost' rule by contributing to the transparency in asset value and balance sheets. However, an important assumption underlying the accounting rule is that the 'fair value' of assets can be identified. Indeed, in situations where an asset market exists and functions well, the fair value of the asset can be identified by its market price. However, over the business cycle, the market tends to overreact to reality, displaying irrational exuberance and thus overpricing the asset value in an upturn, while underpricing asset value in a downturn. In other words, the 'mark-to-market' accounting rule is procyclical in the sense that it leads financial institutions to overextend credit in an upturn and to excessively tighten credit in a downturn, thus amplifying cycles in the financial sector, with repercussions through the entire economy. The lending capacity destroyed by the accounting rule has been substantial, according to some estimates.[8]

The Basel accords further compounded the procyclical bias of the accounting rule. Basel II, while it improves on Basel I by requiring banks to set aside more capital for more risky exposures, is considered procyclical because risks are underestimated in a good time and overestimated in a bad time. The Basel accords and the 'mark-to-market' accounting rule together deepened the current global crisis by overestimating the risk and capital needs while destroying large amounts of the lending capacity of financial institutions.[9]

Investment banks have been responsible for the rapid expansion of securitization. Securitization, together with overdependence on leverage and on unstable short-term financing of long-term investments, in turn causes their demise. The demise of large investment banks suggests that systemic stress comes not just from the failure of commercial banks that receive deposits from the public but also from the failure of large, interconnected financial institutions such as investment banks and insurance companies. However, every investment bank, regardless of its size, is under the more lax supervision of the US Securities and Exchange Commission rather than under the Fed. It is not surprising that Goldman Sachs and Morgan Stanley were forced to become bank holding companies by the US Treasury Department so that they could be supervised by the Fed.

## 1.4  REGULATORY IMPLICATIONS OF THE GLOBAL FINANCIAL CRISIS

The first lesson to learn from the global financial crisis is that under the existing regulatory framework, market mechanism and self discipline are not effective in preventing the financial sector from taking systemic risks. Thus, it is timely to review the regulatory weaknesses, of which some are common to all, while others are unique to Taiwan. A large literature and many policy debates have focused on supervisory integration, capital adequacy and investor protection. For Taiwan, the review should also involve the role played by the government-controlled banks, which dominate Taiwan's banking sector, and Taiwan's recent globalization efforts in its drive to become a regional asset-management and fundraising hub.

**Regulatory Integration**

Despite the trend towards the integration of financial services, financial supervision and regulation have been fragmented, thus inducing regulatory arbitrage and slowing responses to crises. To consolidate supervision, the Obama financial reform plan adopts a soft approach. Instead of putting all financial regulators under one roof, the Obama plan is to establish a new financial services oversight council of regulators with broader coordinating responsibility across the financial system. The plan gives the Fed additional consolidated supervisory power over all large, interconnected firms whose failure could threaten the stability of the financial system. However, the establishment of an oversight council, while it avoids the Fed becoming too powerful to control, may risk handicapping the independence of the Fed. It remains to be seen how the Obama plan strikes a proper balance between them.

Since the Asian financial crisis in 1997, Taiwan has realized the need to integrate its fragmented regulatory functions and to upgrade their independence. The consolidation efforts resulted in the establishment of the Financial Supervisory Commission (FSC) within the Executive Yuan in 2004. The FSC puts banking, securities (and futures) and insurance regulations under one roof. The FSC also gains greater independence, as its nine commissioners all have a fixed term rather than serving at the pleasure of the premier. The chairperson is appointed at the ministerial level and its nine commissioners collectively resist pressure from interest groups.

There is a proper division of labor between the FSC and the Central Bank. The Central Bank is responsible for supervision at the macro level and with respect to the foreign exchange market, while the FSC is responsible for supervision and regulation of institutions, markets and products. The FSC and the Central Bank hold joint meetings on a regular basis to examine changes in financial markets in order to pre-warn and thereby avoid any possibility of a systemic crisis.

However, the supervisory integration remains incomplete in the sense that the current Banking Act, Securities and Exchange Act, and Insurance

Act still apply differential regulatory intensities on banks, securities firms and insurance companies in the belief that commercial banks that accept deposits from the public are more likely than others to cause systemic crises and therefore require more rigorous supervision. For example, the Banking Act provides more thorough protection of customers and imposes more severe penalties on violations than do the Securities and Exchange Act and the Insurance Act. The crisis proves incorrect the belief that only commercial banks can cause systemic crisis.

The reason the three Acts remain to be harmonized is that it will require a lengthy and cumbersome process to amend each of them separately. To speed up the legislative process, the FSC has drafted a Financial Services Act that would harmonize regulations across the board, and remedy the shortcomings and discrepancies of the current Banking, Securities and Exchange, and Insurance Acts in protecting investors and consumers. On this basis, the proposed Act will also provide a legal foundation for liberalizing investment banking activities, patterned after Japan's Financial Product Exchange Act and Korea's Capital Market Integration Act. If finally passed by the legislature, the proposed Act would help close the loopholes in regulation and in investor protection. In view of the crisis, the proposed Act should aim at achieving harmonization of regulations across the board in terms of investors and consumer protection, while applying differential regulatory intensities based on the possibilities of systemic risks due to size and interconnectedness, rather than on the business nature of the financial institutions. There should also be a review of the scope of supervision, particularly with respect to such institutions as hedge funds, private equity firms and credit-rating agencies.

Although Taiwan still does not have world-ranked national champions among its financial institutions, some are already large enough to cause systemic stress should they fail. As Taiwan continues its consolidation efforts and the liberalization of its investment banking activities, there will be an increasing number of systemically important financial institutions. They should receive special regulatory attention with respect to capital adequacy, risk-management capability and corporate governance.

**Investor Protection and Securitized Assets**

The losses suffered by individual investors from their investment in securitized assets (and others that are not traded in exchanges), to the detriment of their retirement, highlight the fact that, unlike consumer products that are heavily regulated for health and safety, financial products are only weakly regulated by a fragmentation of laws that are slow to respond to changing market conditions (Bar-Gill and Warren, 2008). It should be noted that financial markets are a platform for risk-sharing. A higher rate of return entails a greater risk-bearing. Thus, financial-product regulation is not to prevent individual investors from taking risks, but rather to provide them with correct and useful information, so that they know in their decision-making how much risk they are taking. Equally important, it should prevent financial institutions that issue or originate products from profiting from information asymmetry. There is also the view that individuals have 'cognitive limitations'. Taking this view into account, the Obama reform plan is to encourage financial institutions to design financial products for retail markets that are like 'plain vanilla', simple and easy to understand (Posner, 2009). Shiller (2009) likewise suggests that investors should be protected from 'overzealous innovators who might disregard public safety and take improper advantage of nascent [financial engineering] technology'.

The Obama reform plan is also to impose robust reporting standards on the issuers of asset-backed securities, and to reduce investors' and regulators' reliance on credit-rating agencies. It ensures greater accountability by requiring the originator, sponsor or broker of a securitization to retain a financial interest (i.e., an equity tranche) in its product.

Taiwan's additional problem with securitized assets is that many sold there are issued overseas and therefore contain greater information asymmetry. When Lehman Brothers filed for bankruptcy, there was very little investors could do to protect their investment. Furthermore, financial institutions suffered losses that defied common sense, indicating a necessity to improve their risk-management capabilities and knowledge about securitized and other new financial products. The FSC has proposed a set of guidelines to remedy the above situations. Specifically, offshore financial institutions are required to have a branch in Taiwan, or to set up there a general agent (distributor), which satisfies a minimum capital requirement to take operational and financial responsibility before they are allowed to distribute their financial products there locally. And their structured products to be sold to non-professional investors there must be only those which are allowed to be sold to individual investors in overseas retail markets; they must also be approved by the relevant industry associations in Taiwan (FSC, 2009).

To enhance protection of consumers and investors, the Obama reform plan is to set up a consumer financial protection agency with authority over such consumer financial products as mortgages and credit cards. Taiwan already has a Consumer Protection Commission, headed by the vice premier, which studies, reviews and supervises the implementation of the basic consumer protection policy. There is also an Investor Protection Center to protect shareholders against the wrongdoings of corporate management and securities firms and to compensate them for any abuse.

The Lehman Brothers disputes, however, point to the loopholes in the current investor protection structure. The Consumer Protection Commission is vested with authority by the Consumer Protection Act, which defines consumers narrowly as those who conduct transactions, use products and receive services for the purpose of consumption, and businesses as those organizations that design, produce, manufacture, import or sell products, or provide services. Under this charter, the Commission provides protection only to individuals who use credit cards or sign loan contracts in junction with consumption purchases, and not to those individuals investing in financial products.

On the other hand, the Investor Protection Center is vested with authority by the Securities Investor and Futures Trader Protection Act only to protect shareholders from the wrongdoings of corporate management and securities firms and to compensate them for abuse. The securitized products sold or distributed in Taiwan are approved on the authorization of the Trust Act, and are not considered 'securities' as defined by the Securities and Exchange Act. Consequently, the Investor Protection Center does not have authority to intervene in disputes over securitized assets, or to take class legal actions on behalf of investors against the wrongdoings of the originators, issuers or distributors of such products.

Because of the lack of a mechanism for protecting individual investors, the disputes over structured products are currently handled by the bankers and other relevant industry associations. Despite their best efforts, the industry associations' involvement invites suspicion of conflict of interest, fairness and impartiality. Possibly because of public pressure, the Legislature passed in May 2009 the amendment of the Securities Investor and Futures Trader Protection Act to include protection provided under the Securities Investment Trust and Consulting Act. However, a complete review of the Act to remove any remaining loopholes and the coordination between the Investor Protection Center and the Consumer Protection Commission are highly desirable.

**Executive Compensation**

Many scholars and the Obama administration have blamed executive compensation that emphasizes short-term profitability and large upfront fees and commissions from securitization for encouraging imprudence and excessive risk-taking by financial institutions (Caprio et al., 2008; Kashyap et al., 2008). US Treasury Secretary Timothy Geithner claimed, 'I don't think the government should set caps on compensation. We'll make it less likely that people take large amounts of short-term risk at the expense of their firm and the system as a whole.' The US Securities and

Exchange Commission has proposed new rules on executive compensation that would link pay and risk. The rules require public companies to disclose information about how compensation policies would lead to increased risk-taking, and explain how those risks are managed, if the risks could have a material effect on the business, such as steep losses (*Wall Street Journal*, 3 July 2009). The US House of Representatives likewise passed a bill giving shareholders more say about executive compensation.

Taiwanese executives, particularly those of government-controlled financial institutions, are on average underpaid compared with their US counterparts. Thus, the 'fat cat' problem is not serious there. Taiwan's problem is in transparency and disclosure, and in its frequently criticized lack of accountability. The FSC has encouraged full disclosure of executive pay and the setting up of a compensation committee in corporate boards to review the pay of directors and top management. It is highly desirable for executive pay to include a stock option or dividend, with a lock-in period to avoid short-sighted behavior.

Another problem is in the sales end, where many disputes have taken place in Taiwan. The current bonus system appears to encourage short-sighted aggressive sales behavior. It is a challenge to make sure that sales commission is consistent with accountability. The sales staff should be encouraged to follow the principles of 'Know your products', 'Know your customers (KYC)', and 'Treat your customers fairly (TCF)'. A remedy is to pay the sales commission over the life of the sale contract rather than the moment of sale, so as to increase the accountability of the salesperson. Furthermore, the salesperson should have appropriate professional certifications and should be required to know the products he handles.

## Capital Adequacy

The demise of investment banks reflects the social cost of excessive leverage and capital inadequacy. However, any talk of capital adequacy will not be meaningful until the off-balance-sheet problem associated with securitization is resolved.

The crisis provides evidence that the stress tests on capital adequacy undertaken by individual institutions have been inadequate. In the wake of the financial crisis, the Fed (2009) and the US Treasury Department have run stress tests to ensure that the 19 largest bank holding companies (those with year-end 2008 assets in excess of US$100 billion) have a sufficient capital cushion to continue lending in a 'more adverse' scenario in the short term (by the end of 2010).[10] The reactions to the stress tests suggest that improved transparency is an important step in crisis management as it provides the assurance that investors need to keep their confidence in the financial markets.

As mentioned above, the Basel II accord and the mark-to-market accounting rule are both procyclical to the extent that they can potentially lead us to underestimate risk and overestimate asset value in a good time and overestimate risk and underestimate asset value in a bad time, when recapitalization is difficult. Thus, there have been calls by European Union finance ministers and the US Government Accountability Office for studying the possibility of a change in the rules to dampen cycles in financial markets.[11] An alternative is to make the capital-adequacy requirement a time-varying (countercyclical) rather than a fixed ratio: in other words, that a higher requirement be imposed in good times (to save for rainy days) and a lower requirement be allowed in a crisis scenario. Obviously, a higher capital-adequacy ratio reduces the possibility of a crisis but increases the efficiency cost to the economy (Greenspan, 2010). A challenge is to strike an appropriate balance between risk and cost. Kashyap et al. (2008) suggest that financial institutions be allowed to opt out of raising capital by acquiring a capital insurance policy. Through capital insurance, during crises when the private sector is unwilling or unable to recapitalize, the government can be involved directly in recapitalization via transfers. The capital insurance approach may be used as a supplement in achieving the capital-adequacy requirement.

Since the Asian financial crisis, Taiwan has achieved an improvement in the capital-adequacy ratio of its banking sector. In December 2008, the Legislative Yuan passed an amendment to the Banking Act, allowing the FSC to classify bank capital-adequacy ratios as adequate, inadequate, significantly inadequate, and seriously inadequate, respectively, and apply differential regulatory intensities to banks based on capital adequacy, including an authority to force the market exit of those with serious capital inadequacy. The amendment greatly strengthens the regulators' ability to avoid, and to manage, a financial crisis.[12] However, as Taiwan strives for financial consolidation, there will be an increasing number of systemically important financial institutions. These systematically important financial institutions should be subject to a tougher capital adequacy requirement. Importantly, the regulators should have tools and resources for risk management and for disposing of zombie institutions.[13]

**Government-Controlled Banks**

The global financial crisis not only teaches a regulatory lesson common to all economies, but also provides a good opportunity for Taiwan to re-examine problems that are unique to the economy. In particular, it is timely to reexamine the role played by government-controlled banks in financial markets and the extent to which a mid-sized open economy like Taiwan should globalize its financial markets.

It has long been a topic of heated public debate as to how far government-controlled banks, which have dominated Taiwan's banking sector, should be privatized to improve efficiency by overcoming the layers of cumbersome administrative and legislative oversight. In an economic development conference held in August 2001, convened by the president's office and attended by opposition parties, scholars and industry representatives, a consensus was reached that in the interest of efficiency, all government-controlled banks should be completely privatized in an orderly manner, and the government's share of government-controlled banks (and other financial institutions) should be lowered to less than 20 per cent in five years. In the financial reform efforts embarked on in 2004, this consensus on bank privatization was redefined as a policy goal of reducing the number of government-controlled banks by half (from 14 to 7) by the end of 2006.

On the other hand, in the last few years, it has become clear that government-controlled banks could be instrumental in implementing the government's financial-market policy. In particular, in the takeover of zombie banks, they have provided the needed manpower and professional support to allow smooth completion of the task. In the current global financial crisis, government-controlled banks also served as a stabilizing force in financial markets and a safe haven for small investors to park their cash in. In the meantime, a number of recent events in the financial sector have caused the public to cast doubts about the soundness of the bank privatization policy. In particular, the public is concerned that the corporate governance of at least some private financial institutions remains to be enhanced. Unless private banks strengthen their corporate governance and the regulatory agencies exercise effective supervision, there will be concern about the possibility of big private banks turning into monsters and the implications of privatization for financial stability.

An alternative, that seems to have been adopted by the government, is to reduce the government's share while maintaining control over government-controlled banks, so that the banks can continue implementing government policy. There is a dilemma here, however, because the relevant corporate laws require that the board directors of government-controlled banks are, like their private counterparts, to fulfil their fiduciary duty to all their shareholders, not just the government. Note that of all government-controlled banks, only three are 100 per cent owned by the government. Implementation of government policy by banks partially owned by the government at the expense of private shareholders is not only inconsistent with the principle of good corporate governance preached by the government but also in violation of the relevant laws that require fiduciary duty. The global financial crisis provides an opportunity for policymakers to reexamine the privatization policy, taking into account the dual policy objectives of maintaining financial stability and promoting the competitiveness of the economy.

**Globalization**

Recent financial globalization efforts have greatly expanded Taiwanese investors' exposure to foreign assets as well as foreigners' exposure to Taiwanese assets. In particular, foreign ownership of Taiwan's stocks has concentrated on ICT companies and on financial institutions. Despite its financial globalization, Taiwan's contagion of the global financial crisis came primarily through the decline in exports rather than through the financial channel.

Obviously, expanded globalization presents policymakers with a challenge as it increases the difficulty of stabilizing the financial sector in a crisis situation when hot money flows rapidly in and out of the country. With a huge foreign exchange reserve in hand to maintain liquidity, the Central Bank has passed the challenge. Despite increased globalization, Taiwan's financial markets remained relatively stable during the crisis. However, Iceland is a vivid example of an open economy going wrong. It is highly desirable to reexamine how well Taiwan's early-warning system works, and whether the regulators have enough resources, legal power and tools both to deal with the rapid flow of hot money and to manage a crisis should either one happen.

The above preliminary evidence suggests that financial globalization did not lead to financial instability or the worsening of economic downturn in this crisis. Instead, financial globalization allowed Taiwan to diversify the risks of the concentration of production and trade in the ICT sector. This provides some confidence for Taiwan's continued drive to become a regional asset-management center. However, Taiwan should reevaluate whether the global financial crisis has altered its comparative advantage in becoming such a center, and map out the appropriate strategy, including how it is to engage in tax and regulatory competition with Hong Kong and Singapore.

## 1.5   CONCLUSIONS

The current financial crisis reminds us that as Taiwan consolidates its financial sector it must beef up its capability for risk management and strengthen regulation of systemically important financial institutions whose failure might cause financial stress. Furthermore, the focus of regulatory reform should be on further integrating fragmented regulatory functions, as well as on enhancing risk management, accountability and transparency, particularly with respect to new financial products. On the other hand, one should be reminded that in the aftermath of a crisis it is too easy to get overzealous in tightening regulation.

There is also the realization that capital adequacy is important for preventing a financial crisis. Taiwan's government-dominated banking system provides an alternative way of stabilizing public confidence in a crisis situation. It is important that there be a critical review of the soundness of corporate governance of private banks, and the role to be played by government-controlled banks in implementing financial policy.

The financial losses that investors suffered in this crisis to the detriment of their retirement remind us that investor protection is important not only for the development of the financial sector but also for the establishment of a sound safety net, and its enhancement should receive the priority attention of the regulators.

Taiwan is a mid-sized open economy that is heavily dependent on trade. Unavoidably, such an economy is easily subject to external shocks, both real and financial. In the aftermath of the global financial crisis, there will undoubtedly be structural changes in the world economy. To prepare for such changes, the administration has now identified a number of industries, including biotech, boutique agriculture, health and long-term care, green energy, tourism, and cultural and creativity industries, as the direction for future development. As a mid-sized economy highly dependent on trade, Taiwan has no choice but to concentrate on sectors in which it has a comparative advantage. Taiwan's success lies in taking advantage of the externality of ICT in these new industries. In the area of financial markets, it appears that the development of Taiwan as a regional hub for fundraising and asset management will involve further financial globalization. The global financial crisis provides a timely lesson and an opportunity to review and adjust the strategy for achieving this policy objective.

## NOTES

1. Of the five largest investment banks in the US, Bear Stearns and Merrill Lynch were acquired by Morgan Stanley and the Bank of America, respectively, while Lehman Brothers filed for Chapter 11 protection. Morgan Stanley and Goldman Sachs were forced to become bank holding companies under the supervision of the US Federal Reserve System.
2. 14 September 2008 was the D-day on which the Fed decided not to rescue Lehman

Brothers, but to provide assistance to Merrill Lynch and, a few days later, also to AIG. With these decisions, the US government practically drew a line that defines what institutions are systemically important, or 'too big to fail'.

3. The Obama plan was approved in July 2010 by the US Congress as the Wall Street Reform and Consumer Protection Act.

4. *The Economist* (2009b) used current account surplus as a percentage of GDP, short-term debt as a percentage of reserves and banks' loan-to-deposit ratio as indicators to rank the vulnerability among emerging-market economies to the global credit crunch. Taiwan ranked the third least vulnerable country, next to China and Malaysia.

5. The global saving-glut argument implicitly places blame on China, which has a saving ratio near 60 per cent. Of course, the Chinese government does not agree with this reasoning. Zhou Xiaochuan, governor of the Chinese central bank, argues that while China's saving ratio needs to fall and its consumption needs to rise, focusing too much on macro issues like savings imbalance risks diverting the needed attention from micro factors such as financial regulation (Batson , July 2009).

6. The direct losses on subprime mortgages are estimated to be US$243 billion by Goldman Sachs (Remolona, 2009), US$265 billion by S&P (Lin Che-Chun, 2009) and between US$200 billion and US$400 billion by Calomiris (2008). Using the Calomiris figures, the subprime losses are around 0.14 per cent to 0.28 per cent of the US GDP of US$14.5 trillion, and 18.2 per cent to 36.4 per cent of the total volume of subprime mortgages of US$1.1 trillion (S&P data, Lin Che-Chun, 2009). In comparison, in Taiwan's credit-card problem in 2005, the losses of credit-card debts were, based on the data from the FSC, between NT$280 billion and NT$370 billion, or between 2.4 per cent and 3.4 per cent of Taiwan's GDP, larger than the subprime mortgage losses in the US. The credit-card crisis lowered Taiwan's GDP growth rate by around 0.5 per cent, but did not cause an economy-wide crisis. If we measure a housing bubble by the excess of the market housing prices over their fundamentals (constructed from either income or house rents), the current housing bubble is of about the same magnitude as the one in the early 1980s, which caused the S&L debacle – around 20 per cent in both cases (Lin Chu-Chia, 2009).

7. In July 2009, California Public Employees' Retirement System (Calpers) filed suit against three rating agencies (Moody's, Standard and Poor's and Fitch Ratings), accusing them of issuing 'wildly inaccurate and unreasonably high ratings' on mortgage-based securities that cost the Fund huge losses (*Wall Street Journal*, 16 July 2009). See also Mizen (2008) and Caprio et al. (2008).

8. William Isaac, former chairman of the US Federal Deposit Insurance Corporation (FDIC) claimed, in a testimony before the US Congress (12 March 2009), that in this crisis the 'mark-to-market' accounting rule has destroyed well over US$500 billion of capital and thus over US$5 trillion of lending capacity in the US financial system (assuming that banks are allowed to lend up to ten times their capital), contributing significantly to a severe credit contraction. The IMF and the BIS estimate the 'mark-to-market' write-downs to be US$4 trillion by financial institutions and US$4.1 trillion of traded debt, respectively (Remolona, 2009).

9. See Repullo and Surez (2008) for analysis of the procyclical effect of Basel II; and Saurina and Persaud (2008) for a debate about whether Basel II deepens or prevents crises. Note that even without the procyclical nature of Basel II, a binding and stringent capital requirement alone could weaken the monetary mechanism and contribute to credit crunch, although it ensures the financial soundness of individual institutions (Yilmaz, 2009).

10. The 'more adverse' scenarios outlined in the stress test conducted by the US Treasury Department include: (1) How much additional tier-1 capital the institutions would need today to be able to have a tier-1 risk-based capital ratio in excess of 6 per cent: (2) How much additional tier-1 common capital the institutions would need to have a tier-1 risk-based common capital ratio in excess of 4 per cent.

11. See the report in the *Wall Street Journal*, 8 July 2009, and US Accountability Office

12. (2009). The German Ministry of Finance went further, proposing to European Union finance ministers that the Basel II accord be suspended. The recommendation was not adopted by EU finance ministers, although they criticized the accord and agreed that the issue should be studied.
12. Prior to the amendment, an ROC Grand Justice's interpretative order, in the interest of protecting bank shareholders, prevented the FSC from taking over a zombie bank without giving shareholders sufficient time to replenish its capital.
13. In August 2009, the FSC for the first time took over without a bank run a zombie insurance company that had a negative net worth. The FSC was not able to act earlier only because it did not have enough resources for the takeover.

## REFERENCES

Akerlof, George A. (1970), 'The Market for "Lemons": Quality Uncertainty and the Market Mechanism,' *Quarterly Journal of Economics*, **84** (3), 488–500.

Bar-Gill, Oren and Elizabeth Warren (2008), 'Making Credit Safer,' *University of Pennsylvania Law Review*, **157** (1), 3–101.

Batson, Andrew (2009), 'Asian Officials Reject Focus on Saving Glut,' *Wall Street Journal,* 6 July.

Blanchard, Olivier (2008), 'The Tasks Ahead,' IMF Working Paper WP/08/262, Washington, DC, November.

Calomiris, Charles (2008), 'Not (Yet) a "Minski Moment",' in Andrew Felton and Carmen Reinhart (eds), *The First Global Financial Crisis of the 21st Century*, http://www.voxeu.org, July.

Caprio, Gerard Jr, Asli Demirgüç-Kunt and Edward J. Kane (2008), 'The 2007 Meltdown in Structured Securitization: Searching for Lessons Not Scapegoats,' World Bank Policy Research Working Paper WPS4756, Washington, DC, September.

Cooper, Richard N. (2007), 'Living with Global Imbalances,' Brookings Papers on Economic Activity 2007 (2), 91–107.

Coulibaly, Brahima and Jonathan Millar (2008), *The Asian Financial Crisis, Uphill Flow of Capital and Global Imbalance: Evidence from A Micro Study*, Washington, DC: Federal Reserve Board, August.

DGBAS (Director-General of Budget, Accounting and Statistics, Executive Yuan, ROC) (2010), *National Income Account Statistics and Domestic Economic Outlook*, February (in Chinese).

*Economist* (2009a), 'Taiwan Economy: Mirror, Mirror on the Wall,' http://www. economist.com, 12 February.

*Economist* (2009b), 'Domino Theory: Where Could Emerging-Market Contagion Spread Next?' http://www.economist.com, 26 February.

Fed (Board of Governors of the Federal Reserve System, USA) (2009), *The Supervisory Capital Assessment Program: Overview of Results*, Washington, DC, 7 May.

Freedman, Charles, Michael Kumhof, Douglas Laxton and Jaewoo Lee (2009), 'The Case for Global Fiscal Stimulus,' IMF Staff Position Note SPN/09/03, Washington, DC, March.

FSC (Financial Supervisory Commission, Executive Yuan, ROC) (2009), *Supervisory Guidelines for Offshore Structured Products*, Taipei, 23 July.

Goswami, Mangal, Andreas Jobst and Xin Long (2009), 'An Investigation of

Some Macro-Financial Linkages of Securitization,' IMF Working Paper, WP/09/06, Washington, DC, February.

Greenspan, Alan (2009), 'The Fed Didn't Cause the Housing Bubble,' *Wall Street Journal*, 12 March.

Greenspan, Alan (2010), 'The Crisis,' Greenspan Associates, LLC, 9 March 2010, second draft, presented at the Brookings Institution.

IMF (International Monetary Fund) (2009a), *Global Financial Stability Report: Navigating Challenges Ahead*, October.

IMF (International Monetary Fund) (2009b), 'The State of Public Finances Cross Country Fiscal Monitor: November 2009,' IMF Staff Position Note SPN/09/25, Washington, DC, November.

Kashyap, Anil, Raghurm Rajan and Jeremy Stein (2008), 'Rethinking Capital Regulation,' paper prepared for the Federal Reserve Bank of Kansas City Symposium on Maintaining Stability in a Changing Financial System, Jackson Hole, Wyoming, August 2008.

Lin, Che-Chun (2009), 'Credit Risk of Exotic Mortgage Products,' paper presented at the Conference on the Financial Storm in the Early 21st Century, National Cheng-Chi University, Taipei, May 2009.

Lin, Chu Chia (2009), 'A Study of the US Housing Bubbles,' paper presented at the Conference on the Financial Storm in the Early 21st Century, National Cheng-Chi University, Taipei, May 2009 (in Chinese).

Loser, Claudio M. (2009), 'Global Financial Turmoil and Emerging Market Economies: Major Contagion and a Shocking Loss of Wealth?' Asian Development Bank (ADB) Research Report, Mandaluyong, Philippines, March.

Miline, Alistair and Geoffrey Wood (2008), 'Banking Crisis Solution New and Old,' *Federal Reserve Bank of St. Louis Review*, **90** (5), 517–30.

Mizen, Paul (2008), 'The Credit Crunch of 2007–2008: A Discussion of the Background, Market Reaction, and Policy Response,' *Federal Reserve Bank of St Louis Review*, **90** (5), 531–67.

Posner, Richard (2009), 'Treating Financial Consumers as Consenting Adults,' *Wall Street Journal*, 24 July.

Remolona, Eli (2009), 'How the Crisis Got So Big: The Contagion in Asia,' paper presented to the Dr Sam-Chung Hsieh Memorial Conference, Chung-Hua Institution for Economic Research, Taipei, Taiwan, 9–10 July.

Repullo, Rafael and Javier Suarez (2008), 'The Procyclical Effects of Basel II,' paper presented at the Ninth Jacques Polak Annual Research Conference, hosted by the International Monetary Fund, Washington, DC, November.

Saurina, Jesús and Avinash Persaud (2008), 'Will Basel II Help Prevent Crises or Worsen Them?' *IMF Finance and Development*, **45** (2), June.

Shiller, Robert (2009), 'Financial Invention vs. Consumer Protection,' *New York Times*, 19 July.

Sommer, Martin (2009), 'Why Has Japan Been Hit So Hard by the Global Recession?' IMF Staff Position Note SPN/09/05, Washington, DC, March.

Taylor, John (2009), 'The Financial Crisis and Policy Responses: An Empirical Analysis of What Went Wrong,' National Bureau of Economic Research Working Paper 14631, Cambridge, MA, January.

US Accountability Office (2009), *Financial Markets Regulation: A Report to Congressional Committees*, Report GAO-07-739, Washington, DC.

US Department of the Treasury (2009), *Financial Regulatory Reform, A New Foundation*, June.

Yilmaz, Ensar (2009), 'Capital Accumulation and Regulation,' *The Quarterly Review of Economics and Finance*, **49** (3), 760–71, August.

# 2. A perspective on the US dollar after the current financial crisis: lessons from the fall of the pound sterling and the gold standard after World War I[1]

**Lee-Rong Wang**

Global imbalances have been one of the important and puzzling policy issues in the international policy arena since 2003. A global imbalance consists of a number of related and remarkable developments primarily in the United States (the US hereinafter) and East Asia, namely, large US current-account deficits, large Chinese current-account surpluses, a large accumulation of foreign reserves among the Asian countries, low global real interest rates, and the large current-account surpluses of oil-producing nations. Such imbalances might be expected to point to substantial dollar depreciation and Chinese currency appreciation. Many economists have predicted (or wished for) a fall in the dollar, but all have been disappointed – at least so far.

Clearly a number of different actors are present in the global imbalance phenomenon, and it is difficult to pinpoint a single cause that is most important. Dooley et al. (2008) examine one view of an important minority regarding the origin and sustainability of global imbalances. They argue that the current situation of large US current-account deficits and large East Asian surpluses can be expected to continue for some time, since it is in the interest of all the relevant parties. Fukuda and Kon (2008) argue that a preference for dollar assets exhibited by East Asian countries can help explain the flows of Asian capital to the US.

This chapter, by examining the history of the great powers, explores the possibility of a dying-away of such global imbalances following the current financial crisis. Based on the experiences of the pound sterling in the 1920s after World War I, it is projected that the decline in the US's fundamental economic strength and the rise of China caused by the current financial crisis are expected to have a marked impact on the perceptions regarding the US dollar in the future. Much as the US economy avoided the impact of World War I, China will become another great power owing to her being largely unscathed by the impact of the current financial crisis.

## 2.1   THE BRITISH EXPERIENCE FOLLOWING WORLD WAR I

The United Kingdom had intended to restore its currency to the gold standard in the 1920s following World War I. Realizing that a low interest rate would reduce the value of the pound, the governor of the Bank of England, Montagu Norman, insisted on lifting the rate even though this resulted in severe unemployment and the subsequent depression. In addition, the estrangement of the central banks that was brought about by the war also eroded the credibility of each country to commit to the gold standard. The Bank of England thus ceased to base the pound on its convertibility for gold and hence discarded the gold standard system in 1931. Willingness to hold the pound, both on the part of investors in the form of assets and by central banks as foreign reserves, was accordingly sharply reduced.

In fact, Britain's restoration of the pound's convertibility in 1925 is taken to mark the gold standard's resurrection and the devaluation of sterling in 1931 its demise (Eichengreen, 1992). Fearing that the capital flight from England and the devaluation of the pound sterling would harm Britain's status as an international financial center, the Bank of England raised the discount rate from 2.5 per cent to 6 per cent in 1925 to attract foreigners to hold sterling. This action significantly reduced the international competitiveness of Britain's industries, which finally led to a swelling of Britain's imports and a shrinking of her trade surplus. The gold reserve accordingly declined very quickly. It was obvious that the British government regarded defending sterling as its first priority, leaving behind that the numbers of unemployed rose and economic conditions deteriorated. The unemployment rate in the UK was around 21.3 per cent at the end of 1929. Shortly afterwards, the profits earned and wages paid by the industries plummeted and workers started to protest. When the public started to panic, they began to withdraw currency and gold deposits from the banks. On one occasion, within the space of less than one week, the Bank of England lost gold reserves amounting to £40 million. The bank was forced to terminate its obligation to exchange the pound sterling for gold bullion from the public. In 1931, the British government therefore announced it was relinquishing the gold standard system which had been in existence since the 1870s.

*Table 2.1*   *How the economic strength of the UK declined in the early*
             *1900s (per cent)*

|         | Share in world industry | | | Share in world trade | | |
|---------|------|------|------|------|------|------|
|         | 1900 | 1920 | 1930 | 1900 | 1920 | 1930 |
| UK      | 18   | 14   | 9    | 19   | 15   | 14   |
| US      | 31   | 47   | 39   | 12   | 14   | 12   |
| Germany | 16   | 9    | 11   | 13   | 8    | 10   |
| France  | 7    | 5    | 7    | 9    | 7    | 7    |

*Source:*   Huang (2002).

It is difficult to say, as pointed out by Eichengreen (1992), how long
these arrangements would have persisted in the absence of World War I.
The war destroyed and distorted industrial capacity across Europe while
stimulating manufacturing on other continents. London's position was
already eroding in the face of rapid growth abroad and the associated
decline in Britain's share of international trade. Table 2.1 shows that the
shares of the UK in world trade gradually declined from 19 per cent in
1900 to 15 per cent and 14 per cent in 1920 and 1930, respectively. The
share of the UK in world industry dropped by 50 per cent (from 18 per
cent to 9 per cent), while that of the US grew by more than 25 per cent
(from 31 per cent to 39 per cent) over the period 1900 to 1930 (Huang,
2002).

In fact, ever since the outbreak of the Civil War, the US has become
an economic giant. In 1860 the ratio of the US industrial output in the
world, even though it was still far behind that of the UK, almost reached
that of France and exceeded those of the German Confederation and
Russian Empire (Table 2.2). From 1860 to 1914, the exports of the US
increased seven times (from US$0.334 billion to US$2.365 billion). At
that time, however, most of the trade was still denominated in pounds
sterling (Kennedy, 1987). Owing to the outbreak of World War I, which
was fought mainly in Europe, the economic strength of the US eventually
surpassed that of the UK. The exports of the US grew 2.6 times over the
period from 1913 (US$2.8 billion) to 1918 (US$7.7 billion), and the trade
surplus rose on average, from 1914 to 1917, to five times what it had been.
Other than that, although the US still owed US$3.6 billion in foreign debt
in 1914 right before the war, it replaced the UK as the biggest creditor in
the world in 1918, its second year in the war (Yamada, 2000). At that time,
global financial assets, international reserves and international settlements
were expanding more rapidly than the resources of the London market

*Table 2.2    Shares of world industrial output, 1800–1900 (per cent)*

| Year / Nation | 1800 | 1830 | 1860 | 1880 | 1900 |
|---|---|---|---|---|---|
| United Kingdom | 4.3 | 9.5 | 19.9 | 22.9 | 18.5 |
| France | 4.2 | 5.2 | 7.9 | 7.8 | 6.8 |
| German Confederation | 3.5 | 3.5 | 4.9 | 8.5 | 13.2 |
| Kingdom of Italy | 2.5 | 2.3 | 2.5 | 2.5 | 2.5 |
| Russian Empire | 5.6 | 5.6 | 7.0 | 7.6 | 8.8 |
| USA | 0.8 | 2.4 | 7.2 | 14.7 | 23.6 |
| Japan | 3.5 | 2.8 | 2.6 | 2.4 | 2.4 |
| China | 33.3 | 29.8 | 19.7 | 12.5 | 6.2 |
| India/Pakistan | 19.7 | 17.6 | 8.6 | 2.8 | 1.7 |

*Source:*    Kennedy (1987).

and the Bank of England. This rendered foreigners hesitant to concentrate their foreign exchange reserves in sterling. This phenomenon is similar to the status of the US dollar recently, which is explored in the next section. In addition, mounting diplomatic tension in Europe after the turn of the century also heightened the risks of concentrating reserves in London.

Some sets of wartime changes actually had profound implications for the world economy of the 1920s and 1930s (Eichengreen, 1992). For instance, the wholesale liquidation of foreign assets and the accumulation of new foreign liabilities transformed the structure of international finance. In addition, international trade was redirected, with European exports declining at the expense of the products of other parts of the world. Finally, domestic politics were restructured by the rise of labor, the extension of the franchise and the reform of electoral systems. After World War I, the traditional basis for international cooperation became increasingly tenuous. The outbreak of hostilities caused by the war ended the gold standard system abruptly. In combination, these changes promised to transform fundamentally the international monetary system and the world economy once peace was restored.

## 2.2    THE FALL OF THE US AND THE RISE OF CHINA AFTER THE CRISIS

Europe was not able to be restored after the war without the assistance of the US. The US swept over all the world not only through foreign direct investment but also through portfolio investment. Americans bought

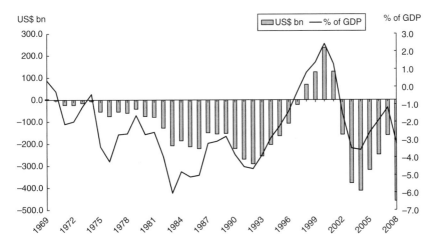

*Source:* Congressional Budget Office, USA.

*Figure 2.1  US budget balance.*

huge amounts of European government bonds at that time, just as China now holds tremendous amounts of US Treasury bonds. Owing to the current financial crisis, the US now needs sufficient capital to finance her enormous fiscal deficit, which is spent on bail-outs, unemployment benefits, stimulus plans etc. The American fiscal deficit will quadruple this year, from US$459 billion in 2008 to US$1.85 trillion (from 3.2 per cent of GDP to 13.1 per cent), according to the Congressional Budget Office (CBO) (Figure 2.1). This vast fiscal deficit is also twice the highest previously recorded fiscal deficit since World War II, i.e. the 6 per cent in the Reagan era. The CBO reckons the deficit will still be running at more than US$1 trillion in 2019. It estimates that the accumulated debt of the US will hit almost US$19 trillion by then. It is obvious that it is hard for the US to recover from the current financial crisis without the support of other countries with excess capital. Those countries with the largest amounts of foreign exchange reserves, including China, Japan and Russia, are also the countries holding most of the US Treasury securities. China surpassed Japan to become the biggest foreign holder of US Treasury securities in September 2008 (Figure 2.2).

Around 90 years ago, during the period after World War I, the state of the world was transformed from peace under the control of the UK to peace under the control of the US. By contrast, as analysed below, China will probably catch up with the US as the great power following the present financial crisis.

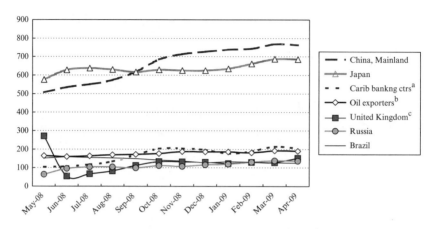

*Notes:*
Estimated foreign holdings of US Treasury marketable and non-marketable bills, bonds, and notes reported under the Treasury International Capital (TIC) reporting system are based on annual surveys of foreign holdings of US securities and on monthly data.
[a] Caribbean banking centers include the Bahamas, Bermuda, the Cayman Islands, the Netherlands Antilles and Panama. As from June 2006 they also include the British Virgin Islands.
[b] Oil exporters include Algeria, Bahrain, Ecuador, Gabon, Indonesia, Iran, Iraq, Kuwait, Libya, Nigeria, Oman, Qatar, Saudi Arabia, the United Arab Emirates and Venezuela.
[c] The United Kingdom includes the Channel Islands and the Isle of Man.

*Source:*   Department of the Treasury/Federal Reserve Board, USA, 15 June 2009.

*Figure 2.2   Major foreign holders of US Treasury securities (billions of dollars, at end of period).*

*Table 2.3   Economic growth rate of China (per cent)*

| Period | Average growth rate |
| --- | --- |
| 1978–87 | 10.14 |
| 1988–97 | 9.99 |
| 1998–2007 | 9.95 |
| Average (1978–2007) | 10.03 |

*Source:*   CEIC Data China.

Since 1978, when China's Open-Door Policy reform was implemented, China has become the economy with the fastest growth in the world. Her economic growth rate within the 30 years to 2007 has been more than 10 per cent (10.03 per cent) on average (Table 2.3), which has made her share

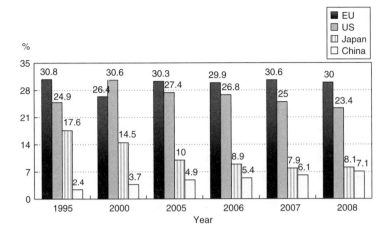

*Source:*    Global Insight, May 2009.

*Figure 2.3    Shares of world nominal gross domestic income.*

*Table 2.4    World shares of trade amounts and export amounts (per cent)*

|  | US | | Germany | | Japan | | China | |
|---|---|---|---|---|---|---|---|---|
|  | Trade amount | Export amount | Trade amount | Export amount | Trade amount | Export amount | Trade amount | Export amount |
| 1997 | 14.90 | 12.99 | 8.99 | 9.67 | 7.13 | 7.94 | 3.05 | 3.45 |
| 1998 | 15.46 | 13.04 | 9.64 | 10.39 | 6.35 | 7.42 | 3.08 | 3.51 |
| 1999 | 16.14 | 12.97 | 9.31 | 10.03 | 6.67 | 7.72 | 3.30 | 3.60 |
| 2000 | 16.60 | 12.89 | 8.51 | 9.07 | 6.98 | 7.90 | 3.86 | 4.11 |
| 2001 | 16.33 | 12.68 | 9.05 | 9.94 | 6.44 | 7.02 | 4.36 | 4.63 |
| 2002 | 15.55 | 11.50 | 9.08 | 10.22 | 6.19 | 6.92 | 5.10 | 5.40 |
| 2003 | 14.31 | 10.34 | 9.57 | 10.73 | 6.03 | 6.74 | 6.00 | 6.25 |
| 2004 | 13.57 | 9.60 | 9.43 | 10.69 | 5.90 | 6.63 | 6.68 | 6.96 |
| 2005 | 13.46 | 9.35 | 8.97 | 10.08 | 5.66 | 6.13 | 7.25 | 7.85 |
| 2006 | 13.09 | 9.26 | 9.05 | 10.01 | 5.44 | 5.80 | 7.79 | 8.65 |
| 2007 | 12.19 | 8.96 | 9.16 | 10.23 | 5.10 | 5.47 | 8.33 | 9.38 |

*Source:*    Ministry of Finance, ROC.

in world nominal GDP grow steadily from 2.4 per cent in 1995 to 7.1 per cent in 2008 (Figure 2.3). In 2007, China outstripped Germany to become the third-largest economy in the world. Furthermore, the Cabinet Office of Japan announced in August 2010 that the GDP of China surpassed that of Japan in the second quarter of 2010. China is now the world's second-largest economy. By contrast, the US share in world nominal GDP has slipped gradually during this period, from 24.9 per cent to 23.4 per cent, as shown in Figure 2.3. Although the gap between China and the US in terms of the respective amounts of GDP is still big, the amount of China's exports has already exceeded that of the US in 2007, and the amount traded will also soon exceed that by the US (Table 2.4).

The close relationship between the UK and the US in the early twentieth century was similar to that between the US and China today. At that time, Britain exported her capital and industrial goods to the US, while she imported raw materials from the US. The close interaction between these two countries significantly stimulated the US's economic growth. Towards the end of the nineteenth century and during the early stages of the twentieth century, the rise of the US became the most critical transformation within the equilibrium of global power (Kennedy, 1987). By contrast, the US has consumed large quantities of products from China in the past decade. China has then used the money earned from these exports to the US to purchase US government notes and bonds, which have provided the production capital needed by the Americans. A new word, 'Chimerica', has emerged to symbolize the tight mutual dependence between these two countries.[2]

Many people expect, following the outbreak of the current financial crisis, that the national strength of the US will decline and the influence of China will rise in its place. China has been requested, especially by the US, to enlarge her domestic demand while decreasing her exports to the world. Previous mutual dependence will probably fall apart once China successfully diversifies her reliance on exporting to the US and enhances her trading relationship with other partners. More than that, China has also tried very hard to diversify her huge foreign exchange reserves by engaging in more outward foreign direct investment (FDI) and portfolio investment (FPI) in other countries. China has become active in adopting transnational mergers and acquisitions since 2005. In 2007, transnational mergers and acquisitions in the world slowed down owing to the outbreak of the subprime crisis. China's amounts of overseas mergers and acquisitions, however, surpassed those of her inward mergers and acquisitions for the first time in 2007. The spreading of the crisis in the middle of 2008 further speeded up China's activities on global mergers and acquisitions. Once China shows less interest in US Treasury bonds, owing perhaps to a weaker US dollar and a straitened fiscal situation in the US, the Chimerica phenomenon will finally disappear. Until then, the equilibrium of global power will readjust.

After the financial crisis, whether or not the Chinese yuan will replace the US dollar will depend on the speed of the change in the national strength and financial development of the US and China. Concern about rising government deficits and debt levels across the world together with a wave of downgrading of European government debt and the depreciation of the euro, for example, has created alarm on financial markets. Although the leaders of the sixteen-nation eurozone gave formal approval in May 2010 to a 3-year, €110bn rescue plan to help Greece avoid a restructuring of its sovereign debt, market tensions remained high, as the premium that investors ask to buy southern European 10-year government bonds soared to 973 basis points for Greece, 354 for Portugal and 173 for Spain. This turmoil caused by the European sovereign debt problem may also occur in the US in the future, where the ratio of national debt to GDP is even higher than in the eurozone countries as a whole. The strength of the US dollar will have to face the challenge of the US sovereign debt problem in the future.

For the Chinese yuan to become an international currency, however, three preconditions have to be fulfilled. The Chinese yuan must flow freely, the width and depth of China's domestic capital markets must grow to some extent, and the circulation of the Chinese yuan all over the world must improve drastically. The Chinese yuan nowadays, however, is not convertible. China's exchange rate and interest rates do not yet float freely. In addition, China's financial account and capital movements are still restricted. These circumstances lead us to conclude that apparently the internationalization of the Chinese yuan has not yet come true. However, its tempo is speeding up. The internationalization of the Chinese yuan will definitely and continuously catch people's eyes in the near future.

## 2.3 THE FALL OF THE GOLD STANDARD AND THE RISE OF THE DOLLAR STANDARD

Apart from analysing the changes in the relationship between the great powers during the two above-mentioned periods, this chapter attempts to explore whether the dollar standard system will reach its demise after the current financial crisis, just like the gold standard did following World War I. The evolution of each of these two international monetary systems is therefore examined carefully in this section.

In the mid 1800s, countries began adopting the gold standard as a way to standardize transactions in a blossoming world trade market. The gold standard is a monetary system in which a region's common medium of exchange is paper currency that is normally freely convertible into preset, fixed quantities of gold. By World War I, most countries were on the gold standard. Between 1914 and 1919, most countries suspended the gold standard so that they could print enough money to pay for their involvement in the war. After the war, countries returned to a modified gold standard, but abandoned it during the Great Depression.

Under the dollar standard system, the US dollar was used by most countries as the primary reserve asset, in contrast to the gold standard in which gold played this role. The dollar's role was formalized under the Bretton Woods monetary agreement of 1944. Other nations set official exchange rates against the dollar, while the US agreed to exchange dollars for gold at a fixed price on demand by central banks. This system, also called the quasi-gold standard, functioned well for a brief period. However, by about 1958, the initial worldwide dollar shortage had turned into an overabundance. With the too rapid growth of dollar credits around the world, gold backing of the dollar proved unsustainable. The Bretton Woods agreement collapsed in 1973, but it enthroned the dollar as the international medium of exchange. This unique role of the dollar continues to the present day.

Some characteristics of these two international monetary systems are now discussed to clarify their evolutionary process.

**The deposit insurance mechanism was not established until the Great Depression**

To respond to the banking crisis caused by the Great Depression, the US established the world's first deposit insurance corporation, the FDIC, in 1934. Since the UK and the US abandoned the gold standard in 1931 and 1933, respectively, there was basically no deposit insurance mechanism in the era of the gold standard. However, deposit insurance has played a very important role in subsidizing bank runs under the dollar standard system in recent decades. The mechanism of deposit insurance did give rise to stabilization effects during the current financial crisis while one by one many countries announced the provision of full coverage from deposit insurance institutions. It is thus reasonable to conclude that the mechanism of deposit insurance in each country prevented the further spread of the current crisis.

**Is there an automatic adjustment mechanism for the trade imbalances?**

Regardless of whether the gold standard or the quasi-gold standard system (i.e. the Bretton Woods system) was used, a large trade deficit was impossible to sustain because of the innate auto-adjustment mechanism. Under the gold standard/quasi-gold system, central banks retained discretion over when and how to intervene. However, the basic rules of the game

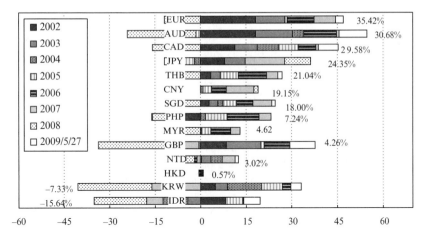

The percentage for each currency indicates the accumulated appreciation (+)/depreciation (−) for each currency vis-à-vis the US dollar since 2002. For example, the euro (EUR) appreciated vis-à-vis the US dollar by 35.42% between 2002 and 27 May, 2009.

*Figure 2.4   Exchange rate between the US and other countries.*

were more or less followed: restricting credit in response to gold/US dollar outflows and loosening it in response to inflows. Under the dollar standard system, by contrast, the US borrowed from the rest of the countries in the world by printing money or issuing securities in terms of US dollars, such as Treasury bonds. The previous auto-adjustment mechanism, which was capable of avoiding imbalance, lost its function when the US discarded the convertibility of the US dollar for gold in 1972. It was no longer necessary for the US to face strict tests with respect to her trade deficit problem. In other words, the US was, from 1972 onwards, able to pay for her import purchases by printing the same amount of currency bills or bonds without any required reserves. The amount of US dollars in circulation all over the world thus began to surge tremendously. Once the national strength of the US declines for sure, the value of the US dollar will promptly start to fall. The gradual depreciation of the US dollar since 2002 (Figure 2.4) has brought some forewarning of its long-run decline, which is likely to deteriorate further with the impact of the current crisis.

**The global money supply is not easily controlled under either one of these international monetary systems**
Under the gold standard system, the authorities were not able to control the global money supply owing to the limited supply of gold in the

world. Since the monetary base under this system consists mainly of gold, it was not possible for the global money supply to grow unless extra gold was dug from the ground. That is to say, gold reserves did not increase until new goldmines were found. It was argued at that time that the shortage of gold had severely restricted the growth of many economies.

Under the dollar standard system, the global money supply could not be controlled, because of the US trade deficit and fiscal deficit. Huge amounts of foreign exchange reserves, mostly accumulated through trade surpluses, propelled the purchasing power of the exporting countries and then flowed back to the US to purchase US assets. These inflows of capital further benefited the US economy. Since the dollar standard is a paper money system, the world supply of money will be explosive as long as the US does not control the growth rate of US dollars. The trade imbalance and complicated capital flows caused the system to go out of control and gave rise to an imbalance in the global money supply that still prevails today.

### The credibility of the commitment to the gold standard or dollar standard system rested on international cooperation

The gold standard system was established in the 1870s. International cooperation, already important as early as 1890, became increasingly frequent in the first decade of the twentieth century. Britain once played a central role in the organization of these cooperative ventures under the gold standard system. Britain's prominence in international financial markets permitted her to play a critical coordinating role and to exert a stabilizing influence in normal periods. The Bank of England served as international lender of last resort at that time. The bank's ability and willingness to orchestrate the operation of the prewar system had been responsible for its success. The International Monetary Fund (IMF), the Bank for International Settlements (BIS) and the central banks of the G7/G20 under the dollar standard system played the same role as the Bank of England under the gold standard system. The central banks and related authorities of the G20 worked closely during the crisis. However, the central bank of China as well as the central banks of some emerging economies, including Brazil and the members of the Gulf Cooperation Council (GCC), have already expressed their hesitance to hold more US dollar assets. Once international cooperation in supporting the US dollar begins to shake, the future of the dollar standard system will be greatly threatened via the contagion effect and the global free flow of capital.

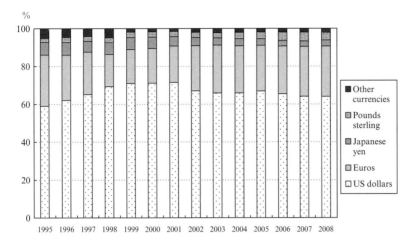

*Source:* IMF.

*Figure 2.5* *Currency composition of official foreign exchange reserves (COFER).*

## 2.4 POSSIBLE PERSPECTIVES OF THE INTERNATIONAL RESERVE SYSTEM

**Intra-regional trading will become much more prevalent owing to several factors**

1. First, climbing oil prices, which will raise transportation costs, together with environmental protection considerations will induce people to choose to purchase and sell within their region. If this is the case, the role that the regional currencies play will become more and more significant. Three big currency blocs, those of the US dollar, the euro and the Chinese yuan (renminbi), are expected to shape the balance of power in the future.

2. As indicated in Figure 2.5, after climbing to a peak of 71.52 per cent in 2001, the share of the US dollar in the currency composition of official foreign exchange reserves declined steadily to 64 per cent in 2008. China, as the biggest foreign holder of US Treasury securities since September 2008,[3] actually started to diversify her portfolio of foreign exchange reserves several years ago, as mentioned in the previous section. China has, for instance, increased its holding of gold by three-fourths since 2003. US Treasury securities have also been less emphasized in the Chinese portfolio content.

*Table 2.5　GDP components of China, 2000–2020 (per cent)*

| Year | 2000 | 2005 | 2010 | 2015 | 2020 |
|---|---|---|---|---|---|
| Private consumption | 47.8 | 45.7 | 49.6 | 51.2 | 52.2 |
| Investment | 36.5 | 41.2 | 37.2 | 35.7 | 34.8 |
| Government expenditure | 13.0 | 12.6 | 12.8 | 12.9 | 12.9 |
| Domestic demand | 97.3 | 99.5 | 99.6 | 99.8 | 99.9 |
| Exports | 26.0 | 30.5 | 32.3 | 34.3 | 34.9 |
| Imports | 23.4 | 30.1 | 31.9 | 34.1 | 34.7 |
| Foreign demand[a] | 49.4 | 60.6 | 64.2 | 68.4 | 69.6 |

*Note:* [a]Exports fulfill the demand from abroad. Imports, while they provide some demand from domestic markets, mostly fulfill the demand derived from re-exports, which basically provide the demand from abroad.

*Source:* Wang (2005).

### Suggestions as to how to prevent the collapse of global monetary and financial systems include the following

1. Countries with trade surpluses should increase their domestic demand (for instance, increase consumption and investment), whereas countries with trade deficits should reduce their domestic demand (for instance, decrease consumption and increase saving). The former countries include most Asian countries such as China, Japan, Singapore, Taiwan etc. The latter include the US, Australia and so on. Faced with the current financial tsunami, however, each country has taken whatever measures have been necessary, mostly by lifting government expenditure to carry out stimulation programs, to counter the severe local recessions. US Treasury Secretary Timothy Geithner recently emphasized that a sustained global recovery depends on the efforts of both the US and China in overhauling their economies. His focus on the mutual dependence of the two countries has reinforced the shift in the US–China relationship since the financial crisis. US pressure on China to boost its domestic demand – and, Washington hopes, buy more US goods – as well as to move to more market-based interest rates and prices has taken on increased urgency as the damage from the financial crisis has left the world with fewer likely sources of growth.

In fact, by putting forth its Tenth Five-Year Plan during the 2001 to 2005 period, China promoted a new strategy to propel its economic growth. That is, it switched from relying mainly on investment and exports to focusing more on consumption and then on domestic demand. During the first 4 years of China's Eleventh Five-Year Plan, China's exports and imports grew at a similar pace, which caused her external demand (i.e.

net exports) to increase moderately. Up to 2005, however, the growth of China's exports (28.4 per cent) significantly exceeded that of her imports (17.59 per cent). In January 2009, China promised a US$120 billion effort to give citizens better access to healthcare, which could very much reduce households' need to save. Establishing a sound social security protection mechanism as well as improving government efficiency is also necessary to reduce China's high saving ratio.

According to the projections made by Wang (2005), the ratio of consumption in China's GDP will gradually climb to more than 50 per cent after 2010, whereas that of investment will remain at around 35 per cent (Table 2.5). This will cause the sum of domestic demand, which includes consumption and investment, to increase slightly towards 99.9 per cent. The share of exports in GDP, even though it will steadily rise to 35 per cent in 2020, will not result in a significant increase in the net exports ratio owing to the simultaneous improvement in Chinese imports. Allowing the Chinese yuan to rise would be an important sign that China is serious about boosting domestic demand, as has long been claimed by the US. A stronger currency could hurt China's exporters but would also raise her buying power in international markets, thereby encouraging imports. The ratio of net exports to total GDP is expected to be lower if China's government focuses more attention on increasing domestic demand following the financial crisis.

On the other hand, US personal saving jumped abruptly after the outbreak of the financial crisis and has reached a 15-year high (Figure 2.6). Overspending via undue borrowing induced US housing markets to slump, which then triggered the spread of the current financial crisis. Americans have been forced to adjust their consumption behavior to allow them to escape the impasse. Many economists expect US personal saving to increase continuously, which is just the beginning of the current adjustment in American consumption behavior. The decline in consumption, which for long contributed more than 60 per cent of US GDP, will definitely delay the recovery of the US economy. Lower consumption will, however, be helpful in reducing US imports from abroad, which will then be beneficial for the US economy. It will probably take 3 to 4 years, or at most 5 to 6 years, for Americans to fill the production gap caused by the current recession.

2. In the 1930s John M. Keynes proposed imposing financial punishments on countries in possession of unbalanced current accounts, in order to ensure that such countries adopt the necessary measures to restore their balance of payments to equilibrium. The amount of the punishment was proposed as being 1 per cent of each country's deficit/surplus. This measure was supposed to bring about an effect through intimidation.

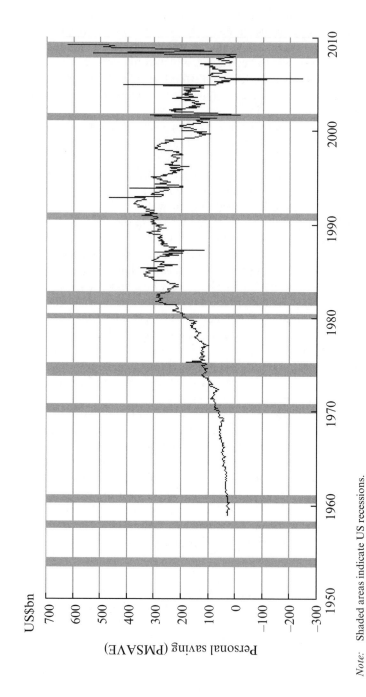

*Note:* Shaded areas indicate US recessions.

*Sources:* St Louis Federal Reserve Bank; data of personal saving from US Department of Commerce, Bureau of Economic Analysis.

*Figure 2.6   How American personal saving jumped after the financial crisis.*

Were such a measure to have no effect then the punishment percentage could be raised each year until equilibrium was restored.

3. The governor of the People's Bank of China, Zhou Xiaochuan, proposed enhancing the special drawing rights (SDR) mechanism within the IMF in order to moderate international reserves. Nobel prize laureate Robert Mundell, who is also well known as the father of the euro, indicated that the Chinese yuan should become an international currency. Mundell has suggested an international foreign exchange reserve be established that includes the Chinese yuan, with an 11 per cent to 16 per cent share, into the SDR's basket of currencies. The Chinese yuan has in fact infiltrated Southeast Asia, is increasingly accepted internationally, and may one day directly challenge the status of the US dollar.

## 2.5   CONCLUDING REMARKS

Whether or not the Chinese yuan will replace the US dollar after the financial crisis depends on the speed of the change in the national strength and financial development of the US and China. For instance, the current turmoil caused by the European sovereign debt problem after the financial crisis may also occur in the US, where the ratio of national debt to GDP is even higher than that in the eurozone countries as a whole. The strength of the US dollar will have to face the challenge of the US sovereign debt problem in the future.

For the Chinese yuan to become an international currency, however, three preconditions have to be fulfilled: the Chinese yuan must flow freely, the width and depth of China's domestic capital markets must grow to some extent, and the circulation of the Chinese yuan all over the world must improve drastically. Developments to date lead us to conclude that the internationalization of the Chinese yuan has not yet come about, though its progress will definitely and continuously catch people's eyes in the near future.

## NOTES

1. This chapter was prepared originally as a paper for the Samuel Shieh Memorial Conference held at the Chung-Hua Institution for Economic Research, Taipei, on 9 July 2009.
2. The Chimerica theory was put forth in 2009 by Professor Niall Ferguson of Harvard University and Visiting Professor Moritz Schularick of Cambridge University.
3. China held $767.9 billion in US Treasury securities at the end of the first quarter of 2009, accounting for 6 per cent of the $10.9 trillion total amount of US Treasury securities.

# REFERENCES

Bernstein, L. Peter (2000), *The Power of Gold: The History of an Obsession*, New York: John Wiley & Sons.

Dooley, Michael P., David Folkerts-Landau and Peter Garber (2008), 'Life on the Tri-Polar Sphere: How Should Interest and Exchange Rates Realign Next?' in T. Ito and A.K. Rose (eds), *International Financial Issues in the Pacific Rim: Global Imbalances, Financial Liberalization, and Exchange Rate Policy* (NBER-EASE, vol. 17), University of Chicago Press, pp. 13–37.

Eichengreen, Barry (1992), *Golden Fetters – The Gold Standard and the Great Depression, 1919–1939*, New York: Oxford University Press.

Fukuda, Shin-ichi and Yoshifumi Kon (2008), 'Liquidity Risk Aversion, Debt Maturity, and Current Account Surpluses: A Theory and Evidence from East Asia,' in T. Ito and A.K. Rose (eds), *International Financial Issues in the Pacific Rim: Global Imbalances, Financial Liberalization, and Exchange Rate Policy* (NBER-EASE, vol. 17), University of Chicago Press, pp. 39–70.

Huang, An-Nein (2002), *The Development and Crisis of Contemporary Capitalism in the First Half of the 20th Century: The Thirty Theses of Global Modern and Contemporary History*, Shung-Shi: North-West University Publisher (in Chinese).

Kennedy, Paul (1987), *The Rise and Fall of the Great Powers: Economic Change and Military Conflict from 1500 to 2000*, New York: Random House.

Wang, Mong-Kue (2005), *Key Issues in China's Development – 2006–2020*, Beijing: China Development Publishing House (in Chinese).

Yamada, Shinji (2000), *The Global Economic Depression*, Taipei: Yazi Publishers (in Chinese).

# 3.  De-privatization? Case studies of government banks' performance in developing countries during the financial crisis

**Chung-Hua Shen and Chih-Yung Lin**

## 3.1  INTRODUCTION

The financial crisis of 2008–09 raises the issue of the performance of government-owned banks (GOBs). Because most of the privately-owned banks (POBs) were hit severely by the crisis, governments started injecting funds to rescue them and thus nationalizing them. This de-privatizing action seems to go against the privatization tide that has run since the 1980s. Because of this nationalization process, researchers are wondering whether this de-privatizing process implies that GOBs perform better than privately owned banks.

This issue is interesting because empirical studies argue typically that private banks perform better regardless of profitability measures, regions and sample periods. For simplicity, the underperformance of government-owned banks is termed 'the GOB effect'. For example, Mian (2003), using 250 GOBs from 71 emerging economies, found that government banks uniformly underperform private banks. Iannotta et al. (2007), using an enlarged sample, found that government banks have lower profitability and loan quality, and a higher insolvency risk, than private banks. Furthermore, Cornett et al. (2008) found that government banks are significantly less profitable than private banks. Micco et al. (2007) also identified government bank underperformance in less-developed countries (LDCs)[1] but not developed countries (DCs).

So how could a well-accepted concept be suddenly refuted by the evidence observed during the financial crisis of 2008?

We argue that the typical conclusion that government banks perform worse arises from cases where the GOB is requested to purchase a distressed bank. We thus propose a political hypothesis to explain why GOBs perform worse than private banks. Political situations arise in which a government bank is mandated to purchase a distressed bank,[2] often a local bank, to avoid a bank run or to restore public confidence.[3] In addition this suggests that the motivation of a government bank to acquire a distressed bank is most likely a government request. For example, because the management skills, asset quality and corporate governance of distressed banks are usually suspect, government banks acquire such banks only when asked to do so by the authorities, in order to avoid media criticism. In our study, to identify whether government banks perform this political policy role, we have searched the global M&As of each government bank, then identified whether the target bank was distressed, and specifically whether its net worth or return on assets (ROA) was negative. At the same time, we have referred to local newspapers to examine whether the M&As were government-mandated. Government banks involved heavily in political intervention through undertaking strong policy roles are termed 'strong-policy banks'.

Our hypothesis (the *policy role hypothesis*) is that GOBs, before they undertake a strong-policy role, perform similarly to private banks. By contrast, GOBs underperform private banks after they undertake such a policy role. This hypothesis suggests that GOB performance deteriorates after GOBs undertake the strong-policy role, but not before. Furthermore, this is not the case with private banks. Thus the taking-over of distressed banks is in fact a policy role of GOBs, which can also explain why the GOB effect is commonly observed in emerging countries.

To investigate this hypothesis, we examine four strong-policy banks and one private acquirer bank, from Hungary, Morocco, the Czech Republic, Tunisia and Japan, respectively. We compare the performance of strong-policy banks with the average of all the banks in the same country (hereafter the country average). The country average differs between countries. We use the purchase year as the event year and then examine the dynamic patterns before and after it. Based on our hypothesis, we expect GOBs to perform no worse than the country average before the event year but worse than the country average after the event year, though this result may not occur for private bank acquirers.

The remainder of this chapter is organized as follows. Section 3.2 presents the literature on the performance of government-owned banks, and the political connections. Section 3.3 discusses the construction of strong- and weak-policy roles. Subsequently, Section 3.4 presents four case studies and their descriptive results. Finally, Section 3.5 presents the conclusion.

## 3.2 LITERATURE REVIEW

Two streams in the literature are often applied to examine whether there is an underperformance of a GOB. The first stream directly compares performance between GOBs and POBs, while the second examines government bank performance after privatization. The present survey demonstrates that the GOB effect typically exists in developing countries, but reveals mixed results for developed countries.

Regarding the direct comparison, Mian (2003) confirmed the GOB effect in developing countries using commercial banks from 100 emerging economies, and found that GOBs underperform POBs in emerging economies. Cornett et al. (2008) found that GOBs are significantly less profitable than POBs. Moreover, they found that the performance of GOBs deteriorated more than that of POBs during the Asian economic crisis in 1997 and 1998, and that these differences were most acute in countries whose governments intervened frequently in the banking system. Unlike the above studies, Micco et al. (2007) demonstrated that GOBs located in developing countries tend to exhibit lower profitability and higher costs than their private counterparts, but that this phenomenon does not exist in developed countries.

Next, numerous studies compare the performance between GOBs and POBs from the perspective of privatization. The GOB effect is supported if the performances of government banks improve after privatization. Verbrugge et al. (1999) identified increased profitability and capital adequacy among privatized banks even in OECD countries. Moreover, Beck et al. (2005), examining a sample of Nigerian banks, found that performance improved in nine privatized banks but failed to surpass that of the country's existing private banks. Boubakri et al. (2005) found that several, but not all, performance measures improved after privatization in developing countries. Furthermore, Weintraub and Nakane (2005) examined the privatization experience of Brazilian banks and found that GOBs are significantly less productive than private banks. Moreover, Megginson (2005) surveyed the effects of bank privatizations around the world, finding that the empirical evidence supports the 'privatization effect', indicating that GOBs are less efficient than POBs.

## 3.3 DATA

We first defined the GOBs in situations where the government had a shareholding exceeding 20 per cent of total shares. The detailed government ownership data for each bank were obtained mainly from the ownership structure presented in Bankscope. Additionally, because Bankscope provides only current ownership, which is a dynamic process, we tracked ownership changes using the privatization databases of the World Bank, Verbrugge et al. (1999), Megginson (2005), Bonin et al. (2005), Beck et al. (2005) and Clarke et al. (2005). These databases contain information on shareholding changes for some government banks. We also checked individual bank websites and other publications for verification purposes.[4] Accordingly, we obtained information on the full bank ownership history.

## 3.4   FIVE CASES

This section describes the four cases to investigate our hypothesis. We compare those GOBs that purchased a distressed bank with the country average. The performance variables can be categorized into four groups based on capital, management, earnings, and liquidity performances, respectively. Capital is proxied by the equity ratio ($E/A$); management is proxied by the net interest margin ($NIM$), the non-interest expense ratio ($NIE/A$) and the cost-to-income ratio ($C/I$); earnings are proxied by the return on assets ($ROA$), the return on equity ($ROE$), the net interest revenue ratio ($NIR/A$) and the other operating income ratio ($OOI/A$); liquidity is proxied by the liquidity ratio ($L/A$). Table 3.1 gives the detailed definitions and source of the above variables.

### Case 1: Kereskedelmi & Hitelbank RT (Hungary)

Kereskedelmi Bank RT was established in 1987. On 1 January 1996, Kereskedelmi Bank RT acquired Ibusz Bank RT (a distressed bank) and changed the name to Kereskedelmi & Hitelbank RT (K&H). Kereskedelmi Bank, with 74 branches, has been working on the integration of its wholly owned subsidiary, Ibusz Bank, with 85 branches, to turn the latter into its retail arm. This is planned to be handled by government resources. So far, Kereskedelmi & Hitelbank RT is the only major bank not to have attracted foreign investor interest.

Tables 3.2 and 3.3 show the basic conditions of K&H and the country average, respectively. In particular, Table 3.2 lists the descriptive statistics of the characteristic and performance variables for K&H. In addition, Table 3.3 lists the average descriptive statistics of the characteristic and performance variables in Hungary.

In Table 3.2's panel A, all the characteristic variables of K&H are larger than those of the country average in Hungary. That is, the K&H has

*Table 3.1   Definitions of characteristic and performance variables*

| Variable | Definition | Expected sign after executing policy |
|---|---|---|
| *Characteristic variables* | | |
| *ASSETS* | Total assets | |
| *EQUITIES* | Total equities | |
| *LOANS* | Total loans | |
| *DEPOSITS* | Total deposits | |
| *Performance variables* | | |
| Capital performance | | |
|   *E/A* | Total equities/Total assets | − |
| Management performance | | |
|   *NIM* | Net interest income to total assets | − |
|   *NIE/A* | Non-interest expense/assets | + |
|   *C/I* | Cost-to-income ratio | + |
| Earnings performance | | |
|   *ROA* | Net income to total assets | − |
|   *ROE* | Net income to total equity | − |
|   *NIR/A* | Net interest revenue/assets | − |
|   *OOI/A* | Other operating income/assets | − |
| Liquidity performance | | |
|   *L/A* | Liquid assets/assets | − |

*Source:*   Bankscope.

larger *ASSETS*, *EQUITIES*, *DEPOSITS* and *LOANS* than the country average. In particular, the *ASSETS* of K&H is around a triple multiple of other banks in the period $t = 1$. Thus, larger sizes of government banks are more likely to purchase the distressed banks.

Regarding the performance variables, when *NIE/A* and *C/I* are used as the performance measures, K&H increases greatly against the mean of Hungarian banks during the post-event years, especially in periods $t = 2$, 3 and 4. For instance, the values of K&H in periods $t = 2$, 3 and 4 for *C/I* are 109.91 per cent, 127.61 per cent and 106.86 per cent. Moreover, when using *ROA* and *ROE* as the performance measures, during the pre-event years, K&H performs similarly to the country average. However, during the post-event years, the performances of K&H are overwhelmingly negative in periods $t = 2$, 3 and 4. For example, in periods $t = 2$, 3 and 4 K&H's values of *ROA* are −0.76 per cent, −3.41 per cent and −0.07 per cent and those of *ROE* −11.71 per cent, −96.88 per cent and −1.98 per cent. In addition, other variables of K&H do not show substantial change.

*Table 3.2    Performances of Kereskedelmi & Hitelbank RT (K&H)*

| t | −2 | −1 | 0 | 1 | 2 | 3 | 4 |
|---|---|---|---|---|---|---|---|
| Year | 1994 | 1995 | 1996 | 1997 | 1998 | 1999 | 2000 |
| *Panel A: Characteristic variables* (US$m) | | | | | | | |
| ASSETS | 2 739 | 2 473 | 2 209 | 2 237 | 2 400 | 3 949 | 3 939 |
| EQUITIES | 78 | 84 | 90 | 163 | 138 | 93 | 168 |
| DEPOSITS | 2 372 | 2 164 | 1 973 | 1 971 | 2 130 | 3 186 | 3 020 |
| LOANS | 983 | 844 | 882 | 847 | 1 020 | 1 664 | 2 033 |
| *Panel B: Performance variables* (%) | | | | | | | |
| Capital performance | | | | | | | |
| E/A | 2.87 | 3.41 | 4.05 | 7.29 | 5.75 | 2.35 | 4.27 |
| Management performance | | | | | | | |
| NIM | 7.47 | 5.37 | 5.10 | 4.05 | 3.19 | 4.36 | 4.20 |
| NIE/A | 7.55 | 5.66 | 4.94 | 5.42 | 5.38 | 14.00 | 7.00 |
| C/I | 40.95 | 73.2 | 88.15 | 93.74 | 109.91 | 127.61 | 106.86 |
| Earnings performance | | | | | | | |
| ROA | 0.52 | 1.00 | 0.58 | 0.53 | −0.76 | −3.41 | −0.07 |
| ROE | 25.36 | 31.82 | 15.41 | 9.05 | −11.71 | −96.88 | −1.98 |
| NIR/A | 6.28 | 4.56 | 4.32 | 3.49 | 2.81 | 3.79 | 3.64 |
| OOI/A | 2.59 | 1.57 | 2.06 | 2.41 | 2.01 | 6.10 | 2.96 |
| Liquidity performance | | | | | | | |
| L/A | 23.11 | 20.17 | 22.18 | 23.60 | 21.37 | 24.15 | 18.91 |

*Note:*   $t = 0$ denotes the year of merging distressed banks, $t = -1, -2$ denote the number of years before the event date and $t = 1, 2, 3, 4$ denote the number of years after.

Thus, during the pre-event years, the performance of K&H and the mean of Hungary banks are roughly equal. However, upon acquiring the distressed banks, the management and earnings performances of K&H immediately deteriorated in periods $t = 2$, 3 and 4.

**Case 2: Crédit Agricole du Maroc SA (Morocco)**

Caisse Nationale de Crédit Agricole was established in 1961. In June 2003, Caisse Nationale de Crédit Agricole acquired Banque Marocaine pour l'Afrique et l'Orient (a distressed bank). On 11 November 2003 Caisse Nationale de Crédit Agricole changed its name to Crédit Agricole du Maroc SA (CAM).

Tables 3.4 and 3.5 show the basic conditions of CAM and the country average, respectively. In particular, Table 3.4 lists the descriptive statistics of the characteristic and performance variables for CAM. Table 3.5

*Table 3.3  Average performances of all banks in Hungary*

| t | −2 | −1 | 0 | 1 | 2 | 3 | 4 |
|---|---|---|---|---|---|---|---|
| Year | 1994 | 1995 | 1996 | 1997 | 1998 | 1999 | 2000 |
| *Panel A: Characteristic variables* (US$m) | | | | | | | |
| *ASSETS* | 115 | 102 | 123 | 707 | 861 | 1 585 | 1 853 |
| *EQUITIES* | 6 | 7 | 32 | 141 | 104 | 199 | 252 |
| *DEPOSITS* | 92 | 75 | 73 | 263 | 99 | 1 157 | 1 412 |
| *LOANS* | 40 | 36 | 35 | 324 | 646 | 593 | 892 |
| *Panel B: Performance variables* (%) | | | | | | | |
| Capital performance | | | | | | | |
| *E/A* | 10.93 | 9.76 | 9.17 | 10.39 | 9.27 | 10.24 | 9.94 |
| Management performance | | | | | | | |
| *NIM* | 5.93 | 6.18 | 5.14 | 4.55 | 4.35 | 4.08 | 5.08 |
| *NIE/A* | 6.04 | 6.27 | 5.52 | 4.81 | 5.34 | 7.00 | 5.53 |
| *C/I* | 72.13 | 67.15 | 61.30 | 70.80 | 80.77 | 85.50 | 76.48 |
| Earnings performance | | | | | | | |
| *ROA* | 0.98 | 1.96 | 1.60 | 0.90 | 0.51 | −0.56 | 0.90 |
| *ROE* | 15.74 | 28.48 | 14.64 | 13.42 | 4.08 | −3.17 | 10.13 |
| *NIR/A* | 5.15 | 5.39 | 4.52 | 4.03 | 3.85 | 3.57 | 4.43 |
| *OOI/A* | 3.05 | 4.76 | 3.91 | 2.70 | 4.31 | 2.84 | 2.49 |
| Liquidity performance | | | | | | | |
| *L/A* | 14.08 | 11.15 | 10.50 | 12.02 | 9.80 | 11.56 | 10.29 |

*Notes:*
Numbers here are averages of the variables during the sample periods.
$t = 0$ denotes the year of merging distressed banks, $t = -1, -2$ denote the number of years before the event date and $t = 1, 2, 3, 4$ denote the number of years after.

lists the average descriptive statistics of the characteristic and perform-ance variables in Morocco. Additionally, in panel A, the characteristic variables *ASSETS, EQUITIES, DEPOSITS* and *LOANS* of CAM are all similar to those of other banks in Morocco.

Regarding the performance variables, when using *E/A* as the perform-ance measure, the performances of CAM decrease greatly against the country averages during the post-event years, especially in periods $t = 2$, 3 and 4. For example, in periods $t = 2$, 3 and 4, the values of CAM are 0.70 per cent and 1.57 per cent and 1.84 per cent for *E/A*. Moreover, when using *ROA* and *ROE* as the performance measures, CAM performs worse than the country average during the pre-event years. However, the worse performances of CAM are overwhelmingly enlarged during the post-event years, especially in periods $t = 2$. For instance, in periods $t = 2$, the values of CAM are −8.58 per cent for *ROA* and −304.36 per cent for *ROE*. In

*Table 3.4　Performances of Crédit Agricole du Maroc (CAM)*

| $t$ | −2 | −1 | 0 | 1 | 2 | 3 | 4 |
|---|---|---|---|---|---|---|---|
| Year | 2001 | 2002 | 2003 | 2004 | 2005 | 2006 | 2007 |
| *Panel A: Characteristic variables* (US$m) | | | | | | | |
| *ASSETS* | 1 938 | 2 286 | 2 855 | 3 421 | 3 721 | 5 026 | 7 865 |
| *EQUITIES* | 163 | 162 | 182 | 185 | 26 | 79 | 145 |
| *DEPOSITS* | 1 448 | 1 732 | 2 178 | 2 568 | 3 574 | 4 764 | 7 248 |
| *LOANS* | 1 379 | 1 596 | 2 069 | 2 342 | 2 384 | 2 881 | 4 226 |
| *Panel B: Performance variables* (%) | | | | | | | |
| Capital performance | | | | | | | |
| $E/A$ | 8.42 | 7.09 | 6.36 | 5.41 | 0.70 | 1.57 | 1.84 |
| Management performance | | | | | | | |
| *NIM* | 4.05 | 3.97 | 3.54 | 3.54 | 4.39 | 3.71 | 3.35 |
| *NIE/A* | 3.67 | 2.59 | 3.30 | 3.34 | 4.07 | 3.90 | 4.07 |
| *C/I* | 60.1 | 61.6 | 64.06 | 60.62 | 49.83 | 45.28 | 45.02 |
| Earnings performance | | | | | | | |
| *ROA* | 0.00 | 0.00 | 0.00 | 0.00 | −8.58 | 0.38 | 0.53 |
| *ROE* | −0.02 | 0.01 | 0.01 | 0.00 | −304.36 | 32.52 | 30.39 |
| *NIR/A* | 3.51 | 3.39 | 3.10 | 3.23 | 3.97 | 3.35 | 2.91 |
| *OOI/A* | 0.19 | 0.16 | 0.17 | 0.23 | 0.41 | 1.00 | 0.63 |
| Liquidity performance | | | | | | | |
| *L/A* | 6.93 | 11.00 | 5.54 | 8.99 | 9.80 | 5.12 | 17.37 |

*Note:*　$t = 0$ denotes the year of merging distressed banks, $t = -1, -2$ denote the number of years before the event date and $t = 1, 2, 3, 4$ denote the number of years after.

addition, when using $L/A$ as the performance measure, CAM decreases greatly against the country average during the periods $t = 0, 1, 2$ and 3. For example, in periods $t = 0, 1, 2$ and 3 CAM's values of $L/A$ are 5.54 per cent, 8.99 per cent, 9.80 per cent and 5.12 per cent. Other variables of CAM do not change substantially on average.

In sum, after acquiring the distressed banks, the capital, earnings and liquidity performances of CAM deteriorated immediately. Thus, our policy role hypothesis that the performances of government banks deteriorate immediately after acquiring distressed banks is once more confirmed.

### Case 3: Investiční a Poštovní Banka AS (Czech Republic)

Investiční Banka Plc was established in 1983. On 1 January 1994, Investiční Banka Plc absorbed Poštovní Banka (a distressed bank) and changed its name to Investiční a Poštovní Banka AS (IPB). The net profit of IPB in

*Table 3.5   Average performances of all banks in Morocco*

| $t$ | −2 | −1 | 0 | 1 | 2 | 3 | 4 |
|---|---|---|---|---|---|---|---|
| Year | 2001 | 2002 | 2003 | 2004 | 2005 | 2006 | 2007 |
| *Panel A: Characteristic variables* (US$m) | | | | | | | |
| *ASSETS* | 3 583 | 4 427 | 5 567 | 7 339 | 7 215 | 9 142 | 10 155 |
| *EQUITIES* | 350 | 413 | 495 | 625 | 635 | 792 | 934 |
| *DEPOSITS* | 3 140 | 3 878 | 4 915 | 6 455 | 6 333 | 8 015 | 8 772 |
| *LOANS* | 1 478 | 1 723 | 2 203 | 2 948 | 3 431 | 4 639 | 5 377 |
| *Panel B: Performance variables* (%) | | | | | | | |
| Capital performance | | | | | | | |
| *E/A* | 9.77 | 9.33 | 8.89 | 8.52 | 8.80 | 8.66 | 9.20 |
| Management performance | | | | | | | |
| *NIM* | 9.62 | 9.36 | 8.91 | 8.42 | 8.96 | 7.93 | 7.61 |
| *NIE/A* | 3.57 | 3.72 | 3.61 | 3.24 | 2.56 | 2.31 | 2.45 |
| *CII* | 60.35 | 59.93 | 61.42 | 57.63 | 62.71 | 54.56 | 48.77 |
| Earnings performance | | | | | | | |
| *ROA* | 1.10 | 0.70 | 0.68 | 0.89 | 1.10 | 1.19 | 1.21 |
| *ROE* | 11.44 | 7.60 | 7.42 | 10.33 | 12.71 | 14.17 | 15.27 |
| *NIR/A* | 3.92 | 3.87 | 3.75 | 3.65 | 3.19 | 3.02 | 3.24 |
| *OOI/A* | 0.87 | 0.87 | 0.82 | 1.04 | 0.84 | 0.94 | 0.81 |
| Liquidity performance | | | | | | | |
| *L/A* | 22.53 | 23.92 | 26.26 | 28.05 | 33.75 | 31.28 | 30.96 |

*Notes:*
Numbers here are averages of the variables during the sample periods.
$t = 0$ denotes the year of merging distressed banks, $t = -1, -2$ denote the number of years before the event date and $t = 1, 2, 3, 4$ denote the number of years after.

1993 exceeded CZK350 millions. It was the fourth-strongest Czech bank, with 120 branches and 3500 outlets in post offices in the Czech Republic. On 1 January 1999, IPB bought substantial amounts of the assets and liabilities of BH Capital AS.

The Czech government drafted new legislation to reform the system of guarantees on bank savings. Savings with Česká Spořitelna, Komerční Banka, Investiční a Poštovní Banka and Živnobanka are currently covered by state guarantees, a situation inherited from the previous regime. The state holding in IPB was 36.6 per cent. The existing situation is causing considerable market distortion in favor of the four banks covered by state guarantees.

Tables 3.6 and 3.7 show the basic conditions of IPB and the country average, respectively. In particular, Table 3.6 lists the descriptive statistics

*Table 3.6   Performances of Investiční a Poštovní Banka AS (IPB)*

| t | −2 | −1 | 0 | 1 | 2 | 3 | 4 |
|---|---|---|---|---|---|---|---|
| Year | 1992 | 1993 | 1994 | 1995 | 1996 | 1997 | 1998 |
| *Panel A: Characteristic variables* (US$m) | | | | | | | |
| *ASSETS* | 3726 | 3918 | 5313 | 7145 | 8025 | 6556 | 9099 |
| *EQUITIES* | 147 | 211 | 371 | 468 | 662 | 201 | 505 |
| *DEPOSITS* | 2941 | 3597 | 4694 | 6106 | 6612 | 5249 | 7210 |
| *LOANS* | 2546 | 2730 | 3690 | 4481 | 5109 | 4032 | 5148 |
| *Panel B: Performance variables* (%) | | | | | | | |
| Capital performance | | | | | | | |
| *E/A* | 3.95 | 5.40 | 6.99 | 6.55 | 8.25 | 3.06 | 5.55 |
| Management performance | | | | | | | |
| *NIM* | 3.19 | 3.30 | 3.40 | 3.19 | 2.49 | 2.60 | 2.92 |
| *NIE/A* | 2.24 | 3.21 | 3.25 | 3.28 | 3.22 | 8.11 | 4.40 |
| *C/I* | 27.53 | 38.24 | 53.76 | 60.36 | 54.94 | 52.21 | 50.07 |
| Earnings performance | | | | | | | |
| *ROA* | 0.44 | 0.31 | 0.51 | 0.59 | 0.43 | −4.98 | 0.19 |
| *ROE* | 9.49 | 6.65 | 8.06 | 8.81 | 5.77 | −88.76 | 4.29 |
| *NIR/A* | 2.91 | 3.06 | 3.14 | 2.95 | 2.23 | 2.31 | 2.60 |
| *OOI/A* | 0.28 | 0.65 | 0.64 | 0.71 | 1.80 | 2.37 | 2.34 |
| Liquidity performance | | | | | | | |
| *L/A* | 1.11 | 1.18 | 0.97 | 0.94 | 1.13 | 1.23 | 1.09 |

*Note:*   $t = 0$ denotes the year of merging distressed banks, $t = -1, -2$ denote the number of years before the event date and $t = 1, 2, 3, 4$ denote the number of years after.

of the characteristic and performance variables for IPB. In addition, Table 3.7 also lists the average descriptive statistics of the characteristic and performance variables in the Czech Republic.

In panel A, the characteristic variables of IPB are all larger than those of other banks in the Czech Republic. That is, IPB has larger *ASSETS*, *EQUITIES*, *LOANS* and *DEPOSITS* than those of other banks in the Czech Republic. Also, the *ASSETS* of IPB are around triple those of other banks in periods $t = 0$. Thus, it is confirmed again that larger-sized government banks are more likely to purchase distressed banks.

With regard to the performance variables, when using *ROA* and *ROE* as the performance measures, we see that during the pre-event years IPB performed similarly to the country average. However, the performances of IPB in the period $t = 3$ were negative, the values being −4.98 per cent for *ROA* and −88.76 per cent for *ROE*. Moreover, other variables of IPB did not change substantially on average. So the earnings performances of IPB

*Table 3.7    Average performances of all banks in the Czech Republic*

| t | −2 | −1 | 0 | 1 | 2 | 3 | 4 |
|---|---|---|---|---|---|---|---|
| Year | 1992 | 1993 | 1994 | 1995 | 1996 | 1997 | 1998 |
| *Panel A: Characteristic variables* (US$m) | | | | | | | |
| *ASSETS* | 1 645 | 1 676 | 1 670 | 1 969 | 2 044 | 1 756 | 2 304 |
| *EQUITIES* | 94 | 86 | 119 | 139 | 123 | 128 | 158 |
| *DEPOSITS* | 1 433 | 1 467 | 1 347 | 1 575 | 1 631 | 1 442 | 1 754 |
| *LOANS* | 530 | 905 | 793 | 919 | 949 | 794 | 964 |
| *Panel B: Performance variables* (%) | | | | | | | |
| Capital performance | | | | | | | |
| *E/A* | 15.05 | 9.40 | 10.83 | 7.96 | 7.94 | 8.30 | 9.97 |
| Management performance | | | | | | | |
| *NIM* | 3.39 | 3.98 | 3.82 | 3.53 | 2.55 | 3.22 | 4.67 |
| *NIE/A* | 3.79 | 4.94 | 4.87 | 6.11 | 6.99 | 5.03 | 4.12 |
| *C/I* | 63.44 | 60.18 | 72.52 | 62.58 | 78.12 | 61.14 | 69.82 |
| Earnings performance | | | | | | | |
| *ROA* | 0.43 | −0.04 | 0.17 | −0.16 | −2.12 | 0.01 | 0.24 |
| *ROE* | 8.11 | 3.71 | 6.07 | 6.45 | 9.99 | 2.83 | 2.36 |
| *NIR/A* | 3.12 | 3.63 | 3.41 | 3.17 | 2.33 | 2.86 | 3.88 |
| *OOI/A* | 1.56 | 1.93 | 1.94 | 1.98 | 2.45 | 2.86 | 1.93 |
| Liquidity performance | | | | | | | |
| *L/A* | 2.43 | 5.02 | 4.43 | 7.18 | 7.61 | 13.78 | 17.34 |

*Notes:*
Numbers here are averages of the variables during the sample periods.
$t = 0$ denotes the year of merging distressed banks, $t = -1, -2$ denote the number of years before the event date and $t = 1, 2, 3, 4$ denote the number of years after.

deteriorated immediately after acquiring the distressed banks, supporting our policy role hypothesis.

### Case 4: Société Tunisienne de Banque (Tunisia)

Société Tunisienne de Banque (STB) was founded in 1957, the first indigenous bank to be established following Tunisia's independence. Initially begun as a development bank, it is now a full-service commercial bank. The Republic of Tunisia and quasi-government institutions own 44.69 per cent of the bank, and its objectives include support of official economic and social policies.

As part of the central bank's plan to consolidate the domestic banking sector, Société Tunisienne de Banque was nominated to merge with two development banks, Banque de developpement economique de Tunisie

*Table 3.8   Performances of Société Tunisienne de Banque (STB)*

| t | −2 | −1 | 0 | 1 | 2 | 3 | 4 |
|---|---|---|---|---|---|---|---|
| Year | 1998 | 1999 | 2000 | 2001 | 2002 | 2003 | 2004 |
| *Panel A: Characteristic variables* (US$m) | | | | | | | |
| *ASSETS* | 2014 | 1931 | 2757 | 2693 | 3170 | 3315 | 3575 |
| *EQUITIES* | 117 | 135 | 277 | 280 | 307 | 354 | 353 |
| *DEPOSITS* | 1699 | 1620 | 1648 | 1623 | 1959 | 1983 | 2241 |
| *LOANS* | 1013 | 973 | 1830 | 1821 | 2207 | 2482 | 2671 |
| *Panel B: Performance variables* (%) | | | | | | | |
| Capital performance | | | | | | | |
| *E/A* | 5.80 | 6.96 | 10.06 | 10.39 | 9.69 | 10.69 | 9.86 |
| Management performance | | | | | | | |
| *NIM* | 2.71 | 2.82 | 2.77 | 2.22 | 1.57 | 1.48 | 2.03 |
| *NIE/A* | 2.94 | 3.21 | 3.75 | 3.79 | 2.75 | 2.08 | 2.71 |
| *CII* | 58.77 | 57.79 | 57.81 | 66.95 | 75.77 | 80.92 | 74.92 |
| Earnings performance | | | | | | | |
| *ROA* | 0.97 | 1.08 | 1.47 | 1.07 | 0.48 | 0.45 | 0.13 |
| *ROE* | 19.28 | 16.91 | 16.62 | 10.44 | 4.78 | 4.42 | 1.25 |
| *NIR/A* | 2.09 | 2.46 | 2.41 | 1.97 | 1.42 | 1.34 | 1.84 |
| *OOI/A* | 1.45 | 1.64 | 1.78 | 1.34 | 1.46 | 1.35 | 1.20 |
| Liquidity performance | | | | | | | |
| *L/A* | 25.99 | 17.85 | 13.45 | 13.53 | 11.16 | 8.413 | 9.00 |

*Note:*   $t = 0$ denotes the year of merging non-distressed banks, $t = -1, -2$ denote the number of years before the event date and $t = 1, 2, 3, 4$ denote the number of years after.

and Banque Nationale de developpement Touristique (distressed banks) in 2000. The merger was part of a Tunisian financial sector restructuring program supported by a US$400 million loan from the World Bank, the European Union and the African Development Bank.

Tables 3.8 and 3.9 discuss the basic conditions of STB and the country average, respectively. In particular, Table 3.8 lists the descriptive statistics of the characteristic and performance variables for STB. In addition, Table 3.9 lists the average descriptive statistics of the characteristic and performance variables in Tunisia.

In panel A, the characteristic variables *ASSETS*, *EQUITIES*, *DEPOSITS* and *LOANS* of STB were larger than the country average. In particular, the *ASSETS* of STB were around triple those of other banks in period $t = 0$. Thus, larger government banks were also more likely to purchase non-distressed banks.

Turning to the performance variables, when using *ROA, ROE, NIM*

*Table 3.9   Average performances of all banks in Tunisia*

| $t$ | −2 | −1 | 0 | 1 | 2 | 3 | 4 |
|---|---|---|---|---|---|---|---|
| Year | 1998 | 1999 | 2000 | 2001 | 2002 | 2003 | 2004 |
| *Panel A: Characteristic variables* (US$m) | | | | | | | |
| *ASSETS* | 924 | 822 | 914 | 1025 | 1057 | 1018 | 835 |
| *EQUITIES* | 41 | 42 | 46 | 87 | 93 | 90 | 95 |
| *DEPOSITS* | 633 | 550 | 599 | 645 | 658 | 634 | 625 |
| *LOANS* | 615 | 552 | 624 | 710 | 705 | 686 | 629 |
| *Panel B: Performance variables* (%) | | | | | | | |
| Capital performance | | | | | | | |
| *E/A* | 6.27 | 13.84 | 11.47 | 11.93 | 12.22 | 11.86 | 13.89 |
| Management performance | | | | | | | |
| *NIM* | 3.01 | 3.57 | 3.40 | 3.18 | 3.47 | 3.26 | 3.97 |
| *NIE/A* | 2.80 | 3.37 | 3.51 | 3.20 | 3.80 | 3.69 | 4.00 |
| *C/I* | 54.10 | 53.25 | 53.41 | 54.41 | 51.25 | 48.34 | 53.72 |
| Earnings performance | | | | | | | |
| *ROA* | 0.97 | 1.30 | 1.13 | 1.31 | 1.08 | 1.12 | 1.17 |
| *ROE* | 14.80 | 12.99 | 15.28 | 12.97 | 12.23 | 11.39 | 8.12 |
| *NIR/A* | 2.19 | 2.55 | 2.64 | 2.49 | 2.74 | 2.62 | 3.41 |
| *OOI/A* | 1.47 | 1.86 | 1.87 | 1.97 | 2.25 | 2.19 | 2.04 |
| Liquidity performance | | | | | | | |
| *L/A* | 22.93 | 21.69 | 20.38 | 22.33 | 17.54 | 14.15 | 13.19 |

*Notes:*
Numbers here are averages of the variables during the sample periods.
$t = 0$ denotes the year of merging non-distressed banks, $t = -1, -2$ denote the number of years before the event date and $t = 1, 2, 3, 4$ denote the number of years after.

and *L/A* as the performance measures, during the pre-event years, the performances of STB were similar to the country average. However, during the post-event years the performances of STB clearly deteriorated in periods $t = 2$, 3 and 4. For example, STB's values of *ROE* were 19.28 per cent, 16.91 per cent, 16.62 per cent, 10.44 per cent, 4.78 per cent, 4.42 per cent and 1.25 per cent in periods $t = -2, -1, 0, 1, 2, 3$ and 4. Moreover, when using *C/I* as the performance measure, STB increased greatly against the country average during the post-event years, especially in periods $t =$ 1, 2, 3 and 4. For instance, STB's values of *C/I* in periods $t = 1, 2, 3$ and 4 were 66.95 per cent, 75.77 per cent, 80.92 per cent and 74.92 per cent. Other variables of STB did not change substantially. Hence the management, earnings and liquidity performances of STB deteriorated immediately after acquiring the distressed banks, confirming our policy role hypothesis again.

*Table 3.10*   *Performances of Mitsubishi UFJ Financial Group (MUFJ)*

| t | −2 | −1 | 0 | 1 | 2 | 3 |
|---|---|---|---|---|---|---|
| Year | 2003 | 2004 | 2005 | 2006 | 2007 | 2008 |
| *Panel A: Characteristic variables* (US$m) | | | | | | |
| *ASSETS* | 1861612 | 1890173 | 1817863 | 1803800 | 1861591 | 1930455 |
| *EQUITIES* | 54906 | 61727 | 90322 | 103842 | 94424 | 87366 |
| *DEPOSITS* | 1333498 | 1347703 | 1309041 | 1236034 | 1259875 | 1247930 |
| *LOANS* | 903591 | 855786 | 875224 | 868207 | 905734 | 938531 |
| *Panel B: Performance variables* (%) | | | | | | |
| Capital performance | | | | | | |
| *E/A* | 2.95 | 3.27 | 4.97 | 5.76 | 5.07 | 4.53 |
| Management performance | | | | | | |
| *NIM* | 1.09 | 1.03 | 1.06 | 1.12 | 1.07 | 1.12 |
| *NIE/A* | 1.75 | 1.27 | 1.15 | 1.24 | 1.33 | 1.44 |
| *CII* | 54.29 | 52.30 | 56.83 | 56.81 | 61.58 | 64.56 |
| Earnings performance | | | | | | |
| *ROA* | 0.11 | −0.09 | 0.70 | 0.55 | 0.40 | −0.11 |
| *ROE* | 4.30 | −2.76 | 17.01 | 10.22 | 7.33 | −2.24 |
| *NIR/A* | 1.03 | 0.98 | 1.01 | 1.07 | 1.02 | 1.06 |
| *OOI/A* | 0.85 | 0.86 | 0.96 | 1.03 | 0.93 | 0.70 |
| Liquidity performance | | | | | | |
| *L/A* | 0.05 | 0.07 | 0.06 | 0.05 | 0.07 | 0.09 |

*Note:*   $t = 0$ denotes the year of merging non-distressed banks, $t = -1, -2$ denote the number of years before the event date and $t = 1, 2, 3, 4$ denote the number of years after.

### Case 5: Mitsubishi UFJ Financial Group (Japan)

We discuss finally the case of a private financial institution acquiring a distressed bank. Mitsubishi Tokyo Financial Group was established on 2 April 2001 and on 1 October 2005 it acquired UFJ Holdings Inc., whose equity was US$2684 million in 2004. After the acquisition, the acquirer changed its name to Mitsubishi UFJ Financial Group Inc. (MUFJ).

Table 3.10 lists the descriptive statistics of the characteristic and performance variables for MUFJ. For comparison, Table 3.11 also lists the descriptive statistics of the characteristic and performance variables of Japan.

Panel A shows the characteristic variables, *ASSETS*, *EQUITIES*, *DEPOSITS* and *LOANS*, of MUFJ to have been much larger than the country average. In particular, the *ASSETS* of MUFJ were around 50 times the average in period $t = 0$. Thus, we can say that large private banks purchase distressed banks.

*Table 3.11    Average performances of all banks in Japan*

| t | −2 | −1 | 0 | 1 | 2 | 3 |
|---|---|---|---|---|---|---|
| Year | 2003 | 2004 | 2005 | 2006 | 2007 | 2008 |

| *Panel A: Characteristic variables* (US$m) | | | | | | |
|---|---|---|---|---|---|---|
| ASSETS | 40038 | 40955 | 40006 | 40246 | 41885 | 33430 |
| EQUITIES | 1191 | 1288 | 1787 | 2106 | 1950 | 1656 |
| DEPOSITS | 19268 | 19124 | 18931 | 19576 | 20405 | 30499 |
| LOANS | 30249 | 30936 | 30274 | 30276 | 31403 | 16898 |

| *Panel B: Performance variables* (%) | | | | | | |
|---|---|---|---|---|---|---|
| Capital performance | | | | | | |
| $E/A$ | 6.21 | 6.02 | 6.23 | 6.59 | 6.55 | 6.08 |
| Management performance | | | | | | |
| $NIM$ | 1.83 | 1.85 | 1.86 | 1.89 | 1.82 | 1.73 |
| $NIE/A$ | 2.01 | 1.75 | 1.72 | 1.72 | 1.69 | 1.79 |
| $C/I$ | 71.16 | 69.84 | 69.15 | 68.59 | 73.57 | 75.54 |
| Earnings performance | | | | | | |
| $ROA$ | −0.11 | −0.01 | 0.33 | 0.18 | 0.20 | 0.15 |
| $ROE$ | −0.52 | 1.42 | 3.66 | 0.68 | −1.01 | −1.30 |
| $NIR/A$ | 1.76 | 1.76 | 1.77 | 1.80 | 1.74 | 1.65 |
| $OOI/A$ | 0.47 | 0.33 | 0.34 | 0.35 | 0.32 | 0.46 |
| Liquidity performance | | | | | | |
| $L/A$ | 0.01 | 0.01 | 0.01 | 0.01 | 0.01 | 0.02 |

*Notes:*
Numbers here are averages of the variables during the sample periods.
$t = 0$ denotes the year of merging non-distressed banks, $t = -1, -2$ denote the number of years before the event date and $t = 1, 2, 3, 4$ denote the number of years after.

Turning to the performance variables, when we use *ROA, ROE, NIM, NIR/A, NIE/A, C/I* and *OOI/A* as the performance measures we see that the performances remained similar during the pre- and post-event years. For example, during the post-event years, the performances of MUFJ were similar to the country average in periods $t = 0$, 1, 2 and 3. For example, MUFJ's values of *ROA* were 0.11 per cent, −0.09 per cent, 0.70 per cent, 0.55 per cent, 0.40 per cent and −0.11 per cent in periods $t = -2$, −1, 0, 1, 2 and 3. Also, MUFJ's values of *ROE* were 4.30 per cent, −2.76 per cent, 17.01 per cent, 10.22 per cent, 7.33 per cent and −2.24 per cent in periods $t = -2, -1, 0, 1, 2$ and 3. Some of these values were larger than the average of the bank industry in Japan.

Therefore, the performances of MUFJ did not all deteriorate after it acquired the distressed banks, confirming our policy role hypothesis that the performances of government banks become worse after acquiring distressed banks, but that this is not necessarily true in the case of acquisition by a private bank.

## 3.5   CONCLUSION

During the 2008 financial crisis, most private-owned banks were severely damaged and were nationalized. Researchers are interested in knowing whether the conventional wisdom that government banks underperform the private banks still holds true. We investigated why government-owned banks underperform private-owned banks, the phenomenon referred to as the GOB effect. We proposed a policy role hypothesis to explain this phenomenon. Government banks that acquired a distressed bank for political reasons showed a deterioration in performance, but the performance of a private bank that acquired a distressed bank did not necessarily decline.

We presented five cases taken from Hungary, Morocco, the Czech Republic, Tunisia and Japan to examine this issue. The basic statistics of the first four cases all showed overwhelmingly that, in terms of profitability, the GOB effect did not exist before the acquisition of the distressed banks, but did exist afterwards. Accordingly, the purchase of distressed banks tends to be one of the possible causes of the observed worse performance of government banks, which supports the policy role hypothesis. That is, government banks, after being mandated to merge with a distressed bank, suffer adverse performance. Furthermore, the last case showed that private banks, after merging with a distressed bank, do not suffer adverse performance. These results can also explain why GOB effects are commonly observed in emerging countries.

## NOTES

1.  The terms of 'developing countries' and 'less-developed countries' are used interchangeably in this chapter.
2.  'Distressed' means the net income of the bank is negative during the merger period.
3.  For example, in April 2009, Taiwan Bank, 100 per cent of its shares owned by the government, was asked by the minister of finance to take over a distressed private-owned Bank, ChinFon bank, when its net worth became negative.
4.  These were *Bankers Almanac, American Banker, Bank Director* and *ABA Banking Journal*.

# REFERENCES

Beck, T., R. Cull and A. Jerome (2005), 'Bank Privatization and Performance: Empirical Evidence from Nigeria,' *Journal of Banking and Finance*, **29**, 2355–79.

Bonin, J., I. Hasan and P. Wachtel (2005), 'Privatization Matters: Bank Efficiency in Transition Countries,' *J. Banking Finance*, **29**, 2155–78.

Boubakri, N., J.C. Cosset, K. Fischer and O. Guedhami (2005), 'Privatization and Bank Performance in Developing Countries,' *J. Banking Finance*, **29**, 2015–41.

Choi, S. and I. Hasan (2007), 'Bank Privatization and Performance: What Really Counts,' Working Paper, Rensselaer Polytechnic Institute.

Chong, B.S., M.H. Liu and K.H. Tan (2006), 'The Wealth Effect of Forced Bank Mergers and Cronyism,' *J. Banking Finance*, **30**, 3215–33.

Clarke, G., R. Cull and M. Shirley (2005), 'Bank Privatization in Developing Countries: A Summary of Lessons and Findings,' *J. Banking Finance*, **29**, 1905–30.

Cornett, M.M., L. Guo, S. Khaksari and H. Tehranian (2008), 'The Impact of Corporate Governance on Performance Differences in Privately-Owned Versus Government-Owned Banks: An International Comparison,' Working Paper, Boston College.

Iannotta, G., G. Nocera and A. Sironi (2007), 'Ownership Structure, Risk and Performance in the European Banking Industry,' *J. Banking Finance*, **31**, 2127–49.

Megginson, W.L. (2005), 'The Economics of Bank Privatization,' *J. Banking Finance*, **29**, 1931–80.

Mian, A. (2003), 'Foreign, Private Domestic, and Government Banks: New Evidence from Emerging Markets,' mimeo, University of Chicago.

Micco, A., U. Panizza and M. Yañez (2007), 'Bank Ownership and Performance. Does Politics Matter?' *J. Banking Finance*, **31**, 219–41.

Verbrugge, J.A., W.L. Megginson and W.L. Owens (1999), 'State Ownership and the Financial Performance of Privatized Banks: An Empirical Analysis,' paper presented at the World Bank/Federal Reserve Bank of Dallas Conference on Bank Privatization, Washington, DC, March.

Weintraub, D.B. and M.I. Nakane (2005), 'Bank Privatization and Productivity: Evidence for Brazil,' *J. Banking Finance*, **29**, 2259–89.

# PART II

Impacts, consequences and policy responses

# 4. Why world exports are so susceptible to the economic crisis: the prevailing 'export overshooting' phenomenon, with particular reference to Taiwan

**Bih Jane Liu**[1]

## 4.1 INTRODUCTION

In the years leading up to the summer of 2007 when the US subprime crisis began to unfold, the world saw a period of relative calm and prosperity after the recovery from the dot-com bubble-burst in the early 2000s. While the major industrialized nations grew at a modest pace of 1 to 3 per cent per annum, the rise of the BRIC and other emerging markets gave great impetus to the world's economic progress and spurred high growth in world trade. But the subprime loan problem gave way quickly to a broad global crisis marked by slowing economies and dried-up liquidity with unprecedented reach. The scope and devastating impacts of the global financial crisis were greater than anyone had anticipated. Like a game of dominos, the financial crisis started in the United States and spread to the rest of the world. It first lacerated the world's financial systems, then jolted and knocked out the real economy. No country was immune to it. Not the 'Wealthy Country Club' with member countries such as the United States, Germany and Japan. Not the usually resilient East Asian NICs. Not even the up-and-coming powerful BRIC group. Among all these, countries with a strong export orientation and opened up most to the world, especially Japan and the East Asian NICs, were hit the hardest.

Figure 4.1 and 4.2 show clearly the impacts of the financial crisis of 2008 on the volume of world exports for a sample of eleven countries consisting of major advanced industrialized countries, the Asian NICs and the emerging market economies. World exports began to fall in the second half of 2008 and quickly rebounded towards the end of the first half of 2009, forming a narrow V-shaped pattern-of-growth trajectory. The

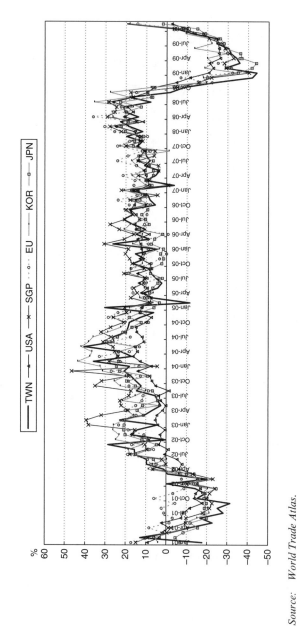

*Source: World Trade Atlas.*

*Figure 4.1   Export growth, 2000–2009.*

68

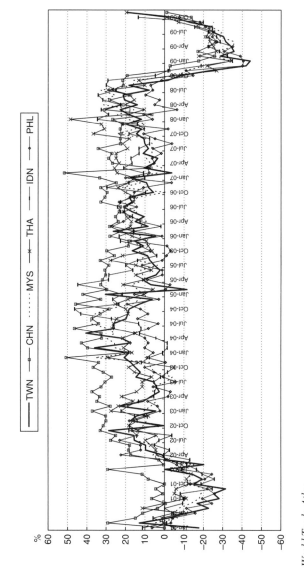

*Source: World Trade Atlas.*

*Figure 4.2 Export Growth, 2000–2009.*

*Table 4.1    Growth rates 2000–2009 of GDP for OECD, non-OECD and world (per cent)*

| Year | OECD | Non-OECD | World |
|------|------|----------|-------|
| 2000 | 4.02 | 5.69 | 4.30 |
| 2001 | 1.32 | 3.74 | 1.77 |
| 2002 | 1.58 | 4.15 | 2.07 |
| 2003 | 1.90 | 5.86 | 2.67 |
| 2004 | 3.05 | 7.62 | 3.97 |
| 2005 | 2.59 | 7.09 | 3.53 |
| 2006 | 2.96 | 7.92 | 4.03 |
| 2007 | 2.64 | 8.26 | 3.89 |
| 2008 | 0.42 | 5.96 | 1.71 |
| 2009 | −3.41 | 1.84 | −2.14 |

*Source:*   Global Insight. Annual growth rates were calculated using the quarterly real GDP series.

dramatic collapse in world exports is not without historical precedence as the same V-shaped pattern was also observed during the dot-com crisis around 2001. In effect, both crises had led to economic downturns which in turn resulted in high levels of unemployment and a sharp fall in global demand and international trade.

It is worth noting that during the economic downturns around 2001 and 2008, the contraction in world exports was far greater than that of world GDP, as revealed in Tables 4.1 and 4.2. In 2001, while real world GDP still grew at 1.77 per cent, growth of total exports for the countries in our sample had already turned negative and contracted at a rate of 6.21 per cent. In contrast, the overall export performance was much worse in the recent economic downturn, with the total exports shrinking at an astounding rate of 25.68 per cent a year after the crisis broke out. Meanwhile real world GDP suffered only a mild decline and growth slowed down to −2.14 per cent in 2009.

Another noteworthy observation was that Taiwan appeared to exhibit a relatively narrower V-shaped export growth pattern than the others in the group. That is, Taiwan was amongst the first to contract and also the first to recover in exports. Even though all of the eleven nations studied had displayed a similar pattern of ups and downs in export growth and were highly influenced by the two economic crises, the crises seemed to have a greater impact on Taiwan's export performance (Figure 4.1 and 4.2). In fact, the contractions in Taiwan's exports were the most severe both in terms of timing and magnitude, and Taiwan's recovery was also among

*Table 4.2   Growth rates 2001–2009 of exports by country (per cent)*

| Year | Whole sample | TWN | CHN | USA | SGP | MAS |
|---|---|---|---|---|---|---|
| 2001 | −6.21 | −16.87 | 6.89 | −6.58 | −11.65 | −10.14 |
| 2002 | 4.46 | 7.13 | 22.24 | −4.94 | 2.85 | 5.86 |
| 2003 | 15.06 | 11.29 | 34.65 | 4.57 | 27.93 | 7.22 |
| 2004 | 21.34 | 21.10 | 35.39 | 12.43 | 24.15 | 26.50 |
| 2005 | 12.73 | 8.81 | 28.41 | 10.58 | 15.54 | 11.83 |
| 2006 | 15.14 | 12.89 | 27.15 | 13.86 | 18.39 | 13.56 |
| 2007 | 15.76 | 10.12 | 25.67 | 11.91 | 10.11 | 9.62 |
| 2008 | 12.82 | 3.63 | 17.30 | 12.13 | 12.94 | 13.30 |
| 2009[a] | −25.68 | −24.10 | −18.70 | −20.12 | −26.22 | −29.52 |

| Year | EU | THA | KOR | IDN | PHL | JPN |
|---|---|---|---|---|---|---|
| 2001 | 1.42 | −5.28 | −12.67 | −9.34 | −15.57 | −15.83 |
| 2002 | 6.56 | 5.68 | 8.00 | 1.49 | 9.13 | 3.45 |
| 2003 | 16.73 | 17.00 | 19.29 | 6.82 | 2.78 | 13.12 |
| 2004 | 20.16 | 20.99 | 30.97 | 17.24 | 9.78 | 19.98 |
| 2005 | 10.20 | 13.13 | 12.04 | 19.66 | 3.59 | 5.14 |
| 2006 | 11.61 | 18.91 | 14.43 | 17.67 | 14.70 | 8.60 |
| 2007 | 16.83 | 24.88 | 14.14 | 13.20 | 6.88 | 10.47 |
| 2008 | 12.88 | 9.03 | 13.60 | 20.09 | −2.48 | 9.50 |
| 2009[a] | −22.76 | −17.36 | −17.06 | −22.01 | −26.91 | −28.61 |

*Note:*   [a]Up to the third quarter of 2009.

*Source:*   *World Trade Atlas.* Statistics were calculated using the monthly merchandise trade series.

the most speedy, particularly in the 2008 crisis. Importantly, in the two economic crises, Taiwan delivered one of the worst export performances among the nations.

A number of papers have identified that fluctuations in exports are highly correlated with the changes in worldwide demand, effective exchange rates, the volatility of exchange rates (see for example, Boug and Fagereng, 2010; Sapir and Sekkat, 1995) and FDI (Zhang and Song, 2000). These determinants (hereafter referred to as the fundamental factors) are shown to be able to govern adequately the behavior of the export growth performance of a country in the long run. The fact that the decline in world exports was much greater than the decline in world GDP suggests that the force causing exports to deviate from their long-run trend may have been further magnified by some other factors not accounted for in the short-run dynamics. In other words, the surprisingly large declines in exports could not have been predicted by the historical relationships linking exports to the fundamental factors.

Based on what we have observed, we formulate several testing hypotheses. Specifically, we look for evidence that addresses the 'export overshooting phenomenon' (i.e. the unusually large deviation of exports from their long-run level) during times of economic duress as well as evidence that shows that the extent of overshooting was larger in Taiwan than in other countries. Moreover, we offer some explanations for why overshooting occurs and why Taiwan might be especially susceptible to shocks when compared with other countries.

The group of countries being studied in this chapter includes three Asian NICs, namely Taiwan, Korea and Singapore; several Asian emerging market economies, namely China, Indonesia, Malaysia, the Philippines and Thailand; and Taiwan's major trading partners, namely the US, the EU and Japan. The data are monthly data for the period 2000–2009.

The structure of the chapter is as follows. Section 4.2 begins with a comparison in terms of causes and economic impacts of the two economic crises. Section 4.3 describes the structural changes in Taiwan's exports over time and explains what produced the changes. In addition, several testable hypotheses are derived in Sections 4.2 and 4.3 based on the revealed trends and patterns of exports during the crisis periods. These hypotheses are then tested in Section 4.4 using an error correction panel regression model, and we examine in a dynamic context how the response of exports to adverse external shocks may vary across different groups of countries and industries. Some explanations are provided in Section 4.5 as to why, when facing economic crisis, exports will overshoot their long-run trend and why Taiwan's export performance is among the worst. Finally, in the last section we summarize our findings and offer conclusions.

## 4.2   IMPACT OF ECONOMIC CRISIS ON EXPORTS

The two economic crises were triggered by different events. The first economic crisis occurred during 2000–02 and was a direct result of the internet bubble (also referred to as the dot-com bubble) bursting in 2000 and the 9/11 terrorist attacks on US soil in 2001. The second crisis was the recent 2008 global financial crisis which originated from the subprime crisis and led to a massive global economic downturn. But the two economic crises may be interconnected, as is argued by Lin (2008). This is because the easy-credit monetary policy adopted by developed countries is believed to have been an important catalyst of the subprime crisis, in order to minimize the duration and depth of the recession following the 2001 crisis.

In retrospect, the internet bubble, a speculative bubble covering roughly the period 1998–2001, originated from the accelerated growth in internet sectors and related industries. Because of the 'get-big-fast' strategy adopted by the new internet-based companies and the market confidence on the profitable future of these companies, the internet bubble saw rapid run-ups in market valuations of these companies (Valliere and Peterson, 2004). When the bubble burst in 2000, it was followed by an equally rapid collapse of the markets and led to bankruptcy of many internet firms and huge losses in stock markets. The United States, in particular, suffered from a severe economic downturn with unemployment reaching new heights.

The bubble had an important impact on the wealth and the spending habits of consumers, especially those in the developed countries. People spent more because they felt richer with their overvalued assets; but when their wealth was suddenly reduced once the bubble burst, they scaled back on discretionary spending. Changes in discretionary spending are a result of the so-called 'wealth effect', which turns out to have important implications for the growth of international trade and the global economy. For many export-oriented countries, this surge in discretionary spending in developed countries, especially in high-tech products, was for a long time a major source of global demand for their exports. After the 9/11 attacks, countries with a heavy reliance on the exports of high-tech products such as Japan, Singapore, South Korea and Taiwan saw the global demand for ICT products slowing in a weak economic outlook. Similarly, the exports of other Asian countries such as Malaysia and the Philippines, which are part of the integrated ICT production–supply chain system in the region, were also negatively affected. China, meanwhile, still managed to experience a positive growth in exports as the volume of Chinese high-tech exports constituted only a small part of its external trade at that time and hence the impacts were limited.

Unlike the export contractions seen in 2001, which were due largely to a collapse in external demand for ICT output, a shrunken export demand in 2008 was truly global as a result of a great economic recession unlike any seen since the early 1930s. In varying degrees, this great economic recession affected virtually every industry and business sector. The reason why the recent economic downturn has had far-reaching consequences lies in the rapid proliferation of speculative financial innovations fueled by a torrent of cross-board capital flows that further quickened the speed of contagion worldwide (Hu, 2011). As a consequence, the economic impacts of a lowered level of world income were felt around the globe, and a collapse in export demand across the board quickly followed. This included a plunge in global demand for Chinese output.

Although the causes of the two crises are different, exports contracted largely because of the decline in worldwide demand, an important growth predictor that has been identified in the trade literature as one of the most significant fundamental factors underlying exports. As shown in Tables 4.1 and 4.2, world trade fell more rapidly than output in varying degrees across nations. In the 2001 crisis, the growth rate of world GDP slowed to 1.77 per cent from 4.30 per cent in the previous year, while the exports in Japan and Taiwan fell by 16.87 per cent and 15.83 per cent, respectively. In the meantime, growth in the Chinese and European exports remained strong, reaching as high as 6.98 per cent and 1.42 per cent, respectively. In contrast, in the 2008 crisis world GDP fell 2.14 per cent from the previous year but exports fell more rapidly within a range of from 17.36 per cent to 28.61 per cent. With these observations and the distinct V-shaped patterns in exports, we suspect that exports may have fallen much more rapidly to an extent far exceeding what can be entirely attributed to the changes in fundamental factors. Thus, we have the following hypothesis:

*Hypothesis 1: During crisis, exports overshoot the deviation bands allowed by the long-run equilibrium relationship governed by the fundamental factors.*

In the two episodes of fast-falling export demand, the impacts were much greater in the 2008 crisis, for the contagion was more severe and truly global, leading to a much weaker global demand (Sun, 2009). The drying up of trade credit and traders' overreaction to a possible collapse in demand made the situation even more serious in the 2008 crisis (Athukorala and Kohpaiboon, 2009). However, a variety of economic stimulus packages were put in place in a timely manner to lessen the negative impact, thanks to the quick and coordinated responses from the world's governments in containing the spread and further worsening of the crisis. It is therefore reasonable to believe that exports would rebound more quickly in the 2008 crisis than in the 2001 crisis. And in fact they did, as observed in Figures 4.1 and 4.2. Thus, we have:

*Hypothesis 2: Although the degree of export contractions was much sharper in the 2008 crisis than in that of 2001, exports also bottomed out much quicker in 2008 than in 2001.*

Moreover, because industries were affected to varying degrees by the two crises and their recovery dynamics were also different, we examine how exports were impacted at the industry level by classifying a country's manufacturing industries into two groups, Group A and Group B, based on their industry characteristics. Group A consists of industries whose production activities tend to be capital- or technology-intensive in nature. Specifically, Group A includes chemicals, metals, electronics, machinery, electrical equipment, ICT (information, communications and technology), transportation, and precision instruments. The demand for Group A is highly income-elastic, and consumer spending on such products tends to follow the ebb and flow of the economy. Spending decreases during economic downturns and increases when the economy expands. Notice that developed countries are the major buyers of Group A. On the other hand, Group B, consisting of all remaining industries,[2] tends to be labor-intensive and of necessity in nature. While developing countries are the major consumers of Group B, developed countries may reduce their consumption as a result of an increase in income. With this in mind, we postulate:

*Hypothesis 3: Group A's capital- or technological-intensive exports tend to increase with the levels of OECD income, while Group B's labor-intensive exports tend to increase with the levels of non-OECD income.*

## 4.3 FDI, OUTSOURCING, INDUSTRY STRUCTURES AND TAIWAN'S EXPORTS

Over the last few decades, Taiwan has achieved miraculous growth and has since been roundly lauded for being one of the East Asian Tigers that also include South Korea, Hong Kong and Singapore. Its successful export-led economic growth model has been well documented and followed by many developing countries. But things appear to have changed over the course of the last decade. The average compound growth rate for Taiwan's exports for the period of 2000–07 was only 7.17 per cent, a marked slowdown from the growth rates of 12.87 per cent and 8.5 per cent achieved during the high growth periods of 1981–90 and 1990–2000. A rapid increase in the nation's outward direct investment (FDI) and the prevalence of export outsourcing practice by the Taiwanese exporters, as well as the nation's being excluded from the deepening regional economic integration process within Asia, may all contribute to a worsening of Taiwan's export performance.

From the 1980s onwards, Taiwan saw a wave of overseas investment expansion, with the United States and the Southeast Asian countries the major recipients of Taiwan's FDI.[3] But after the lifting of the ban on indirect investment in China by the Taiwanese government in the early 1990s, the vast majority of Taiwan's FDI flooded into China for reasons of low-cost labor and cultural proximity. In 1993, China became the largest recipient of Taiwan's FDI; and by 2005 China had already attracted more than half of Taiwan's accumulative outward investment over the decades.

Prior to 1995, almost all of Taiwan's export orders were processed locally and exported out of Taiwan directly. However, because of the rising labor and land costs at home, the Taiwanese firms gradually lost their competitive edge in labor-intensive goods. To regain competitiveness, many Taiwanese firms chose to relocate the production of their labor-intensive goods and low-end production processes to low-wage countries in Southeast Asia and China, while keeping under the control of the parent firms in Taiwan other activities such as R&D, upstream production, marketing and export order processing. Part of the export orders received was therefore filled by (or outsourced to) the parent firms' overseas affiliates and local firms in the third countries. As Taiwan's FDI started to multiply, the outsourcing ratio increased. Since this practice is limited mainly to export orders, it is referred to as export outsourcing, a term coined by Liu et al. (2007).

The increasing reliance on export outsourcing is evident in an ever shrinking proportion of export orders filled at home. Indeed, the proportion of orders filled by domestic sources had decreased over time, from 85.37 per cent in 2000 to 53.87 per cent in 2007. As a consequence, not only has Taiwan's export growth slowed down but its export structure has also shifted toward upstream industries over time.[4] Having upstream firms as the dominant type of firms in Taiwan may have important implications for Taiwan's increasing sensitivity to external shocks in exports.

Like those of other countries, Taiwan's exports exhibited a V-shaped pattern during the crisis period. For 8 months before the crisis broke, with the exception of July 2008 (only 7.9 per cent), the nation's exports had shown double-digit growth. But in September 2008 the situation was quickly reversed, and in just a short time the export markets deteriorated rapidly. The nation saw its export revenues fall almost by half in just 4 months. By January 2009, the contraction finally let up and the slide came to a stop at −44.1 per cent. While still posting in the red, the Taiwanese export sector gradually improved its position in the following months. And by November, export growth had turned positive for the first time since the crisis began, rising to 19.35 per cent. In terms of export orders, as the impacts of the crisis propagated through the economy, export orders showed a similar decline and fell to their lowest point in January 2009 at −41.67 per cent, after which the sharp decline in export orders also began to slow down.

From the foregoing discussion, it is clear that the fall in Taiwan's total exports was rather dramatic and larger in magnitude than the fall in its export orders. In effect, export growth recovered more slowly than export orders. By December 2009, when export orders had already bounced back to the pre-crisis level (102 per cent of December 2007), exports were only stabilizing around 15 per cent below their level in December 2007. This suggests that the Taiwanese exporters may have relied more on export outsourcing to weather the financial storm.

To sum up, there are notably differences in how Taiwan was affected by the 2008 crisis, compared with other countries' experiences (Table 4.3). The differences are summarized as follows: (1) In terms of the timing of experiencing negative growth since the crisis broke out, Taiwan was affected by the crisis much earlier than any other country in the group. Taiwan reported negative growth in exports in September 2008 but neither the European Union nor Singapore was affected until a month later; and for that matter, the United States, Japan and China did not begin to contract until November. (2) In terms of the degree of export contractions, Taiwan had the most severe decline among the countries in the group. Its growth rate of exports dropped to −44.1 per cent, the lowest point in 8 years, while Japan reported a comparable decline of −43.92 per cent 2 months later. The contractions were evidently far worse than those of United States (−26.33 per cent), South Korea (−34.53 per cent) and China (−26.34 per cent). (3) In terms of the timing of bottoming out, Taiwan started its recovery the earliest, after bottoming out in January 2009, while Japan's recovery did not begin until March. The rest of the group was on a slow track to recovery: notably, the export slide did not bottom out until April for the United States and European Union and until May for China and Malaysia.

In fact, the above-mentioned differences were also observed in Taiwan's export performance during the dot-com crisis, although in a somewhat less clear picture (Figures 4.1 and 4.2). Thus, we have:

*Hypothesis 4: Compared with the other countries in the group, Taiwan's export performance during the crisis periods is characterized by a quicker and sharper drop in exports. Nevertheless, its exports bounced back more quickly than those of the others in the group.*

## 4.4   EMPIRICAL MODEL AND RESULTS

To examine how exports adjust to shocks, we need to model their adjustment explicitly by introducing an a-priori long-run equilibrium

*Table 4.3  Variation in timing and duration of impacts across countries*

| | TWN | | USA | | EU | | JPN | | SGP | | KOR | |
|---|---|---|---|---|---|---|---|---|---|---|---|---|
| First recorded negative growth rate after crisis | Sep-2008 | −1.64% | Nov-2008 | −4.76% | Oct-2008 | −3.73% | Nov-2008 | −16.11% | Oct-2008 | −5.19% | Nov-2008 | −19.45% |
| Bottom out | Jan-2009 | −44.11% | Apr-2009 | −26.33% | Apr-2009 | −35.76% | Mar-2009 | −43.92% | Jan-2009 | −40.38% | Jan-2009 | −34.53% |
| First recorded positive growth rate after bottoming out | Nov-2009 | 19.35% | n.a. | n.a. | Nov-2009 | 14.35% | Nov-2009 | 1.83% | n.a. | n.a. | Nov-2009 | 18.14% |
| Compound growth rate, 2000–2008 | | 6.72% | | 6.46% | | 11.90% | | 6.32% | | 11.88% | | 11.85% |

| | CHN | | MYS | | THA | | IDN | | PHL | | VNM | |
|---|---|---|---|---|---|---|---|---|---|---|---|---|
| First recorded negative growth rate after crisis | Nov-2008 | -2.24% | Oct-2008 | -6.73% | Oct-2008 | -4.19% | Nov-2008 | -1.81% | Oct-2008 | -14.57% | Nov-2008 | -7.23% |
| Bottom out | May-2009 | -26.34% | May-2009 | -35.89% | Jan-2009 | -34.44% | Jan-2009 | -34.95% | Jan-2009 | -40.64% | Jul-2009 | -28.21% |
| First recorded positive growth rate after bottoming out | n.a. | n.a. | n.a. | n.a. | Nov-2009 | 19.53% | Oct-2009 | 13.46% | n.a. | n.a. | n.a. | n.a. |
| Compound growth rate, 2000–2008 | | 24.39% | | 9.29% | | 12.66% | | 10.39% | | 3.21% | | 19.77% |

*Note:*  n.a. = not available at time of writing.

*Source:*  *World Trade Atlas.*  Statistics were calculated using the monthly merchandise trade series.

79

relationship, with the hypothesis that there exists an error correction mechanism that makes the short-run deviations converge on a long-run trend. Therefore, modeling a long-run export performance in the context of adjustment to external shocks is inherently dynamic.

Assume export performance $E_{it}$ is affected by a set of fundamental factors and some global shocks, denoted as $Z_{it}$ and *Crisis*, respectively. Let the short-run relationship among $EX_{it}$, $Z_{it}$ and *Crisis* follow an autoregressive-distributed lag model:

$$EX_{it} = \alpha_0 + \alpha_1 Z_{i,t} + \alpha_2 Z_{it-1} + \alpha_3 EX_{it-1} + \alpha_4 Crisis_t + \varepsilon_{i,t}, \quad (4.1)$$

where $EX_{it}(i = 1, \ldots, N, t = 1, \ldots, T)$ is country $i$'s exports in log form at time $t$, $\alpha_0$ is the constant term, and $Z_{it}$ includes some fundamental variables for country $i$ at time $t$. *Crisis*, which includes *Crisis2001* and *Crisis2008*, is a period dummy used to capture the common shocks from the 2001 and 2008 crises. $\varepsilon_{it}(= v_i + u_{it})$ includes country-specific variables $v_i$ and the stochastic error term $u_{it}$, where the former is to reflect country-specific effect stemming from cross-country differences in endowment, technology, and so on.

Two problems may arise when using panel data regression techniques to determine the dynamic relationships between $EX_{it}$ and $Z_{it}$ as indicated in equation (4.1).[5] First, we run into the endogeneity problem caused by the difficulty of identifying the unobserved country-specific effects such as technological progress in a dynamic setting, in which case the right-hand-side variables are not orthogonal to each other. Second, the problem of persistence occurs because $EX_{it}$ and $Z_{it}$ tend to be highly persistent over time with their respective lagged values and are often jointly determined, which is often the case for economic research using time series of macroeconomic variables.[6]

An error correction model is therefore adopted, which can be used to solve for these two problems. Most importantly, it has the advantage of allowing us to examine the short-run and long-run dynamics of the relationship between $EX_{it}$ and $Z_{it}$, and this feature becomes very useful, especially in the context of examining how exports behave when an external shock is present.

$$\Delta EX_{it} = \alpha_1 \Delta Z_{it} + \eta ERROR_{it-1} + \alpha_4 Crisis_t + \varepsilon_{it}, \quad (4.2)$$

where $\Delta$ indicates first difference, $ERROR_{it-1}(= EX_{it-1} - \varphi_0 - \varphi_1 Z_{it-1})$ is the error correction term, $\varphi_0 = -\alpha_0/(1 - \alpha_3)$, $\varphi_1 = -(\alpha_1 + \alpha_2)/(1 - \alpha_3)$, and $\eta = -(1 - \alpha_3)$. In equation (4.2), $\Delta Z_{it}$ captures the short-run effects while $ERROR_{it-1}$ describes the long-run dynamics. Exports could deviate from the long-run equilibrium relationship owing to random shocks in the short run, but eventually converge to the equilibrium when shocks are absent. The error correction coefficient $\eta$, which is negative for such a convergence to occur, therefore measures the speed of adjustment toward the long-run equilibrium.

*Crisis* is used to see whether there exists excessive adjustment in exports that cannot be explained by the effects of short-run and long-run dynamics. If the coefficient of *Crisis* is significantly different from zero, then there exists the so-called 'export overshooting' phenomenon. We indicate the beginning of a crisis using the timing of export growth once it turns negative. That is, a crisis begins once negative export growth is present in any of the countries in our sample. For example in the 2001 crisis, Taiwan was the country whose exports fell earlier than those of the others, so the month when Taiwan's export growth first turned negative is defined as the starting month of the downturn, which was January 2001. The subsequent months of the crisis period are defined as follows: *Crisis2001* = 2 if February 2001, *Crisis2001* = 3 if March 2001, . . ., and *Crisis2001* = 18 if June 2002, when the US was the last country to resume positive growth in exports. By adding *Crisis* and its square term (*Crisis_SQ*), we are able to figure out, on average, how many months it took to reach the trough of the contraction in growth. *Crisis2008* can be similarly defined with the starting month as September 2008 (see Table 4.5).

The set of fundamental factors $Z_{it}$ affecting a country's export performance includes world demand, effective exchange rate, volatility of exchange rate, and FDI flows. Here, world GDP is used to measure world demand. As a larger world GDP is expected to boost a country's exports, we expect a positive relationship between the two variables. The effective exchange rates, which are trade-weight-based measures with weights being time-varying, are obtained from the Bank for International Settlements. Since the appreciation of a country's currency lowers the competitiveness of its exports, we expect the impact of an increase in *EER* on exports to be negative.

The volatility of effective exchange rate $\rho$ is used to capture the impact of exchange-rate uncertainty, where $\rho$ is constructed as the moving average of the deviation of *EER* from its mean over the last 12 months:

$$\rho = \left[ \frac{1}{12} \sum_{j=1}^{12} (EER_{t-j} - \overline{EER_t})^2 \right]^{0.5}. \tag{4.3}$$

Theoretically, the impact of exchange rate volatility on exports may be positive or negative depending on the assumption made with respect to risk preference (De Grauwe, 1988). For risk-averse exporters, higher exchange rate volatility increases the extent of uncertainty and thus negatively impacts exports. On the contrary, for those who are risk-loving, higher exchange rate volatility is often associated with higher exports. Moreover, when exports are considered as an option by exporters, exports may increase with exchange rate volatility (Boug and Fagereng, 2010). Since exporters may be able to reduce or hedge against exchange rate uncertainty, the linkage between exchange rate volatility and exports may be insignificant (Solakoglu, 2008).

*FDI* is another factor affecting exports. Whether or not *FDI* contributes to the export performance depends on the motive of *FDI*. Tariff-jumping *FDI*, which aims at a host market, may not help the host country to expand exports. Export-oriented *FDI*, on the other hand, uses a host country as an export platform and may contribute to the exports of host countries. Since aggregate *FDI* is used, of which motivations cannot be identified, we have no prior expectation of the sign of *FDI*.

To see whether Taiwan has experienced a much deeper impact as compared with other countries, the interactions of a Taiwan dummy with the two crisis variables are included (i.e., *TW\*Crisis2001* and *TW\*Crisis2008*). Also, several square terms (2001*Crisis_SQ*, 2008*Crisis_SQ*, *TW\*Crisis2001_SQ* and *TW\*Crisis2008_SQ*) are added in the regressions to capture the V-shaped nature of the impacts.

We first run the long-run regression $EX_{it} = \phi_0 + \phi_1 Z_{it} + \varepsilon_{it}$ to derive the error correction term ($ERROR_{it-1} = EX_{it-1} - (\hat{\phi}_0 + \hat{\phi}_1 Z_{it-1})$), which is then used to run regression (4.2). The definition and descriptive statistics of the variables are summarized in Table 4.4, while the error correction model results for regression (4.2) are reported in Table 4.5. Three regression results are provided: specification (1) reports the results for the full sample (the Group 11); specifications (2) and (3) summarize the results for Group A and Group B.

**Results for the Full Sample**

Table 4.5 shows that the world GDP and FDI inflows have positive effects, which conform to our expectation. The volatility of effective exchange rates, which has mixed results in the literature (De Grauwe, 1988), is shown to have a positive impact on exports. The real effective exchange rate *EER* is insignificant in the full sample. The error correction term *ERROR* is negative and statistically significant, suggesting that there exists a long-run relationship between export performance *EX* and fundamental factors *Z*, and that the gap between *EX* and those explained by *Z* can be closed through the error correction mechanism. The speed of the short-run correction η is −0.16, indicating that, on average, about 16 per cent of the gap is corrected in each month.

*Table 4.4    Variable statistics and definition – full sample*

| Variables | Definition | Mean | Standard deviation |
|---|---|---|---|
| *EX* | Monthly exports, in log | 9.90 | 1.08 |
| *EX_A* | Monthly exports for Group A, in log; including chemical, metals, electronics, machinery, electrical equipment, ICT (information, communications and technology), transportation, and precision instruments | 9.41 | 1.20 |
| EX_B | Monthly exports for Group B, in log; including textiles, apparel, plywood product, paper, furniture, rubbers and plastics, metal products, nonmetal products, basic metal, printing, chemical materials, chemical products, and petroleum | 8.77 | 1.11 |
| *GDP_world* | World GDP, quarterly, in log | 10.70 | 0.08 |
| *GDP_oecd* | OECD GDP, quarterly, in log | 10.46 | 0.06 |
| *GDP_xoecd* | Non-OECD GDP, quarterly, in log | 9.16 | 0.18 |
| $\rho$ | Volatility of effective exchange rate, in log | −3.47 | 0.58 |
| *EER* | Effective exchange rate, in log | 4.62 | 0.10 |
| *FDI* | Cumulative inward direct investment ($10^6$ billions) | 0.068 | 0.147 |
| *Crisis2001* | $= i$, if the $i$th month of 2001; $= 12+j$, if the $j$th month of 2002, $j = 1, 2, \ldots, 6$; $= 0$ otherwise | 1.54 | 4.08 |
| *Crisis2001_SQ* | Square term of *Crisis2001* | 18.97 | 59.43 |
| *Crisis2008* | $= 1$, if 9/2008; $= 2$, if 10/2008; $= 3$, if 11/2008; $= 4$, if 12/2008; $= 4 + i$, if the $i$th month of 2009; $= 0$, otherwise | 1.11 | 3.17 |
| *Crisis2008_SQ* | Square term of *Crisis2008* | 11.25 | 37.70 |
| *TW\*Crisis2001* | Cross term of Taiwan dummy and *Crisis2001* | 0.15 | 1.37 |
| *TW\*Crisis2001_SQ* | Square term of *TW\*Crisis2001* | 1.90 | 19.64 |
| *TW\*Crisis2008* | Cross term of Taiwan dummy and *Crisis2008* | 0.11 | 1.05 |
| *TW\*Crisis2008_SQ* | Square term of *TW\*Crisis2008* | 1.12 | 12.62 |

*Table 4.5   Error correction model*

| Dependent variable: $\Delta EX$ | Full sample (1) | | Group A (2) | | Group B (3) | |
|---|---|---|---|---|---|---|
| | Coeff. | Standard error | Coeff. | Standard error | Coeff. | Standard error |
| *ERROR* Correction | −0.16 | (0.01)*** | −0.16 | (0.01)*** | −0.37 | (0.02)*** |
| $\Delta GDP\_world$ | 1.18 | (0.35)*** | 2.04 | (0.48)*** | −0.13 | (0.57) |
| $\Delta EER\_volatility/100$ | 0.78 | (0.37)** | 0.17 | (0.50) | 0.02 | (0.61)*** |
| $\Delta EER$ | 0.006 | (0.03) | −0.08 | (0.04)** | 0.24 | (0.05)*** |
| $\Delta FDI$ | 0.12 | (0.04)*** | 0.06 | (0.05) | 0.20 | (0.06)*** |
| *Crisis2001* | −0.05 | (0.003)*** | −0.05 | (0.004)*** | −0.04 | (0.004)*** |
| *Crisis2001_SQ*/100 | 0.28 | (0.02)*** | 0.30 | (0.02)*** | 0.20 | (0.03)*** |
| *Crisis2008* | −0.10 | (0.007)*** | −0.09 | (0.009)*** | −0.12 | (0.01)*** |
| *Crisis2008_SQ*/100 | 0.67 | (0.04)*** | 0.57 | (0.06)*** | 0.76 | (0.07)*** |
| *TW\*Crisis2001* | −0.02 | (0.01)** | −0.02 | (0.01)** | −0.0001 | (0.01) |
| *TW\*Crisis2001_SQ*/100 | 0.12 | (0.05)** | 0.13 | (0.06)** | 0.03 | (0.08) |
| *TW\*Crisis2008* | −0.03 | (0.01)*** | −0.05 | (0.01)*** | −0.01 | (0.01) |
| *TW\*Crisis2008_SQ*/100 | 0.29 | (0.07)*** | 0.37 | (0.10)*** | 0.07 | (0.12) |
| Constant | 0.11 | (0.01)*** | 0.07 | (0.02)*** | −0.16 | (0.02)*** |
| *R*-square: within | 0.8178 | | 0.7007 | | 0.6624 | |
| *R*-square: between | 0.0850 | | 0.0662 | | 0.0008 | |
| *R*-square: overall | 0.2900 | | 0.1916 | | 0.0969 | |
| No. of observations | 1172 | | 1172 | | 1172 | |
| No. of countries | 11 | | 11 | | 11 | |

The signs of *2001Crisis* and *2008Crisis* are negative but the signs of their square terms are positive, indicating that there exist remarkable effects of the two crises on exports, manifested in striking V-shaped growth patterns. This supports Hypothesis 1 that exports had contracted excessively during the economic downturns such that shrinkage in world demand and changes in other fundamental factors were insufficient to explain the fluctuations in exports. The V-shaped pattern, moreover, is significantly deeper and narrower in the 2008 crisis than in the 2001 crisis for the full sample. That is to say, not only did exports contract more rapidly but they rebounded more quickly in the 2008 crisis. The numbers of months it took for the economic crises to bottom out were 9.59 and 7.89 months for the 2001 crisis and 2008 crisis, respectively (see Table 4.8). This supports Hypothesis 2 as discussed in Section 4.2.

Table 4.5 also shows that Taiwan was badly hit by the two economic crises in the sense that the extent of export contraction was larger for Taiwan than for other countries, but its exports also bounced back more quickly than other countries, which is consistent with Hypothesis 4 discussed in Section 4.3. The numbers of months it took for Taiwan's exports to bottom out were 8.75 and 7.33 months for the 2001 crisis and the 2008 crisis, respectively.

**Results for Group A and Group B**

When the sample is divided into two groups, Group A and Group B, the results are somewhat different. World GDP has no significant impact on the exports of Group B, which tends to be of necessity in nature. The real effective exchange rate *EER*, which is insignificant in the full sample, turns out to be negative for Group A but positive for Group B. This suggests that Group A may be more sensitive to price competition than Group B, and the depreciation of *EER* is effective in expanding the exports of Group A.

The adjustment speed η associated with the error correction term is also different across different industry groups; it is much faster for Group B (−0.37) than for Group A (−0.16). This implies that Group B is more stable than Group A in its export trend, which is consistent with the fact that Group A is highly income-elastic and tends to have large oscillations around the trend.

While the exports were hit harder for Group A than for Group B in the 2001 crisis, the opposite is true in the 2008 crisis. This may be due to the fact that the financial crisis was more widespread such that it affected almost every country in the world. In both crises, however, Group A bottomed out more quickly than Group B. Comparing (2) and (3) in Table 4.6 shows that Taiwan, while harder hit than other countries for Group A in both crises, is not significantly different from the rest for Group B.

For the robust check, we divide the full sample into two subsamples, the Asian countries (Table 4.6) and the developed countries (Table 4.7).[7] The results are qualitatively the same in terms of the signs of impact, except *Crisis2001*. It shows that within the group of the Asian countries Taiwan's export contraction in the 2001 crisis is no different from the others. The number of months it took for the export contraction to bottom out for the two subsamples as well as the full sample is summarized in Table 4.8.

To see how demand from OECD and non-OECD countries affects the export performance of Group A and Group B, we also run regressions using OECD GDP and non-OECD GDP in place of world GDP. The results for the Asian sample are reported in Table 4.9. It shows that the demands from OECD and non-OECD countries affect the export performance of each group in a different manner. For Group A, whose output

*Table 4.6    Error correction model – Asian countries*

| | Full sample (1) | | Group A (2) | | Group B (3) | |
|---|---|---|---|---|---|---|
| | Coeff. | Standard error | Coeff. | Standard error | Coeff. | Standard error |
| *ERROR* Correction | −0.19 | (0.02)*** | −0.18 | (0.02)*** | −0.42 | (0.03)*** |
| $\Delta GDP\_world$ | 1.81 | (0.43)*** | 3.00 | (0.61)*** | −0.39 | (0.75) |
| $\Delta EER\_volatility$ | 0.01 | (0.005)** | 0.01 | (0.01) | 0.01 | (0.01) |
| $\Delta EER$ | −0.13 | (0.04)*** | −0.27 | (0.06)*** | 0.21 | (0.07)*** |
| $\Delta FDI$ | −0.17 | (0.39) | −0.90 | (0.56) | 0.12 | (0.66)* |
| *Crisis2001* | −0.06 | (0.003)*** | −0.06 | (0.004)*** | −0.05 | (0.01)*** |
| *Crisis2001_SQ*/100 | 0.31 | (0.02)*** | 0.34 | (0.03)*** | 0.20 | (0.04)*** |
| *Crisis2008* | −0.10 | (0.01)*** | −0.07 | (0.01)*** | −0.12 | (0.01)*** |
| *Crisis2008_SQ*/100 | 0.63 | (0.05)*** | 0.54 | (0.08)*** | 0.76 | (0.10)*** |
| *TW\*Crisis2001* | −0.01 | (0.01) | −0.01 | (0.01) | 0.006 | (0.01) |
| *TW\*Crisis2001_SQ*/100 | 0.07 | (0.05) | 0.06 | (0.07) | 0.004 | (0.09) |
| *TW\*Crisis2008* | −0.03 | (0.01)*** | −0.04 | (0.01)*** | −0.02 | (0.02) |
| *TW\*Crisis2008_SQ*/100 | 0.26 | (0.08)*** | 0.31 | (0.11)*** | 0.14 | (0.14) |
| Constant | 0.10 | (0.04)** | 0.54 | (0.02)*** | 0.18 | (0.03)*** |
| *R*-square: within | 0.8170 | | 0.6843 | | 0.6451 | |
| *R*-square: between | 0.6003 | | 0.3309 | | 0.0482 | |
| *R*-square: overall | 0.3014 | | 0.1879 | | 0.1295 | |
| No. of observations | 851 | | 851 | | 851 | |
| No. of countries | 8 | | 8 | | 8 | |

tends to be more sophisticated and highly income-elastic, OECD demand has a positive impact on the export growth of Asian countries, while non-OECD demand has a negative impact. For Group B, whose output tends to be more labor-intensive and of necessity in nature, the opposite is true; that is, non-OECD demand matters to the export performance of Group B. The results are consistent with the fact that developed countries tend to be big buyers of Group A's output while developing countries are the major consumers of Group B's.

## 4.5   SOME POSSIBLE EXPLANATIONS

Why did the export contraction significantly overshoot its long-run trend when an economic crisis occurred? Why did exports fall much deeper

*Table 4.7    Error correction model – developed countries*

| | Full sample (1) | | Group A (2) | | Group B (3) | |
|---|---|---|---|---|---|---|
| | Coeff. | Stand-ard error | Coeff. | Stand-ard error | Coeff. | Stand-ard error |
| *ERROR Correction* | −0.20 | (0.04)*** | −0.22 | (0.04)*** | −0.27 | (0.04)*** |
| $\Delta GDP\_world$ | 1.08 | (0.55)** | 1.69 | (0.59)*** | 0.74 | (0.53) |
| $\Delta EER\_volatility/100$ | 0.34 | (0.54) | −0.64 | (0.58) | 0.03 | (0.52)*** |
| $\Delta EER$ | 0.38 | (0.06)*** | 0.43 | (0.06)*** | 0.30 | (0.05)*** |
| $\Delta FDI$ | 0.14 | (0.03)*** | 0.09 | (0.034)*** | 0.19 | (0.03)*** |
| *Crisis2001* | −0.04 | (0.004)*** | −0.04 | (0.005)*** | −0.04 | (0.004)*** |
| *Crisis2001_SQ/100* | 0.22 | (0.03)*** | 0.20 | (0.03)*** | 0.18 | (0.03)*** |
| *Crisis2008* | −0.11 | (0.01)*** | −0.10 | (0.01)*** | −0.12 | (0.01)*** |
| *Crisis2008_SQ/100* | 0.70 | (0.07)*** | 0.62 | (0.07)*** | 0.77 | (0.06)*** |
| Constant | 0.09 | (0.02)*** | 0.06 | (0.02)*** | 0.36 | (0.04)*** |
| *R*-square: within | 0.8606 | | 0.8480 | | 0.8499 | |
| *R*-square: between | 0.8004 | | 0.3639 | | 0.3543 | |
| *R*-square: overall | 0.6576 | | 0.7850 | | 0.7848 | |
| No. of observations | 321 | | 321 | | 321 | |
| No. of countries | 3 | | 3 | | 3 | |

*Table 4.8    Number of months to bottom out*

| | Full sample | Group A | Group B |
|---|---|---|---|
| Full sample | | | |
| *Crisis2001* | 9.59 | 9.14 | 11.15 |
| *Crisis2008* | 7.89 | 7.68 | 7.96 |
| *TW*2001Crisis* | 8.75 | 8.49 | – |
| *TW* Crisis2008* | 7.33 | 7.10 | – |
| Asian countries | | | |
| *Crisis2001* | 9.34 | 8.73 | 11.63 |
| *Crisis2008* | 7.71 | 7.24 | 8.11 |
| *TW*2001Crisis* | 9.34 | – | – |
| *TW* Crisis2008* | 7.71 | 7.13 | – |
| Developed countries | | | |
| *Crisis2001* | 10.06 | 10.19 | 10.14 |
| *Crisis2008* | 7.97 | 8.01 | 7.79 |

*Note:*    Asian sample includes China, Indonesia, Korea, Malaysia, Philippines, Singapore, Taiwan and Thailand.

*Table 4.9　Error correction model – Asian countries*

| | Group A (1) | | Group B (2) | |
|---|---|---|---|---|
| | Coeff. | Standard error | Coeff. | Standard error |
| *ERROR Correction* | −0.178 | (0.02)*** | −0.41 | (0.03)*** |
| *ΔGDP_oecd* | 5.03 | (0.77) *** | −6.47 | (0.93)*** |
| *ΔGDP_xoecd* | −1.36 | (0.49)*** | 4.17 | (0.59) *** |
| *ΔEER_volatility*/100 | 1.22 | (0.68)* | 0.70 | (0.82) |
| *ΔEER* | −0.27 | (0.06)*** | 0.17 | (0.07)*** |
| *ΔFDI* | −0.97 | (0.56) * | 0.69 | (0.646) |
| *Crisis2001* | −0.06 | (0.005)*** | −0.03 | (0.01)*** |
| *Crisis2001_SQ*/100 | 0.36 | (0.03)*** | 0.13 | (0.03)*** |
| *Crisis2008* | −0.06 | (0.01)*** | −0.17 | (0.01)*** |
| *Crisis2008_SQ*/100 | 0.45 | (0.08)*** | 1.06 | (0.10)*** |
| *TW*Crisis2001* | −0.01 | (0.01) | 0.006 | (0.01) |
| *TW*Crisis2001_SQ*/100 | 0.06 | (0.07) | 0.007 | (0.09) |
| *TW*Crisis2008* | −0.04 | (0.01)*** | −0.02 | (0.02) |
| *TW*Crisis2008_SQ*/100 | 0.31 | (0.11)*** | 0.14 | (0.14) |
| Constant | 0.12 | (0.03)*** | 0.03 | (0.03) |
| *R*-square: within | 0.6862 | | 0.6711 | |
| *R*-square: between | 0.2963 | | 0.0484 | |
| *R*-square: overall | 0.2259 | | 0.1420 | |
| No. of observations | 851 | | 851 | |
| No. of countries | 8 | | 8 | |

and yet bounce back much more quickly in the crisis of 2008 than that of 2001? What made Taiwan's exports so susceptible to economic crises, to appear more so in 2008 when compared with other countries? All these observations may very well be explained by the so-called Forrester effect on demand variability, a phenomenon well known in the optimization of supply chain and inventory control systems.

The Forrester effect suggests that demand variability increases as one moves up a supply chain. It is a feedback mechanism set forth by external shocks to the supply chain where small fluctuations in demand at the retailer end are dramatically amplified as they proceed up the chain. Such an effect may be caused by the demand forecast updating that reflects not only the need to replenish the stocks to meet the requirements for future demands but also the need for safety stocks which are considered necessary because of the large demand uncertainty and fluctuation (Lee et al., 1997). As a result, the readjustment of demand forecast by the upstream manager is often greater than the change of demand in the downstream. Similarly, periodic ordering (which makes suppliers face a highly erratic stream of orders), special sales promotion (which triggers irregular buying pattern of customers) and rationing (which occurs when demands exceed supply) may all distort demand information (Lee et al., 1997). Inaccuracies and volatility of orders from the retailer to the primary suppliers therefore cause relatively greater readjustments at each point in the chain. Apparently, the amount of safety stock contributes significantly to the Forrester effect. As in the visual metaphor of cracking a bullwhip, demand in the chain fluctuates in a continuous and long-lasting oscillatory movement upstream; it is therefore also labeled the bullwhip effect.

To make things clear, consider a 10 per cent drop in retail sales. In order to deplete the surplus stocks and reduce inventory, given that there is now a weaker sales outlook, orders placed by retailers to wholesalers one step upstream in the chain will thus decrease by more than 10 per cent, say 15 per cent. The decrease in demand amplifies and propagates through the chain as upstream firms react in much the same way as downstream firms do, trying to adjust their stock level and empty the pipeline. Hence the longer the chain is, the more pronounced the upstream demand amplification (or the larger the oscillatory movement) will become. This will result in an even greater decrease, say 20 per cent, in purchase orders to the suppliers further upstream in our example.

The 'export overshooting' phenomenon as seen in the 2001 and 2008 crises, in essence, captures the bullwhip effect. While the real world GDP fell only mildly to 1.77 per cent and −2.12 per cent in 2001 and 2009, exporting countries, constituting the upper stream end of the global supply chain, had experienced a much greater fall in exports (−6.21 per cent and −25.68 per cent, respectively). Apparently, the overcorrection of the demand forecast by every entity in the global supply chain was indeed the force at work that caused manufacturing exports to fall more than the decline in demand at the retailer end of the chain. When the economy recovered, the bullwhip effect also worked in much the same way but in the opposite direction; exports bounced back by a much larger extent than the actual increase in demand as every entity in the supply chain increased its safety stocks to meet unexpected increase in future demand. This can be observed from the 2001 crisis. When world demand recovered, even though world GDP only grew slightly, from 1.77 per cent in 2001 to 2.07 per cent in 2002 and 2.67 per cent in 2003, the exports of our sample of countries had already grown at an astonishing rate of 4.46 per cent and 15.06 per cent, correspondingly. Indeed, the 'export overshooting' phenomenon can therefore be regarded as the magnified version of the bullwhip effect at work, caused by worldwide economic crisis.

Generally, when production becomes more specialized vertically around the world, the length of a supply chain increases, and so does the bullwhip effect (or the extent of overshooting). As already discussed earlier, the bullwhip effect causes modest changes at one end of the chain to be magnified with a fast-cascading impact when they reach the other end. This means literally that the longer the supply chain, the larger the demand swings for the upstream end of the chain. Therefore, as the degree of cross-border vertical specialization increases over time, the demand variability is also increased in an elongated chain, thus enhancing the global supply system's tendency to overcorrect. This helps explain why the overshooting phenomenon was more pronounced in the 2008 crisis than in the 2001 crisis. The findings from Vlasenko (2009) that firms' inventory levels were deteriorating quickly in the 2008 crisis at a faster speed than the average rate in the previous recessions provide some evidence of overcorrection in the supply system. This in turn, we believe, led to an increase in the extent of overshooting (the bullwhip effect), supporting our argument that the recent financial crisis was worse than the previous crisis in terms of the rate of decline in world exports.

Compared with the other Asian countries, Taiwan's export sector is the most vulnerable to such debilitating effects. This is due mostly to a persistent large FDI outflow from the country and as the practice of export outsourcing becomes a standard among Taiwanese firms. Firms that receive international orders subcontract the downstream or labor-intensive assembly processes to overseas Taiwanese firms or firms that are based in a third country. Such process enables these Taiwanese parent firms to concentrate on the manufacture of the upstream intermediate inputs. As a matter of fact, upstream component makers and suppliers now make up a major part of Taiwan's export sector. This structural change has an unintended consequence of exposing Taiwan further to the risks of the bullwhip effect during crisis periods. To put it another way, there is sufficient reason to believe that the bullwhip effect is much enhanced in Taiwan's case, largely as a result of an increasing export outsourcing ratio signaling a process of increased vertical specialization across the border and the positioning of the Taiwanese parent firms as the upstream primary suppliers in an elongated global supply chain.

In addition to the bullwhip effect, Taiwan's export performance is also highly influenced by the type of products it exports. More than 70 per cent of the nation's exports are highly income-elastic and see greater sales volatility when wealth effects become large enough to affect consumption during times of economic upheaval. It is important also to note that not only are these high-tech exports more capital-intensive but they also have a rather sophisticated manufacturing process. This means that compared with labor-intensive manufacture, the supply chain is relatively longer and the exports are therefore more susceptible to the bullwhip effect. A mixture of these factors, as we have seen, contributed to the faster decline in Taiwan's exports as compared with other countries.

## 4.6   CONCLUDING REMARKS

This chapter provides some evidence of the 'export overshooting' phenomenon, i.e. the unusually large deviation of exports from their long-run level. We show that export overshooting occurred in the 2001 and 2008 economic crises. In fact, it prevailed in all of the eleven countries in our sample that represent different income groups: developed countries, Asian NICs, and emerging market countries. All of them experienced an excessive fall in exports. Moreover, the extent of overshooting is shown to have been more severe in Taiwan than in other countries. And it was also more severe in those industries with high income elasticity of demand.

We argue that the bullwhip effect was indeed the driving force behind the 'export overshooting' phenomenon. Because of the overcorrection in demand forecast by every entity of the supply chain, exporting countries, which were at the upstream end of the supply chain, faced a much greater demand oscillation than the demand at the retailer end. As a result, exports fell more than demand at the retail end; but when the economy recovered exports also bounced back by a larger extent than the change in final demand. The export overshooting phenomenon discussed in this chapter may therefore be regarded as a magnified version of the bullwhip effect in world exports, which was triggered by the large negative aggregate demand shocks resulting from the global economic crises.

As production becomes more vertically specialized across countries over time, the supply chain becomes longer accordingly. This helps explain why the extent of overshooting was greater in the 2008 crisis than in the 2001 crisis. And while vertical disintegration of production can also be used to explain the export overshooting phenomena of Taiwan, it alone is insufficient to explain why Taiwan was more susceptible to economic crisis than other Asian countries. It is argued in this chapter that the common practice of export outsourcing has caused Taiwan's production bases to shift towards the upstream end of the supply chain. Such structural shift exposes Taiwan further to the risks of rapid and large demand variability. Moreover, as Taiwan geared towards more high-tech export manufacturing activities for which demand is highly income-elastic, its sensitivity to demand shocks and business cycles also increased.

## NOTES

1. The author would like to thank Yalin Alice Chiang for her excellent research assistance.
2. They are textiles, apparel, plywood products, paper, furniture, rubbers and plastics, metal products, nonmetal products, basic metal, printing, chemical materials, chemical products, and petroleum.
3. By 1990, the United States and the Southeast Asian countries accounted for 43.5 per cent and 35.03 per cent of Taiwan's accumulative FDI, respectively.
4. According to Liu and Lu (2007), more than 80 per cent of Taiwan's export outsourcing was done in China, while the remainder was distributed among countries in Southeast Asia and in other regions. And in order to effectively manage and control overseas production and export activities, a large part of the export outsourcing activity (close to 80 per cent) was carried out by subsidiaries and affiliate firms in the host country. This is distinctly different from the outsourcing practice used by the Western MNEs, which employ mostly local firms or foreign firms in the host country.
5. See Yasar et al. (2006).
6. The Durbin–Watson statistic, which is 0.35 for regression (4.1), suggests the existence of autocorrelation.
7. Developed countries are the US, EU and Japan, and the remaining eight are collected under the 'Asian countries'.

## REFERENCES

Authukorala, P.C. and A. Kohpaiboon (2009), 'Intra-Regional Trade in East Asia: The Decoupling Fallacy, Crisis, and Policy Challenges,' ADB Institute Working Paper no. 177.

Boug, P. and A. Fagereng (2010), 'Exchange Rate Volatility and Export Performance: A Cointegrated VAR Approach,' *Applied Economics*, **42** (7), 851–64.

De Grauwe, P. (1988), 'Exchange Rate Volatility and the Slowdown in Growth of International Trade,' IMF Staff Papers no. 35, 63–84.

Hu, S.C. (2011), 'Global Financial Crisis: Lessons for Taiwan,' in D. Shaw and B.J. Liu (eds), *The Impact of the Economic Crisis on East Asia*, Cheltenham, UK: Edward Elgar Publishing.

Lee, H.L., V. Padmanabhan and S. Whang (1997), 'The Bullwhip Effects in Supply Chains,' *Sloan Management Review*, **38** (3), 93–102.

Lin, J.Y. (2008), 'The Impact of Financial Crisis on Developing Countries', Korea Development Institute, Seoul, at: http://siteresources.worldbank.org/ROMANIAEXTN/Resources/Oct_31_JustinLin_KDI_remarks.pdf

Liu, B.J. and A. Lu (2007), 'The Economic Impact of Export Outsourcing and Policy Implication,' Research Report, Council for Economic Planning and Development, Taipei: Executive Yuan, ROC.

Liu, B.J., A. Lu and A.C. Tung (2007), 'Export Outsourcing: Cost Disadvantage and Reputation Advantage,' in P.A. Yotopoulos and D. Romano (eds), *The Asymmetries of Globalization*, London: Routledge, pp. 108–25.

Sapir, A. and Kh. Sekkat (1995), 'Exchange Rate Regimes and Trade Prices: Does the EMS Matter?' *Journal of International Economics*, **30**, 75–95.

Solakoglu, M.N., E.G. Solakoglu and T. Demirag (2008), 'Exchange Rate Volatility and Exports: A Firm-Level Analysis,' *Applied Economics*, **40**, 921–9.

Sun, M. (2009), 'China: Unscathed through the Global Financial Tsunami,' *China & World Economy*, **17** (6), 24–42.

Valliere, D. and R. Peterson (2004), 'Inflating the Bubble: Examining Dot-Com Investor Behavior,' *Venture Capital*, **6** (1), 1–22.

Vlasenko, P. (2009), 'Have Firms Become Better Equipped to Handle Recession?' American Institute for Economic Research, at: http://www.aier.org/research/briefs/1366-have-firms-become-better-equipped-to-handle-recessions

Yasar, M., C. Nelson and R. Rejesus (2006), 'The Dynamics of Exports and Productivity at the Plant Level: A Panel Data Error Correction Model (ECM) Approach,' in B. Baltagi (ed.), *Panel Data Econometrics: Theoretical Contributions and Empirical Applications*, Amsterdam: Elsevier.

Zhang, K.H. and S. Song (2000), 'Promoting Exports: The Role of Inward FDI in China,' *China Economic Review*, **11**, 385–96.

# 5. The impact of the global financial crisis on the Taiwanese economy and its industrial policy in response

**Jiann-Chyuan Wang and Chia-Hui Lin**

## 5.1 INTRODUCTION

The subprime mortgage crisis in the US was the prelude to a financial and economic crisis the effects of which have been felt all around the world; countries in Europe and the Americas whose financial sectors had been highly internationalized and whose economies were closely linked to the US were particularly badly affected. As the level of financial internationalization in Taiwan is still relatively low, the extent of asset destruction in Taiwan was limited. However, the Taiwanese economy is heavily dependent on exports, and the destruction of wealth in Europe and North America led to reduced demand for imports, which had a severe impact on Taiwan's export performance.

The financial crisis revealed a number of weaknesses in Taiwan's industrial structure and the structure of its foreign trade. The fall in the purchasing power of American consumers had an indirect impact on Taiwan's exports. In the first quarter of 2009, exports fell by over 30 per cent. When to this are added the effects of weak domestic demand, Taiwan's first-quarter economic growth rate was an unimpressive −8 per cent. The question of how the Taiwanese economy has coped with the recent crisis, and how Taiwan can upgrade and transform its industries so as to protect itself from the impact of a similar impact in the future, is an important one.

Under such circumstance, the purpose of this chapter is to analyze the impacts of global financial crisis on Taiwan's industrial structure and overall economy, and explore the industrial policy adopted by the Taiwanese government in response. It is expected that at a later point Taiwan will be able to accelerate its industrial upgrading and create competitive strength.

The chapter is divided into four sections. Following on from this Introduction, Section 2 analyses the impact of the global financial crisis on

Taiwanese trade and industrial structure. Section 3 describes the medium- and long-term strategies that Taiwan has adopted in response to the financial crisis. The final section presents the conclusions and recommendations.

## 5.2 THE IMPACT OF THE GLOBAL FINANCIAL CRISIS ON TAIWAN'S INDUSTRIAL STRUCTURE AND OVERALL ECONOMY

The recent global financial crisis has had a serious impact on Europe and the US, causing their economies to contract and their purchasing power to shrink. Europe and North America are the main export markets for Taiwanese industry, so Taiwan has also been severely affected by the crisis. The manufacturing sector accounts for by far the bulk of Taiwan's exports, and the impact here has been especially pronounced. The largest share of Taiwan's fixed capital investment is concentrated in the IT and electronics industry; this sector's export performance has been severely affected by the worsening of the global economic climate, and manufacturers have responded by cutting back on capital expenditure.

The impact of the global economic downturn has also spread upwards through the value chain to gradually affect the shipment performance of manufacturers of large-sized LCD panel, memory, and PC components. Several cyclical industries that had been expanding vigorously before the crisis – including the chemicals and plastics industry, the iron and steel industry, the cement industry, the shipping industry etc. – have also felt the effects of the global economic downturn.

The banking and insurance industries were the 'epicenter' of the financial crisis. As might be expected, the asset management business and the mutual fund business, which had been growing rapidly in recent years, both contracted. Falls in the value of overseas assets, the need to make increased provision for bad debt, and the reduction in the interest rate spread between deposits and loans, will all have had an impact on earnings in the banking and insurance industry. With business falling off, the relevant departments have been shedding staff. However, the impact of the global financial crisis on Taiwan's financial sector has been mitigated to some extent by Taiwan's relatively low level of financial internationalization.

What with the impact of layoffs and pay cuts, negative growth in real wages, falling house prices and dramatic fluctuations in the stock market, Taiwanese consumers have seen a dramatic contraction in their personal wealth. Consumer spending has fallen as a result, leading to low growth rates in the commercial sector.

The effects of the financial crisis have thrown into sharp relief the

*Table 5.1   Taiwan's economic contribution rate by individual industries*

|  | All industries | Agriculture | Manu-facturing and Mining | Manu-facturing | Information industry | Service industries |
|---|---|---|---|---|---|---|
| Real GDP growth rate (%) | | | | | | |
| 2003 | 3.50 | −0.06 | 4.00 | 5.34 | 9.58 | 3.39 |
| 2004 | 6.15 | −4.09 | 8.94 | 9.74 | 14.51 | 5.28 |
| 2005 | 4.16 | −8.07 | 6.34 | 6.96 | 17.95 | 3.53 |
| 2006 | 4.89 | 6.09 | 7.04 | 7.51 | 18.10 | 3.93 |
| 2007 | 5.72 | −2.91 | 9.31 | 10.29 | 19.17 | 4.30 |
| Growth contribution (%) = Industry's real GDP growth rate (current year) × That industry's share of real GDP (previous year) | | | | | | |
| 2003 | 3.50 | 0.00 | 1.13 | 1.26 | 0.73 | 2.37 |
| 2004 | 6.15 | −0.07 | −2.54 | 2.34 | 1.18 | 3.68 |
| 2005 | 4.16 | −0.13 | 1.85 | 1.73 | 1.57 | 2.44 |
| 2006 | 4.89 | 0.09 | 2.10 | 1.92 | 1.79 | 2.70 |
| 2007 | 5.72 | −0.04 | 2.83 | 2.70 | 2.14 | 2.93 |
| Growth contribution rate (%) = Industry's growth contribution/Growth contribution by all industries | | | | | | |
| 2003 | 100 | 0.00 | 32.29 | 36.00 | 20.86 | 67.71 |
| 2004 | 100 | −1.14 | 41.30 | 38.05 | 19.19 | 59.84 |
| 2005 | 100 | −3.13 | 44.47 | 41.59 | 37.74 | 58.65 |
| 2006 | 100 | 1.84 | 42.94 | 39.26 | 36.61 | 55.21 |
| 2007 | 100 | −0.70 | 49.48 | 47.20 | 37.41 | 51.22 |

*Source:*   Directorate-General of Budget, Accounting and Statistics, Executive Yuan, ROC.

excessive concentration of Taiwan's exports in a handful of industries and the overall weakness of the industrial structure. The main imbalances in Taiwan's industrial structure can be outlined as follows (Wang and Wei, 2009):

First, Taiwan is excessively dependent on the electronics and IT sector. The information and communications technology (ICT) industry, chemical industry and metallurgical industry between them account for around 70 per cent of Taiwan's GDP and 60 per cent of its exports. The 19.17 per cent growth rate that the electronics and IT sector posted in 2007 contributed 2.14 per cent to Taiwan's overall economic growth rate (Table 5.1). However, with the worsening economic climate in Europe and North America leading to lower demand for imports, there was a pronounced deterioration in the export performance of Taiwan's ICT industry; the industry's exports declined by 34.20 per cent in the first half of 2009.

Second, Taiwanese industry is largely engaged in original equipment manufacturing (OEM) and original design manufacturing (ODM) production. Most of the patents that Taiwanese manufacturers secure relate to production process technology; the overall level of value added is low, and Taiwanese companies lack the strong brands that they would need to gain full benefit from their R&D activities. Taiwanese products are concentrated heavily in the midstream and upstream segments of the value chain, with intermediate goods accounting for over 70 per cent of total exports (Figure 5.1). As a result of this situation, Taiwanese companies generally have only limited knowledge of trends in consumer demand for the final goods that are produced using their intermediate goods.

Third, of Taiwan's 'two trillion, twin star' industries, the semiconductor (DRAM) industry and large-sized TFT-LCD panel industry are both cyclical, capital-intensive industries that are highly vulnerable to economic downturns.

A fourth point is that, while the service sector accounts for around 70 per cent of Taiwan's GDP, its level of competitiveness is low, the pace of industry upgrading has been slow, Taiwan's service industries have found it hard to internationalize, and the service sector as a whole has done little to help Taiwan's manufacturing industries add value, or to integrate their operations with those of manufacturers to enhance Taiwan's overall competitive advantage.

The service sector's GDP contribution rate in 2007 was 2.93 per cent, only slightly higher than that of the manufacturing sector (2.70 per cent) (Table 5.1). The small size of Taiwan's domestic market and shortages of human talent and capital and inadequate investment in R&D have combined to impose constraints on the extent to which the service sector has been able to internationalize or grow its exports. Even so, the importance of the service sector to Taiwan's economy should not be underestimated; the financial sector, wholesaling and retailing, changes to distribution, and the restaurant business in particular account for a large share of employment in Taiwan.

## 5.3 THE POLICIES ADOPTED BY THE TAIWANESE GOVERNMENT IN RESPONSE TO THE GLOBAL FINANCIAL CRISIS

As regards the measures adopted by the government in response to the global financial crisis, like many other countries Taiwan has relied heavily on monetary and fiscal policy to cope with the impact of the crisis (Wang

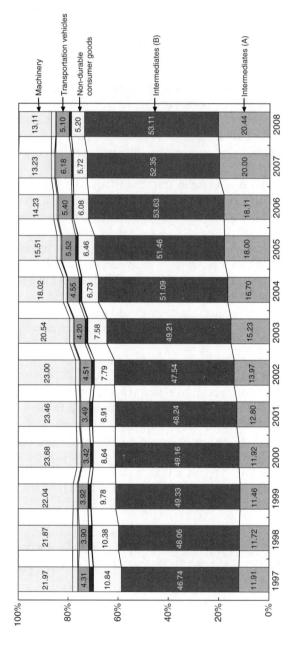

Intermediates (A) include products that require processing before they can be used in the production of consumer goods or producer goods. Intermediates (B) include products that can be used directly in consumer goods or producer goods without processing.

*Source:* Taiwan World Trade Atlas, *Trade Informal System*, Taiwan External Trade Development Council.

*Figure 5.1   Intermediate goods account for the largest share of Taiwan's exports.*

and Wei, 2009). The Taiwanese government adopted a relaxed monetary policy and cut interest rates so as to boost bank liquidity.

In terms of fiscal policy, the government allocated NT$500 billion to support a range of public construction projects over a period of 4 years. The government also distributed consumption coupons worth around US$120 each to every citizen (costing a total of NT$82.5 billion) with the aim of boosting domestic demand. New jobs were created through public investment, and unemployment benefits were provided for the short-term unemployed.

The following subsections examine the short-term and medium- and long-term industrial policies adopted by the Taiwanese government.

**Short-Term Policies**

As regards the short-term policy measures adopted by the government in response to the global financial crisis, the Ministry of Economic Affairs (MOEA, 2009) has focused on four key areas: stimulating consumer spending, helping small and medium enterprises (SMEs) to secure funding, promoting investment and boosting exports (MOEA, 2009).

The main measures adopted to boost consumer spending included programs to encourage consumers to replace old appliances and other consumer durables with new, low-energy-consumption, environmentally friendly appliances. Measures taken to help SMEs secure needed financing included investment promotion and measures to encourage large-scale investment projects.

In terms of export promotion, the MOEA has been working to stimulate exports to China, and also to other emerging markets, with the aim of reducing Taiwanese exporters' excessive reliance on a handful of key markets. The distribution of consumption coupons to boost consumer spending was another important measure that helped to provide a short-term stimulus to the economy.

The government's 'i-Taiwan 12 Projects' initiative also constitutes a key policy. The aim of this is to leverage 12 key public construction projects to stimulate domestic demand and create a new 'economic miracle' for Taiwan. It is anticipated that the i-Taiwan 12 Projects will involve total investment of NT$3990 billion over 8 years, with the government providing two-thirds of this and the remaining one-third deriving from private-sector investment.

The 12 projects are: construction of a fast, convenient island-wide transportation network (NT$1452.3 billion); establishment of the Kaohsiung Free Trade Zone and Eco-Port (NT$57.7 billion); creation of the Taichung Asia-Pacific Sea and Air Logistics Hub (NT$50 billion); development of the Taoyuan International Air City (NT$67 billion); the Intelligent

Taiwan project (NT$225 billion); the Industrial Innovation Corridors project (NT$115 billion); Urban and Industrial Zone Renewal (NT$57 billion); the Farm and Village Regeneration project (NT$150 billion); the Coastal Regeneration project (NT$20 billion); the Green Forestation project (NT$30 billion); the Flood Prevention and Water Management initiative (NT$186 billion); and a Sewer Construction program (NT$240 billion). It is anticipated that the implementation of these 12 projects will create around 120 000 jobs per year.

**Medium- and Long-Term Policies**

With regard to medium- and long-term industrial policies, analysis of the industrial structure shown in Figure 5.2 shows that, first, the financial crisis has revealed serious weaknesses in both Taiwan's industrial structure and the structure of its foreign trade. Effective service sector development and the successful promotion of low-priced products both require the support of a large domestic market; the signing of an 'economic cooperation framework agreement' (ECFA) or similar agreement with China would constitute an important medium-term strategy for expanding access to the China market and stimulating the upgrading and transformation of Taiwanese industry.

The ECFA is a cross-strait free trade agreement that will take effect gradually, using tariff reductions, liberalization of investment and trade, economic collaboration and dispute resolution mechanisms to strengthen cross-strait economic and trading ties between Taiwan and China, creating a win–win situation for both countries (Chu, 2009).

Another important point is that the trend towards regional economic integration – which can be seen in the 'ASEAN + 1' and 'ASEAN + 3' agreements in Asia, the European Union (EU) in Europe and NAFTA in North America – represents a significant threat to the future competitiveness of Taiwan's exports. The ECFA is a key strategy for helping Taiwan to avoid becoming marginalized by this process of regional economic integration (Lan, 2005).

At the same time, Taiwan cannot afford to become excessively dependent on the China market. In the long term, Taiwan will still need to focus on upgrading and transforming its industries and promoting the development of emerging industries, and should attempt to secure membership of the 'ASEAN + 1' and 'ASEAN + 3' groupings so as to enhance the degree of economic autonomy that Taiwan is able to maintain.

The following sections analyze the government's strategy with regard to the ECFA and the six key 'flagship' industries, and consider the role Taiwan will play within the process of Asia Pacific economic integration.

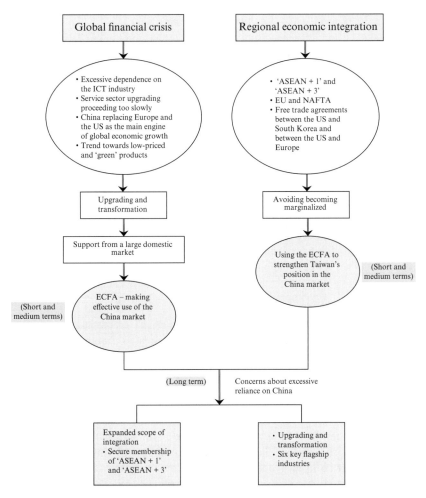

*Figure 5.2    Taiwan's medium- and long-term economic development strategies.*

## The ECFA

The planning for the ECFA agreement with China is based on the fact that current trends in regional economic integration are working to Taiwan's disadvantage. In particular, Taiwan will be excluded from both the 'ASEAN + 1' and 'ASEAN + 3' groupings (ASEAN: Association of Southeast Asian Nations). Another point is that 40 per cent of Taiwan's exports go to China. The signing of the ECFA will help Taiwan to secure its position in the China market, and will help those industries that are

*Table 5.2    Taiwan's six flagship industries plan*

| Industry | Funding | Production value created | Industries that will benefit |
|----------|---------|--------------------------|------------------------------|
| Biotech | NT$60 billion in biotech venture capital funding | Doubling of production value to NT$260 billion within 4 years | Pharmaceuticals and biotech industries |
| 'Green' energy | NT$20 billion over 5 years | NT$1 trillion | Mainly the solar cell and LED industries |
| Healthcare | NT$86.4 billion in investment over 4 years | NT$346.4 billion over 4 years | Medical electronics and medical devices industries |
| High-value-added agriculture | NT$24.2 billion over 4 years | NT$158.9 billion over 4 years | Orchid cultivation, agro-tourism etc. |
| Tourism | NT$30 billion tourism development fund | NT$550 billion within 4 years | Restaurant and hotel industries etc. |
| Cultural and creative | NT$20 billion to establish venture capital funds | NT$1 trillion within 4 years | TV, film, music, handicrafts, design and digital content industries |

*Source:*    Ministry of Economic Affairs (2009).

especially dependent on exports to China – including the petrochemical industry, iron and steel, machinery manufacturing and car parts – to maintain their competitiveness.

The ECFA will also help Taiwanese companies to develop the Chinese domestic market. Finally, the ECFA can be used to encourage Taiwanese businesspeople that have been operating in China to repatriate their earnings and invest in Taiwan, thereby helping Taiwan to reposition itself as an Asia Pacific operations hub.

**The six key 'flagship' industries**
To drive the upgrading and transformation of Taiwan's industries, the Executive Yuan has been implementing the six 'flagship' industries plan, to promote the development of six key emerging industries: biotech; 'green' energy; healthcare; high-value-added agriculture; tourism; and the cultural and creative industry (Table 5.2). The resources made available under the plan will be used to guide and encourage private-sector

investment, helping the industries in question to develop new business opportunities and to upgrade themselves more rapidly.

The main methods that will be used in the six key flagship industries plan are outlined below (Wang, 2009):

*The Diamond Promotion Plan for the Biotechnology Industry*    The Executive Yuan has given its approval for the Diamond Promotion Plan for the Biotechnology Industry, which includes the Biotechnology Venture Capital (BVC) initiative and the Supra Incubation Center (SIC) project as well as various other mechanisms, and which will be implemented in collaboration with the Taiwan Food and Drug Administration (TFDA). The government will also be providing the funding, legal affairs, IP, technology and operational support required by the biomedical technology and biomedical materials industry at the current state of development. In this all-out effort to promote the development of the biotech sector, the government will be working to develop integrated incubation mechanisms and build a world-class legal and regulatory environment for the pharmaceuticals sector as a whole.

*Developing the 'green' energy industry*    The government is aiming to strengthen the competitiveness of the biotech sector and the green energy industry. The green energy industry – including photovoltaics, LED technology, wind power, biomass energy etc. – will be a key focus of the government's promotional efforts in the future.

*Healthcare*    Taiwan possesses advanced medical technology, and has a national health insurance system that is the envy of the world. To transform healthcare from a burden into a valuable industry, the government has initiated the Healthcare Industry Upgrading Plan, which covers the long-term care industry, the spa industry, 'smart' medical services and the internationalization of medical services.

*High-value-added agriculture*    The government will be encouraging the development of those forms of agriculture that have significant market potential, such as flower cultivation and flower markets, tropical fruit production, ornamental fish breeding etc. The government will also be working to develop a high-quality seed cultivation industry, to promote Taiwan's development into an Asia Pacific plant, aquaculture and poultry propagation and breeding center.

*Promotion of the tourism industry and related cross-industry alliances*    The formation of alliances between Taiwan's tourism industry and other emerging industries can help to promote industrial growth and create new jobs. One possible example would be the integration of spa operation with the health and beauty industry. The linking together of industries in this way could create an additional NT$550 billion in tourist revenue, and create an extra 410000 tourism-related jobs, while also attracting at least 10 leading international hotel chains to establish themselves in Taiwan.

*The cultural and creative industry*   Cultural and creative industry development will emphasize design, digital technologies, video, popular music and cultural and creative industry start-ups linked to the National Palace Museum.

**Policy Discussion**

The short-term policies adopted by the Taiwanese government in response to the global financial crisis were intended to minimize the externalities that the crisis created for the Taiwanese economy (through its negative impact on industry and on the financial sector); these policies can be thought of as 'emergency rescue', aimed at reducing the risk of a crisis of confidence. Given the need for these policies to be implemented as quickly as possible, there was little room for making adjustments to them. The focus of the discussion in this chapter is therefore on the government's medium- and long-term strategies, and on the ways in which they could be adjusted.

First, as regards the i-Taiwan 12 Projects, the emphasis in these projects is mainly on 'hardware' infrastructure, and several of the projects derive from the platform adopted in President Ma Ying-Jeou's election campaign; they were not subjected to rigorous evaluation, and will therefore need item-by-item cost–benefit analysis and the establishment of a clear priority order to avoid a situation where public construction is being undertaken for its own sake, drawing off valuable resources from other areas. Some of these resources might be utilized to better effect by investing them in 'software' construction, manpower cultivation and education. Taiwan has already reached a relatively high level of economic development, and has a largely satisfactory basic infrastructure; further large-scale investment in this area is likely to produce only very limited benefits.

Turning to the ECFA, the signing of an FTA or similar agreement with China is a vital step toward strengthening Taiwan's access to its largest export market and preventing Taiwan from becoming marginalized. However, the ECFA is at best a short-to-medium-term policy tool; it is not a panacea (*Commercial Weekly*, 2009). The ultimate goal should be to make effective use of the ECFA to help Taiwanese companies leverage China's resources, establish strong brands, build economies

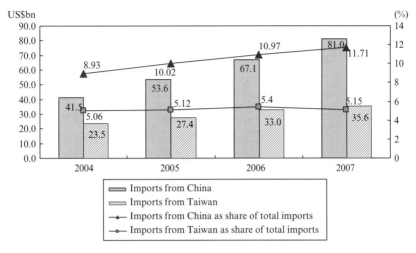

*Source:*   Chu (2009).

*Figure 5.3    China's imports from ASEAN and Taiwan.*

of scale, expand into global markets and boost Taiwan's international competitiveness.

If, on the other hand, the ECFA is just used to protect existing markets, and Taiwanese companies fail to make an active effort to upgrade and transform themselves, then the Taiwanese economy will become ever more dependent on China. Taking the 'ASEAN + 1' and 'ASEAN + 3' agreements as an example, the ASEAN member nations have not seen any significant increase in their share of the China market, but China's share of the Southeast Asian market has grown steadily (Figures 5.3 and 5.4). Signing an FTA with China is at best a short-term protective measure; without a serious effort to upgrade and transform Taiwanese industry, Taiwan will be doomed to see its international competitiveness decline steadily; Taiwan should take the lessons from ASEAN seriously.

Finally, let us go on to consider the six flagship industries plan. As far as the theory behind this is concerned, the idea is for the government to implement a large-scale project to achieve a breakthrough in key industries; the aim is to focus resources, achieve a 'big push' effect, and build economies of scale and economies of scope, so as to speed up economic growth. There are solid theoretical underpinnings for this type of strategy (Thirlwall, 1994).

The choice of biotech, green energy, healthcare, high-value-added agriculture, tourism and the cultural and creative industry as the emerging

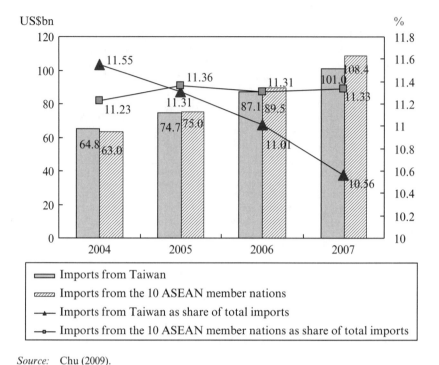

US$bn

%

*Source:*   Chu (2009).

*Figure 5.4    ASEAN's imports from Taiwan and China*

industries to focus on is in conformity with international trends, the need to reduce carbon dioxide emissions, the trend towards smaller families and the aging of the population; overall, the government's strategy in this respect can be said to be broadly correct.

However, there are several suggestions that can be made regarding the planning for the promotion of the six key flagship industries, to avoid distortions during plan implementation:

*1. The key performance indicators (KPIs) that have been set for individual ministries and agencies need to be reconsidered, so as to encourage closer collaboration between ministries and between central and local government, thereby reducing the risk of system failure.*

In the past, the theoretical framework for government promotion of the development of emerging industries and support for innovation and R&D was based largely on the concept of market failure; it was generally held that the government should intervene only in cases where the level of risk was particularly high, or where investment in a particular industry carried high externalities (Arrow, 1962; Rothwell and Zegveld, 1981).

However, developments in theory in this area since around 2000 have stressed that system failure is another major factor that can hinder breakthroughs in technology development, and that governments are justified in helping emerging industries to overcome this problem (Hauknes, 1999). System failure may occur when there is insufficient communication and exchange of information between the different parts of a country's innovation system (including communication between different central government ministries, between central and local government, between government and industry, and between industry and the university sector). Legal and regulatory constraints can also hamper innovation and discourage entrepreneurship, leading to a decline in innovation and productivity in the economy as a whole.

The individual plans for promoting the development of the six flagship industries are all interministerial, interdisciplinary projects, where the extent and quality of interaction between central government agencies, between central and local government, between the government and the private sector, and between industry and academia will have a major impact on each project's success or failure; there is a clear need for communication, the building of consensus and the coordinated use of resources. The question is how to achieve this strengthening of communication and integration. This chapter suggests that the first priority should be to reexamine the KPIs set for each individual government ministry or agency.

First, all ministries (and particularly those with oversight over the service sector) should cease to focus mainly on regulation, and should be tasked explicitly with promoting industrial development; only then will it be possible to achieve the deregulation that is needed to help industries such as healthcare, biotech and communications services, which are currently all tightly regulated, to regain their vitality (Wang, 2009).

Second, the provision of assistance by a ministry to help other ministries complete particular tasks should be listed as a major KPI, so as to promote interministerial collaboration. At the same time, the allocation of funding assistance by central government to local government should take into consideration the needs of both local and central government, in order to facilitate coordinated policy implementation.

Third, the KPIs for individual government employees also need to be reviewed to create new incentive mechanisms, for example by increasing the disparity in pay levels between government employees at different levels so as to provide more incentive for high performance, thereby enhancing overall efficiency. Adjusting KPIs in this way will increase the likelihood of the six flagship industries plan being a success, thanks to the increased focus on deregulation, communication and coordination, and the avoidance of system failure.

*2. Moving away from supply-side thinking and strengthening communication with industry and with universities, so as to build consensus and increase resource allocation.*

Given the difficult financial situation in which the government finds itself at present, the active collaboration of the private sector is vital if the government's policies are to be implemented effectively. So far, efforts to promote and publicize the six flagship industries plan have been limited, and have been very much supply-side-oriented, with little thought given to the question of how to boost demand. What is needed is to gain a thorough understanding of companies' needs and capabilities, supplemented by top-down planning, to ensure a good fit between the measures that the government adopts and its objectives; only then will private-sector companies be willing to allocate resources to support the government's plan.

*3. More investment in service sector infrastructure is needed to support those aspects of the six flagship industries plan that relate to the service sector.*

Two of the industries covered by the six flagship industries plan are service industries. The key element in service sector development is infrastructure, but the kind of infrastructure that the service industries need is significantly different from that required by manufacturing; it includes deregulation, the relaxation of restrictions on the free movement of human talent, establishment of statistical databases and data collection (e.g. data relating to overseas distribution channels, international legal and regulatory issues etc.). Ensuring that adequate service sector infrastructure is in place is a vital prerequisite to ensure success in the six key flagship industries plans and in the development of the service sector as a whole.

*4. The signing of the ECFA will create an enlarged home market for the six key flagship industry plans, making the completion of this agreement an even more urgent task.*

Markets and distribution channels are of great importance in the implementation of the six flagship industries plan. The signing of the ECFA will help to secure Taiwan's access to the Chinese market, making it easier for Taiwanese companies to build economies of scale, grow their brands and expand into international markets, thereby helping them to increase their competitiveness over the long term. The signing of the ECFA is thus an urgent necessity for Taiwan.

## 5.4    CONCLUSIONS AND RECOMMENDATIONS

The aim of the present study has been to explore the problems that face Taiwan in the aftermath of the global financial crisis. These problems include: Taiwanese industry's reliance on ODM/OEM production and its lack of strong brands; insufficient diversification, with excessive reliance on the electronics and IT industry; the highly export-oriented nature of the Taiwanese economy, with exports accounting for around 70 per cent of GDP, and Taiwan's growing dependence on China as its main export market; the slow pace of upgrading and transformation in the service sector; and the mix of opportunities and dangers Taiwan will face following the normalization of cross-strait trading relations between Taiwan and China.

In its response to the global financial crisis, the Taiwanese government's short-term strategy emphasized fiscal and monetary measures to prevent a further deterioration in the state of the economy, accompanied by increased public spending on infrastructure projects to stimulate domestic demand. Medium-term strategies include the efforts to negotiate an 'economic cooperation framework agreement' (ECFA) with China, to secure and improve Taiwan's access to the China market. However, if Taiwan is to achieve sustainable economic growth over the long term it will also need to focus on promoting the development of the six key flagship industries and the transformation and upgrading of Taiwan's other main industries.

In conclusion, the present study puts forward several recommendations to help Taiwan overcome the obstacles that it is facing at present: (1) Strengthen ICT and service sector infrastructure. (2) Develop strong brands and new distribution channels. (3) Strengthen the systems needed to support cross-industry integration. (4) Continue to promote the development of the six flagship industries. (5) Focus more on developing emerging markets. (6) Work to increase practical cross-strait collaboration in industry, so that Taiwan can leverage China's resources in the development of global markets. (7) Aim for a rapid upgrading and transformation of the service sector. (8) Attach more importance to investing in human resources and education (Figure 5.5).

The specific measures that can be taken to achieve these goals are outlined below:

*1. Besides traditional infrastructure investment in bridge-building, highway improvement etc., the government also needs to invest more in ICT infrastructure, undertake 'green' investment, and invest in 'soft' infrastructure such as education and human resources development. This will help both to boost domestic demand and to enhance citizens' quality of life.*

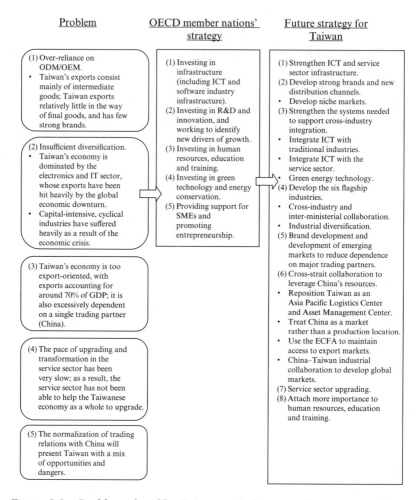

*Figure 5.5    Problems faced by Taiwanese industry, and suggestions for industrial policy in the post-financial-crisis era.*

Judging from Japan's past experience in this area, where an advanced nation continues to focus investment on traditional public works, the rate of return on investment will normally be very low, and there is a risk that political parties will become too heavily influenced by special interest groups. In the future, therefore, when undertaking public spending, the government should direct resources towards innovative 'software' infra-structure investment, such as the strengthening of Taiwan's information and communications technology (ICT) infrastructure.

Investment in education and manpower cultivation in the US, and the promotion of 'green' technology and high-value-added services in South Korea, have succeeded not only in boosting domestic demand but also in improving the rate of return on public sector investment and in improving the quality of life of these countries' citizens.

*2. Helping business enterprises to undertake R&D, innovation, brand development and distribution channel development, and to undertake any necessary restructuring.*

As can be seen from the above analysis, the recent global financial crisis has thrown the fragility of Taiwan's trading and industrial structure into sharp relief. Some of the important tasks that need to be undertaken to remedy this situation include raising the competitiveness of Taiwan's service sector so as to create a more balanced industrial structure, developing strong Taiwanese brands to increase value added, reducing Taiwan's reliance on ODM/OEM production, and furthering the integration of the manufacturing and service sectors.

Strong brands are vital if manufacturers are to be able to turn their investment in R&D into higher profits, and to continue to invest in R&D on an ongoing basis. Having a strong brand can also help companies to achieve greater diversification in terms of their export markets. Of course, creating a powerful brand is no easy task, but the likelihood of success will be substantially increased if the government provides subsidies to help spread the risk, and if companies working to develop their brand exploit the huge market that China offers.

*3. Strengthening cross-industry integration and looking for ways to achieve diversification.*

In the past, when allocating resources to support industrial development, the Taiwanese government has tended to take asset value as the key benchmark. As a result, the industries whose development the government has worked hardest to promote have generally been capital-intensive ones that are particularly vulnerable to the impact of the business cycle.

In future, when deciding how to allocate resources, the government should think in terms not only of asset value but also of value-added, resource integration etc. At the same time, new key performance indicators (KPIs) will need to be set for local government authorities, individual ministries, central government as a whole, and individual government employees, to enhance the productivity of the public sector and strengthen intersectoral and intersystem integration. This should help to make more resources available to support the development of 'green' industries, and should facilitate the wider adoption of ICT in traditional industries and in the service sector, thereby helping to give Taiwan a broader spectrum of industries.

*4. Employing innovative new ways of thinking and new policy tools to support the development of the six key flagship industries, to provide new drivers of growth for Taiwan's economy.*

If the government's goal of building up six major new flagship industries can be made a reality, these industries will constitute an important growth engine for Taiwan in the future. However, before starting to encourage active private-sector participation in this area, the government will need to focus first on ensuring effective inter-ministerial collaboration, and establish new KPIs for government employees, so as to facilitate the coordination of industry development promotion effects between different ministries and agencies.

Other important areas include the development of key technologies and key distribution channels; encouraging companies in the six flagship industries to seek stock market or over-the-counter (OTC) listing so as to benefit from the resources that the capital markets can provide and attract more human talent; and brand and distribution channel development. The government may also wish to consider introducing new incentive measures to stimulate M&A activity in the flagship industries.

*5. Developing emerging markets.*

Currently, government efforts to help Taiwanese industry develop emerging markets are limited largely to ad-hoc, one-off trade missions. In the future, it may be advisable to establish dedicated offices to focus on the development of particular key markets. These offices would be able to collect data on consumer behavior in the markets in question, and play a business-matching role, thereby facilitating the ongoing, continuous development of emerging markets.

*6. Cross-strait collaboration to leverage China's resources and create new growth opportunities.*

The global financial crisis led to a pronounced fall in Taiwan's exports. At the same time, however, China's attitude towards Taiwan has become less hostile. Taiwanese companies were allowed to participate in the special initiative launched by the Chinese government to boost electrical appliance sales in rural areas, and more recently Chinese firms have begun to invest in Taiwan and source products in Taiwan. The prospect of closer economic integration between Taiwan and China has become significantly more likely. South Korean companies are so worried by this possibility that they have coined a new phrase to describe the threat: 'Chaiwan' (China plus Taiwan).

However, both the project to increase the sales of electrical appliances in China's rural areas and the recent wave of Chinese trade missions to Taiwan are only short-term phenomena. The government will need to act as a catalyst to make 'Chaiwan' a reality, ensuring that recent contacts are expanded into practical, meaningful collaboration that can be maintained over the long term; this is a challenge the government should be taking very seriously.

*7. Raising the competitiveness of Taiwan's service sector.*

As regards enhancing the competitiveness of the service sector, given that the service industries account already for around 70 per cent of Taiwan's GDP, but that the small size of the Taiwanese domestic market is making it difficult for the service industries to upgrade and transform themselves rapidly enough, if the service sector is to become the main driver for Taiwan's future economic growth then the government cannot afford to continue to adhere to a manufacturing-oriented mindset when deciding how to allocate resources and when designing policy tools.

The policies that the government formulates should be based on new thinking that takes into account the fundamental differences between the service sector and the manufacturing sector. The key features of the service sector include the difficulty in replicating other companies' service offerings, the fact that services are often experience-oriented, the fact that innovation in the service sector lies in solving problems, the lack of any necessity for ongoing, continuous innovation, the relatively limited amount of capital required to start up a service sector business, and the importance of high-end talent and superior business models, etc.

With these considerations in mind, the government's thinking with regard to the innovative policy tools that can be used to support the development of the service sector in the future can be outlined as follows:

- First, the government will be working to enhance the allocation of resources to the service sector.
- Second, there is a need to establish a higher-level government agency to supervise service sector development.
- A third issue is the question of recruiting overseas talent, and career planning.
- Fourth, the government could plan out the establishment of more service sector development infrastructure.
- A fifth area where the government can provide effective support for service sector development is by selecting priority service industries with significant development potential, and helping these industries to internationalize their operations.

# REFERENCES

Arrow, K. (1962), 'Economic Welfare and the Allocation of Resources for Inventions,' in R.R. Nelson (ed), *The Rate and Direction of Inventive Activity*, Princeton University Press.

Chu, C.Y. (2009), *ECFA Creates Win Win Prospect for Cross Strait*, Taipei: Prospect Interflow Cultural Foundation.

*Commercial Weekly* (2009), 'FTA Is Not a Panacea', *Commercial Weekly* (1138), 130–2.

Hauknes, J. (1999), *Technological Infrastructures and Innovation Policies*, STEP Report, Oslo: STEP Group.

Lan, Wen-Jorng (2005), 'Economic Impact Evaluation on Taiwan and ASEAN Integration,' Taipei: Chung-Hua Institution for Economic Research.

Ministry of Economic Affairs (2009), 'Reaction Plans for Accelerating Economic Recovery' (ppt), Taipei: Ministry of Economic Affairs.

Rothwell, Roy and Walter Zegveld (1981), *Industrial Innovation and Public Policy*, Paris: Frances Pinter.

Thirlwall, A.P. (1994), *Growth & Development – With Special Reference to Developing Economies* (5th edn), Taipei: Mao-Chung Publishing.

Wang, Jiann-Chyuan (2009), 'An Analysis on the Development Strategy of Taiwan's Six New Emerging Industries', *Economic Outlook*, **127**, 35–8.

Wang, Jiann-Chyuan and Tsung-Che, Wei (2009), *Taiwan Industrial Policy in Post Financial Crisis Era*, Taipei: Chung-Hua Institution for Economic Research.

# 6. The American crisis and Korean financial distress[1]

## Un Chan Chung

## 6.1 INTRODUCTORY REMARKS

The global economy has been experiencing wild turbulence coming from the US-born financial crisis since last fall. The media call it an 'unprecedented' phenomenon. In some respects, however, history is merely repeating itself. From the Dutch tulip mania of the seventeenth century to the Great Depression of 80 years ago, and now the recent property-market bust, we have seen that financial markets, especially in the absence of proper regulation, can collapse following the euphoria of bubbles, with devastating results not just for themselves but also for their surroundings as well.

The epicenter of the current crisis happens to be the very heart of the global markets. This is therefore a stark reminder of the fragility of the neo-liberal illusion, or the belief that an unregulated market will always maximize efficiency. Of course, a free market is a good system for the efficient allocation of resources – under normal circumstances. However, like any human endeavor, markets are by no means infallible. On the surface, it was Wall Street's aggressive marketing and greed that triggered the turmoil. However, digging deeper into the roots of the crisis, one will discover that the imbalance of production and consumption in the US, as well as the inequality of income distribution, lie at the heart of the problem. All these observations reveal that the market system may react very slowly to potentially threatening – but not so immediately apparent – structural problems that lurk beneath the water.

The financial crisis that began in the US provides us with an opportunity to reconsider the various imbalances we face. We will examine the deep-rooted structural problems beneath the financial crisis, the risks of market fundamentalism, and issues regarding the current status of the Korean economy.

## 6.2   THE SUBPRIME MORTGAGE CRISIS

Let us start with the US subprime mortgage market, which was the first domino to fall. Subprime mortgages are loan products that enable people with bad credit histories to buy homes. Of course, there is a high level of risk for the banks involved. To manage the risk, mortgage-backed securities were created with those loans as collateral, and financial derivatives based on those securities were developed.

Known as collateralized debt obligations, or CDOs, these derivatives were created from the credit risk of the underlying loans. The likelihood of default on those loans is calculated and traded in the market to manage risk. For example, were a certain subprime mortgage very unlikely to go bad, then the CDO based on it would be valued in the market at a high price, and vice versa. Unfortunately, the market does not always assess the likelihood of a default accurately.

When the housing market becomes strong, only a few loans will go bad. That will raise CDO prices, and investors who have bought those securities will enjoy incredible returns. When house prices fall, however, the delinquency rate will soar above the previously expected levels, and CDO prices will collapse as well. A CDO that was thought to be fairly priced at 90 will find itself devalued to 30 or 40. When that happens, the price becomes quite meaningless. The possibility of this kind of event happening used to be one in a million, according to the previous pricing system.

The mispricing of CDOs was one reason behind the recent subprime crisis. When those financial instruments were created, people were aware of the risks involved but believed that they could be managed through the market. Such a belief has turned out to be mistaken, however.

Together with CDOs, another factor that amplified the chaos in markets was leverage-driven speculation. Back when subprime-backed CDOs were a hot investment, the more you bought, the more you earned. So hedge funds took their investors' money, added funds borrowed from financial institutions and poured everything into subprime. However, the Achilles heel of leverage is that the more you have, the more you stand to lose.

Suppose that a fund invested 100 dollars in subprime CDOs, of which 20 came from its investors and 80 was borrowed. If CDO prices rise to 120, this fund's returns become 100 per cent on its own investment of 20. If CDOs fall to 80, however, the fund loses all its money. This kind of high-risk investment became predominant and eventually triggered the massive losses we have witnessed at global financial institutions.

I must also point out the irresponsibility of subprime mortgage brokers who sold such loans very aggressively without informing their clients of the possible risks. These mortgage brokers would promise low-income clients a house even without money, telling them they could pay back the loan or even make a profit by selling the house after its price rose. This sort of aggressive marketing worked, and subprime mortgages boomed. The brokers themselves collected a windfall in fees, but their poor clients are sliding into bankruptcy as they find themselves unable to repay their debts.

In short, the US subprime crisis that has plunged the global economy into a cloud of uncertainty was born of a mixture of the mispricing of CDOs, leverage-fueled speculation, and predatory lending practices.

## 6.3    THE IMBALANCE OF SAVINGS AND SPENDING, AND INCOME DISTRIBUTION

On the surface, the reason behind the crisis is obvious: financial firms invested heavily in property-related securities. In contrast to their long-term investments, their debts from international financial institutions were short-term – for example, with maturities of one, two, three days or a week. Consequently, there was always the possibility of a liquidity crisis. Firms should have avoided such an excessive mismatch of assets and liabilities.

If everyone thought US home prices would continue to rise forever, the price-mismatch issue would not have expanded into a full-blown crisis. However, as some people started to worry that the property market bubble might burst, problems began to emerge. Once major international financial institutions withdrew their money and did not reinvest it in markets, investment banks melted down quickly.

Beneath the surface of the current financial situation, there lies a more fundamental problem plaguing the economy: the disparity between spending and production. For a long time, Americans consumed more than they produced. The gap was filled with imported goods. Dollars would flow out of the nation to buy those imports but would flow right back in as exporter countries snapped up US Treasuries, thus in effect boosting domestic liquidity. The increased money supply enabled people to continue the spending spree, thus perpetuating a cycle of increasing imports and increasing liquidity. The process continued for several decades while Americans reaped the full benefits of having the world's key currency as their own.

Until the 1970s, the disparity between spending and production was still manageable. It was a period of social stability, as big and small corporations, consumers, the government and the unions maintained a balance that spread the wealth in a fairly even manner throughout society. Robert B. Reich (2007) calls this the period of 'democratic capitalism.'[2]

However, American capitalism began to change after the 1970s. The democratic capitalism that had supported stable livelihoods for most people was replaced by what Reich calls 'supercapitalism', in which the government is reduced to the role of a bystander no matter what happens in the markets.

Under the new system, the US bought massive amounts of goods made by cheap labor in emerging economies, leading to huge trade imbalances. Moreover, to realize even higher returns for investors, financial firms started putting money into riskier securities whose rewards could be very high – or very low. This new system darkened the future of the US. Should foreigners ever decide one day that the dollar has become too abundant, reducing its value, then Americans would become unable to buy imports cheaply like they had before. The world economy would then slide into major chaos, and no one would be able to say for sure what the future held for US-led global capitalism.

In addition, once the rich got richer and the poor got poorer in the US, the economic system became structurally unstable. When inflation is accounted for, middle-class salaries in the US have hardly changed over the past 30 years. In fact, the real wage of the average American male has fallen, including a 12 per cent real decrease for workers in their thirties. While the upper class rode the wave of neo-liberalism, boosting their incomes from the IT boom and the onset of globalization, the majority of Americans saw no real benefit at all, sliding into relative and absolute poverty. Nevertheless, that did not stop them from aspiring to emulate the lavish lifestyles of the rich.

There are a few obvious ways to live big on a small income. The first is for both spouses to work. In the 1970s, 30 per cent of school-age children had working mothers. Recently, that figure had risen to nearly 70 per cent. Another way to make more money is to work longer. Compared with 30 years ago, the average American works 2 weeks more every year. However, both of these methods can only go so far, as there is a limit to a nation's population, as well as the hours in a day. That leaves them with 'debt'.

As home prices soared in the 1990s and the early years of this decade, buoyed by an abundant money supply, consumers took out loans on their homes in order to satisfy their need to spend. This boom in consumption was also fueled by the use of credit cards, which looked like a limitless spring of financial manna. Once Americans got a taste of the bonanzas from property, they began to see houses not as homes but as investments. Ordinary Americans were now seasoned, shrewd investors – or so they thought. To attract even more people to the property markets, real estate firms and mortgage-providing banks, which reaped huge profits during this period, used the bait of a second or third house.

The development of exotic mortgage-backed derivatives led to increasingly bigger profits but also drove up the risks. No one playing in this mother of all casinos paid enough attention to the risks at the time – until everyone started losing. In the end, Wall Street, named after the colonial-era wall erected to fend off attacks from hostile natives, failed to save itself from itself.

By the time Wall Street fell, Main Street was also too weakened to protect itself. How had it been weakened? US households had previously maintained a significant surplus on their balance sheets. Personal saving as a percentage of disposable income averaged 9.1 per cent during the 1980s, compared with a widening government deficit. The situation was reversed in the 1990s as the government turned to a surplus while household debt increased.

In the current decade, both households and the government are back in the red and the savings rate is down to a mere 1.6 per cent. This means the government can't be counted on to help households restructure their balance sheets. So American households are on their own now, and will reduce spending to save more money, putting the brakes on the economy in the short term. That's why the current recession will prove to be a longer downturn than usual.

The US now has little choice but to pour immense amounts of money into its financial sector to avert an even bigger crisis. I sincerely hope the measures have the desired effect. However, there can be no true recovery unless the nation solves its fundamental problems weakening its real economy, namely, the imbalance between income and expenditures and the huge income gap between the rich and the poor.

## 6.4  A KOREAN ECONOMIC CRISIS?

Now, let us turn to the other side of the Pacific, especially Korea. At the moment, the Korean economy is languishing in a state of uncertainty about the future. The extreme currency fluctuations of last fall and winter were a product of such insecurity and investors' mistrust of the economy. While this uncertainty does owe a large part to external factors such as the US crisis, the country's economy had its own homegrown problems.

Here, we can raise a question: were there no crisis in the US, would the Korean economy have kept on growing without any problems? My answer to the question would be negative.

Before getting into the details, let us begin with the changes Korea has gone through during the last 50 years. In the late 1950s, several years after the Korean War, the per capita national income was less than 100 dollars, comparable to that of the poorest countries in the world today. Barely two generations later, with a population of 49 million and a per capita GDP that tops 20000 dollars, Korea has moved itself to the other end of the spectrum. Among the countries that began industrialization after World War II, Korea is arguably the only one with a sizable population that has successfully pulled itself up to the ranks of developed nations.

At the end of November 1997, however, Korea was on the brink of bankruptcy. Having lost confidence in the country, foreign investors were taking flight. In hindsight, one might think of this event as only a temporary liquidity crisis. And it is true that Korea had made a dramatic comeback within just a few years, with the fourth-largest foreign exchange reserves in the world.

However, closer scrutiny shows the crisis was triggered by the underlying economic fracture lines created during the years of rapid growth and exposure to globalization.

Korea's successful growth story was an example of a country having actively participated in the global economy while the government took some steps to intervene and manage. This is the system that many scholars have called a 'state-led growth strategy'.

But the waves of globalization and liberalization that washed through the global markets in the 1990s also triggered a change in paradigm. Korea's capital account liberalization in the first half of the 1990s turned out in retrospect to be one of the most rapid and comprehensive in the developing world.[3] A wide range of deregulations was implemented, particularly on capital inflows, including: the issuance of foreign-currency denominated bonds by domestic firms and financial institutions; export-related foreign borrowing; and general commercial borrowing.

Moreover, the Korean economy had already grown beyond selling low-tech products overseas at cheap prices, and had reached a level of development that made it unable to perpetuate an uneven growth strategy that assumed a large supply of cheap labor. As Korea's standing in the global economy changed, so did the nature of its growth. Its major exports had long before become computer parts, cars and ships. The problem of the chaebols, the nation's family-owned conglomerates, invited some scrutiny, but global companies like Samsung Electronics emerged, and society in general became well associated with the importance of research and development.

What triggered the massive crisis in 1997 was a loss of market confidence, and this in turn was caused by a terrible lack of financial transparency. Large conglomerates' profits were often overstated owing to internal transactions occurring between affiliates in a complicated web of interdependency. In the case of financial institutions, the scale of bad loans was underestimated.[4] Moreover, policymakers refused to admit that the Korean economy had problems, continuing to insist that its fundamentals were sound.

In addition, there were inefficiencies in handling troubled economic entities. For example, the issues surrounding troubled enterprises were not handled by the market system but by the application of the Bankruptcy Prevention Accord (whereby banks could defer the dishonoring of their bills). Nearly all economic players, including enterprises, financial institutions workers and depositors, believed all their losses were implicitly guaranteed by the government.

Faced with the financial crisis, Korea was forced to adopt painful restructuring measures in return for IMF bailout loans. These included monetary tightening and high interest rates that jumped as high as 25 per cent. Moreover, a number of insolvent chaebols were forced to undergo some form of insolvency rehabilitation procedures: out of the 63 largest chaebols, 15 chaebols for in-court procedures and another 15 for informal workout programs. To improve corporate governance, Korea's institutional and legal framework has been overhauled. The nation also had to introduce more market principles into almost all of its economic activities. Several years after the crisis, the economy seemed to be back on track, with GDP growth on the rise – over 6 per cent by 2002. By this time, much had changed for good. Banks and big businesses were no longer 100 per cent protected, and they no longer operated under the illusion that they were 'too big to fail'. Korea was finally becoming better adapted to globalization, and its business practices were closer than ever to the global standard.[5]

But with the boom in the Chinese economy and the tapering off of Korea's own growth, the country faced the task of creating a new economic growth engine to power further development. Between China's size- and cost-competitiveness and Japan's technological competitiveness, it was becoming more difficult for the nation to find and maintain its edge. These challenges, along with the worsening economic imbalances in the world, were increasing the uncertainty in the Korean economy.

As you can see, despite the improvements that had been made in the Korean economy after the 1997 crisis, the story does not have an entirely happy ending. Recently, the economy has suffered from sluggish growth and a polarization of income and worth. It is especially worthwhile to take a look at the problem of increasing inequality. According to the Korea National Statistics Office, the Gini coefficient for income distribution increased from 0.295 in 1998 to 0.325 in 2008 (see Figure 6.1). This increase was due to the restructuring in the corporate and financial sector. Since the end of the Asian financial crisis, those with higher incomes have continued to get richer, but many less-affluent people are beginning to feel

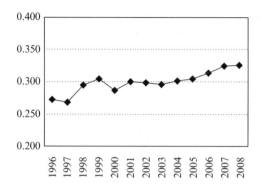

*Source:*    Korea National Statistics Office.

*Figure 6.1    Gini coefficient for income distribution.*

they are even worse off now than they were during the last crisis. Indeed,
the Gini coefficient for total assets also increased from 0.60 in 2000 to 0.64
in 2006. The worsening of wealth distribution was due mainly to the fact
that mortgage loans were relatively concentrated on the high-income class,
and the price of real estate increased steadily during 2001–06, adding to
the wealth of the richest.[6]

Here we are witnessing the beginning of exactly the same problem as
in the US: another kind of supercapitalism is emerging in the Korean
economy. Rich people increased their spending on luxury items, foreign
goods and services, investment funds and houses. The middle class tried
to catch up with such consumption and investment trends, significantly
drying up their savings. As the property bubble swelled, more and more
people got into the risky business of speculation, especially in housing,
relying on financial debt.[7] The result was that the average Korean
household spends about 10 per cent of its disposable income on interest payments, a burden of debt comparable to that of the US. This only
undermines the strength of the Korean economy and its resilience in the
face of economic challenges.

The government and the financial sector certainly had a hand in the
emergence of supercapitalism in Korea. While the nation's manufacturing
industries were restructuring themselves during the last decade, the financial industry was getting more and more bloated. The government had
drawn up a grand plan to grow Korea into a 'financial hub' for Northeast
Asia, similar to what Hong Kong and Singapore had become in the southern parts of the continent.

The media did their part to further the government agenda by helping to drum up public support for a financial-industry boom. Finance was presented as a new, sophisticated alternative to the manufacturing that had driven the nation's previous growth. Many breathtaking reports were produced on the success of the City of London and how it led the UK economy out of a slump, as well as series of articles on the major Wall Street firms.

Of course, everyone, including those in the government and financial sector, knew Korea still had a long way to go before it could lay any legitimate claim to the term 'financial hub'. Government officials were quoted in the press as saying the nation should aim first to create a 'Silverman Sachs' if not a Goldman Sachs, implicitly acknowledging that it was still a rather distant dream for a world-class financial firm to emerge in Korea. Wall Street firms were the template on which Korea's financial companies modeled their futures; the management of many a firm announced that their biggest goal was to become a true investment bank. At the time, the financial markets were still booming, the luster of investment banking had not tarnished and the US model of deregulated markets appeared to be the only path to growth and prosperity.

Perhaps it was the realization that Korean banks had a lot of catching up to do that made the government even more eager to help them grow. According to this ambitious blueprint, lenders were encouraged in various ways to expand a lot, and very quickly at that. To this end, the regulatory oversight of banks was eased to let them freely increase their assets and expand overseas business.

While the regulatory bodies satisfied themselves with perfunctory, document-based audits of financial institutions, the banks intensified competition in lending to households. South Korea's major corporations had no need to take out loans, thanks to their healthy operating profits and cash flow, while smaller companies were considered too risky to lend to. In this situation, banks chose to lend aggressively to households.

This increased lending to households helped spark an increase in consumer spending. People found it easier to take out loans for bigger homes and fancier cars; in effect, they were going down the same road as their American counterparts who had mired themselves in debt trying to copy the lifestyles of the rich.

As their girth expanded, Korean banks also issued large amounts of bonds to fund their growth and borrowed money from overseas.[8] That had worked well previously, but the economic environment has changed dramatically since then. How viable would that kind of expansionary strategy be under the current circumstances? As businesses fail and people lose their jobs, the quality of bank assets will sour as their loans go bad. Once that starts happening, how much of their foreign-currency debt can they keep rolling over?

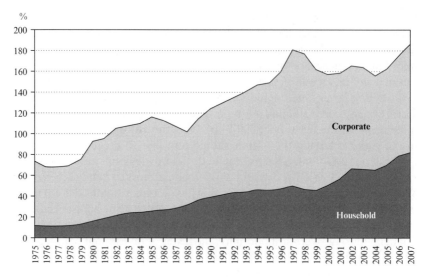

*Source:*   Bank of Korea; quoted from Kim (2009).

*Figure 6.2    Leverage ratio (borrowings/GDP) by private sector.*

Figure 6.2 and Figure 6.3 show the household and corporate sector's borrowing as a percentage of GDP and the share of financial industry in value added out of the whole economy, respectively. It is noteworthy that after 2000 the private sector's leverage has sharply increased mainly owing to the rapid expansion of household debts while the share of value added in financial industry has increased only marginally, implying that Korean financial institutions have managed their asset portfolios loosely.

Therefore, even without the US financial crisis, Korea may have faced its own crisis or crisis-like situation due to its own internal bubbles and imbalances which had worsened throughout the period of rapid globalization.

On the other hand, Korean enterprises have improved their transparency and financial soundness since the Korean financial crisis. Indeed, their debt ratio has fallen more than threefold. However, in the meantime, the Korean economy has become increasingly dependent on external demands, owing to the forces of globalization and its export-oriented growth strategy. Exports now account for more than 40 per cent of GDP, more than 10 percentage points higher than pre-crisis levels. This had the inevitable effect of creating instability within the economy; growth has become extremely sensitive to global business cycles. Thus, the Korean economy now faces challenges from inside and outside at the same time.

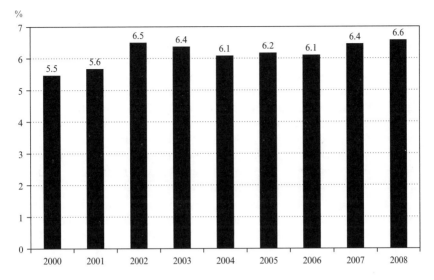

*Source:* Bank of Korea, Economic Statistics System.

*Figure 6.3 Ratio of financial industry's value added/GDP.*

## 6.5 MEASURES TO OVERCOME THE CRISIS

So far, we have examined what caused the problems in the US and Korea. From these two different examples, we can extract a common lesson: imbalances in the economy can create bubbles and crises. Given the source of the crisis, we must focus eventually on structural reform to overcome it, which necessarily requires a long-term perspective. In the meantime, however, liquidity should be properly supplied to prevent the collapse of confidence and more active fiscal policies may be used in the short run to spur growth.

In Korea, the current government is trying to carry out massive construction projects along the nation's major rivers despite many concerns about the plan's effectiveness, let alone the environmental costs. Even though certain short-term measures are necessary to cope with the crisis, as once proposed by John Maynard Keynes (1936), they must be implemented prudently and in a way that enhances productivity in the long run. The government seems to have judged that structural reform is difficult and time-consuming; consequently, it is trying to meet its growth targets by increasing government and corporate spending, especially on construction, through any means possible.

Korea is undeniably suffering from a lack of investment, so an increase in corporate spending is certainly desirable. However, construction is one of the industries in Korea that still harbors the dangers of a bubble burst and is in need of further reorganization. To spend indiscriminately in this sector would only make the problem worse.

The lack of corporate spending is certainly the biggest long-term challenge facing the South Korean economy. But if investment is not accompanied by an improvement in efficiency, the effects will be merely temporary and will soon be worthless in the near future.

Business spending is crucial for maximizing current production and creating future capacity. Therefore a lack of it will hamper the nation's ability to take advantage of the global economic recovery when it comes.

Korea's major corporations won't invest because there's not much to invest in. Until the 1980s, they could make money by investing in mid-level foreign technology, but that's no longer the case now that Korean firms are global leaders in several industries. Those companies won't benefit from investing in anything but the most cutting-edge technology.

Another reason companies won't invest is that a shortage of quality labor has made investment less efficient. We don't have enough of the skilled workers that companies would fight to hire.

As a lack of skilled labor is discouraging companies from investing, we must improve our education. 90 per cent of Korea's education budget goes to primary and secondary education, leaving only 10 per cent for colleges. Not enough funds are going to the institutions that produce our most sophisticated workers.

Koreans are well aware of the important role of people and education in an economy, as its human resources were the driving force behind its remarkable emergence from the devastation of the Korean War. But we came to attach too much importance to size and volume, not only in economic growth but also in education. Too often we have ignored other qualities, such as leadership, steadiness of character and creativity in favor of learning by rote. But Korea has reached a stage where further growth must come from creative innovation in the markets, rather than from government policy as it did in the past. The government should no longer attempt to direct and lead the economy, but focus on nurturing creative innovators and on constructing the best environment for them to unleash their talent in.

Another concern regarding proposed economic policies in Korea is the drive for deregulation, especially in the financial sector. It is interesting to see that these proposals appear to be based on the pre-crisis US system, itself based on a blind faith in markets. It is also interesting that some government officials seem to think deregulation will have immediately observable effects that will play a key role in rapidly overcoming the crisis.

Deregulated does not always mean 'good'. At every opportunity, I have emphasized the importance of financial regulations. The markets have numerous positive functions; but, owing to their very nature, the failure of one institution undermines the stability of the entire system. Such instability eventually causes a contraction in economic activity. The only way to prevent this happening is to introduce and implement the appropriate regulations.

Some rules are made by the regulated party to protect its own interests. Such unnecessary regulations must be eliminated. Others are made, however, to control negative externalities such as pollution, which otherwise would go unchecked in the markets. Still others are needed to make the wheels of the market itself go round. Regulations that encourage fair competition and prevent the abuse of economic power provide the framework for a properly functioning market economy. Therefore, the deregulation, particularly that of the financial industry, requires a special degree of careful consideration. It is difficult to understand why the Korean government clings to deregulation even amid the turmoil brought by it.

In the US, the very heart of deregulation, we are now witnessing a reevaluation of the indiscriminate faith in markets. The regulatory authorities in the US are changing their rules to allow for the stricter policing of markets to maintain their soundness. For example, the US has created a mortgage committee and strengthened the Fed's supervisory role. More long-term measures include bringing state banks under the jurisdiction of federal law and the possible establishment of agencies to stabilize markets and to regulate financial health and business practices.

Criticism of former Federal Reserve Chairman Alan Greenspan, a product of Wall Street, is becoming increasingly common. During his tenure, Greenspan clung to the belief that the 'invisible hand' works almost perfectly in the financial markets. His critics say that his toothless regulations and excessive easing of existing rules encouraged investment banks to take higher risks. Deregulation was supposed to grant greater freedom in financial activity, but the result was rampant, predatory lending. Interest-rate cuts were supposed to spur the economy, but the increase in money supply powered a boom of leverage-driven speculation. The development of derivatives was supposed to help market participants hedge their risks, but their mispricing led to massive losses.

Deregulation is not a panacea for the current problems and should be considered within a long-term framework. A bold 'deregulate first, worry later' approach may be exactly the attitude a company needs when making a decision on a risky investment. However, that kind of attitude can have dire consequences when it comes to changing the rules of the market.

I suggest we remove as much as possible those rules such as entry barriers that protect vested interests, while maintaining or even strengthening those regulations that maintain market order.

## 6.6   CONCLUDING REMARKS

The Korean economy faces both internal and external uncertainties. Nevertheless, there are still opportunities to be seized if we strive to refine the country's economic philosophy and reach a societal consensus. We can learn many lessons from the financial crisis that began in the US. If we cannot break the habit of spending more than we produce, or rectify extreme disparities in income, markets will always harbor the potential for collapse. The desire for cheap goods and high-yielding investments is a part of human nature. However, it can lead to disaster. Several preventative measures need to be taken. Financial markets must not be reduced to speculators' playgrounds through indiscriminate deregulation. Rules that enhance market soundness must be strengthened.

In 10 to 20 years, the world's financial markets may conveniently forget what they have learned this time around and find themselves caught up in another frenzy of speculation. An unrestrained market will always bear the seed of crisis; that is the lesson of history. The situation on Wall Street is sounding a warning about the unconditional belief that the invisible hand will always promote efficiency.

## NOTES

1.  This is a revised and expanded version of the lecture 'Financial Crisis in America and Sustainable Economic Growth in Korea' delivered at the Jackson School of International Studies, University of Washington, 12 February 2009.
2.  Reich (2007).
3.  The Kim Young Sam government that took office in 1993 – the first democratic civilian government since 1961 – aimed at the globalization of the Korean economy. As a means to signify its commitment to globalization, an accession to the OECD was pursued, the target year being set to 1995. It was well understood by the government that capital account liberalization is a necessary condition for Korea to qualify for OECD membership, though its scope and pace are negotiable.
4.  Using the financial statements of the externally audited firms, Kim and Lee (2002) identified the share of financial distressed firms with the interest payment coverage ratio – the ratio of earnings before interest payments and taxes plus depreciation and amortization (EBITDA) to interest expenses – less than one, increasing over time before the financial crisis (20 per cent in 1994, 25 per cent in 1995 and 28 per cent in 1996). However,

according to the official nonperforming loan (NPL) data, the NPL ratio (the ratio of the sum of estimated losses and doubtful and substandard loans to total loans) was low but had been decreasing until 1996 (5.8 per cent in 1994, 5.2 per cent in 1995, 4.1 per cent in 1996). Hence, if the official data were to be believed there would not have been a substantial deterioration in bank balance sheets prior to the crisis (Hahm and Mishkin, 2000).

5.  According to a study by the Korea Development Institute, which examined corporate governance, Korea scored an overall 0.8 out of 1.0, just slightly below the US score of 0.89 (see Table below). Korea's corporate governance scored highest in accountability of managers through shareholders' rights, establishment of a market for corporate control and holding controlling shareholders legally liable. Furthermore, Korea scored relatively well in the areas of disclosure and audit. We should note, however, that the enforcement index is much less than the institutional index in all categories, suggesting that the newly established rules and regulations are yet to be effectively enforced.

Corporate governance and investor protection

| | Institution[a] index[b] (A) | Enforcement[a] index[b] (B) | (A) − (B) |
|---|---|---|---|
| Disclosure and audit | 0.79 | 0.50 | 0.29 |
| Disclosure | 0.88 | 0.47 | 0.41 |
| Audit | 0.63 | 0.53 | 0.10 |
| Supervision and litigation by shareholders | 0.72 | 0.39 | 0.33 |
| Independence of supervisory bodies | 0.50 | 0.47 | 0.03 |
| Power of supervisory bodies | 1.00 | 0.51 | 0.49 |
| Litigation by shareholders | 0.67 | 0.19 | 0.48 |
| Accountability of managers | 0.90 | 0.45 | 0.45 |
| Shareholders' rights | 0.88 | 0.34 | 0.54 |
| Market for corporate control | 1.00 | 0.56 | 0.44 |
| Director/controlling shareholders' liability | 0.83 | 0.45 | 0.38 |
| Overall | 0.80 | 0.45 | 0.35 |

[a]  The institution index is constructed by examining the legal framework; the enforcement index is based on a survey of experts.

[b]  Index score ranges between 0 and 1, with 1 being the perfect score.

*Source:* Youngjae Lim et al. (2004).

6.  Kim (2008).

7.  According to the report made by the Office of National Tax Administration in 2005, 58.8 per cent of households with mortgage purchases in the Kangnam area between 2000 and 2004 already owned three or more houses (Kim, 2008).

8.  Since the Asian finance crisis, Korean government has removed restrictions further on capital inflows along with the liberalization of foreign exchange transactions. Particularly, in 1999 the Foreign Exchange Management Law was replaced with the Foreign Capital Transaction Law, which introduced a negative list system for capital account transactions. With the changes in such laws, Korea's capital market liberalization index reached the level of the most advanced countries in the world (Yoon et al., 2008).

# REFERENCES

Hahm, Joon-Ho and F. Mishkin (2000), 'Causes of the Financial Crisis: Lessons for Policy,' in Inseok Shin (ed.), *The Korean Economic Crisis: Before and After*, Seoul: Korea Development Institute.

Keynes, John Maynard (1936), *The General Theory of Employment, Interest and Money*, London: Macmillan.

Kim, Joon-Kyung (2008), 'Recent Changes in Korean Households' Indebtedness and Debt Service Capacity,' Working Paper 08-23, KDI School of Public Policy and Management, Seoul.

Kim, Joon-Kyung (2009), 'Global Financial Crisis and the Direction for the Korean Economy,' paper presented at the Symposium on 'What are the Problems in Korea's Financial System?' Seoul National University Institute for Research in Finance and Economics, 21 May.

Kim, Joon-Kyung and Chung H. Lee (2002), 'Insolvency in the Corporate Sector and Financial Crisis in Korea,' *Journal of the Asia Pacific Economy*, **7** (2), 267–81.

Lim, Youngjae et al. (2004), 'Developing and Measuring an Evaluation Index for Market Reform,' *OECD Economic Surveys 2004 Korea*, Paris: OECD.

Reich, Robert (2007), *Supercapitalism*, New York: Alfred A. Knopf.

Yoon, Deok Ryong et al. (2008), 'Economic Effects and Policy Implications of Financial Opening in Korea,' Korea Institute of International Economic Policy (KIEP), Policy Reference 08-09, Seoul.

# 7.   Why was Japan hit so hard by the global financial crisis?[1]

## Masahiro Kawai and Shinji Takagi

## 7.1   INTRODUCTION

Japan was hit hard by the global financial crisis of 2008–09; it was the only major advanced economy that experienced negative economic growth in 2008 and continued to contract sharply in 2009 (Figure 7.1). Although most advanced countries experienced recession in 2009, Japan's economic contraction (−5.2 per cent) surpassed the contractions experienced by the United States (US) (−2.4 per cent), the Euro Area (−4.1 per cent),[2] and the United Kingdom (−4.9 per cent), where the financial crisis for the most part originated. In contrast, most of Asia's major economies fared much better, notably with China, India and Indonesia maintaining positive growth during 2009. Though Singapore and Taiwan were hit hard initially by the global financial crisis, they recovered rather quickly to limit the extent of economic contraction to 2 per cent or less for the year as a whole.

When the US subprime loan problem came to the surface in the summer

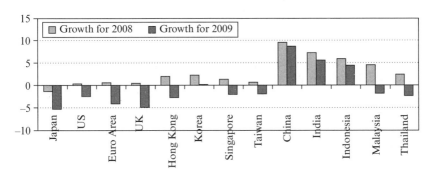

*Source:*   International Monetary Fund (2010).

*Figure 7.1   Economic growth (annual percentage change) for selected countries in 2008 and 2009.*

131

*Table 7.1   Direct impact of the global financial crisis on the US, Europe and Japan*

|  | Credit-related write-downs in the banking sector (billions of US$)[a] | Public outlays for the banking sector (billions of €)[b] |
|---|---|---|
| US | 2712 | 825 |
| Europe[c] | 1193 | 1116 |
| Japan | 149 | 3 |

*Notes:*
[a]  IMF estimates for 2007–10, as of April 2009.
[b]  The magnitude of government actions taken to intervene in the banking sector, up to 10 June 2009.
[c]  Europe means France, Germany, Italy, the Netherlands, Spain, Switzerland and the United Kingdom.

*Source:*   IMF (2009), Table 1.3; BIS (2009), Table 1.2.

of 2007, many observers thought that Japan was immune to the subsequent global deleveraging, given its limited exposure to 'toxic' assets. Indeed, various indicators suggested that the direct financial impact of the global financial crisis on Japan was relatively small. In fact, Japan's banking sector in particular was hardly affected directly, as was evident in the small estimated value of write-downs and the limited cost of public sector support, which were only a fraction of the corresponding amount in the US and Europe (Table 7.1).

When the US and much of Europe went into recession in early 2008 (Bosworth and Flaaen, 2009; Wyplosz, 2009), Japan's real economy did not seem to be affected materially. However, Japan was adversely affected by the large negative terms of trade shock in 2008, with a sharp increase in energy and other commodity prices, but it still maintained positive growth in real GDP and private fixed investment through the second quarter; export growth was steady through the third quarter (Figure 7.2). It was only in the fourth quarter that the evidence of a severe economic contraction was apparent, with a 12.5 per cent (year-on-year) fall in exports. This was followed by a 36.8 per cent fall in the first quarter of 2009. Similarly, industrial production also contracted sharply; it declined by 15.0 per cent, 34.0 per cent and 27.6 per cent (year-on-year) in the fourth quarter of 2008 and the first and second quarters of 2009, respectively. This decline was one of the worst among the major developed countries – in Europe and North America – and Asian economies. When Japan was finally hit, the impact was indeed very severe.

Why was Japan hit so hard by the global financial crisis when its financial

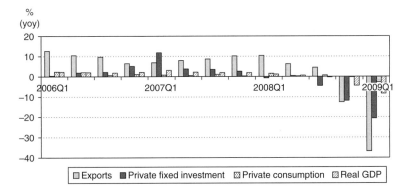

*Source:*     Cabinet Office, Government of Japan.

*Figure 7.2     Growth rates of Japanese GDP and its components.*

system was considered much more robust than those in other developed countries? The rest of this chapter attempts to offer an explanation in the following sequence. Section 7.2 describes what happened in terms of manufacturing production and exports. Section 7.3 argues that the sharp contraction of economic activity occurred largely as a result of the structural changes in the Japanese economy that had taken place over the past decade. Section 7.4 quantifies the impact of the structural changes on the responsiveness of Japanese output to global demand shocks by using a vector autoregression (VAR) model of the world economy. Finally, Section 7.5 offers concluding remarks.

## 7.2   WHAT HAPPENED

Japanese stock prices peaked in the summer of 2007 and, with the outbreak of the US subprime loan crisis, began a gradual but substantial decline through the fall of 2008. The decline in stock prices placed a strain on the balance sheet and capital adequacy ratios of commercial banks and, as a result, limited their willingness to lend by the summer of 2008. The Lehman Brothers shock in September 2008 further depressed the stock market and aggravated the strains on Japanese commercial banks. Bank of Japan data indicate that new loans for equipment funds declined by 9 per cent (year-on-year) in the third quarter of 2008, followed by a 10 per cent decline in the fourth quarter. This, coupled with the lagged impact of the negative terms of trade shock (arising from the sharp rise in oil and other commodity prices until the summer of 2008), may to some extent

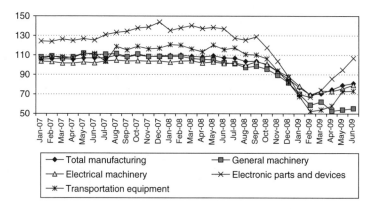

*Source:*    Japan Ministry of Economy and Industry.

*Figure 7.3    Japanese industrial production (2005 = 100).*

explain the sluggishness of industrial activity in some sectors from the summer of 2008 (see below).

Even so, overall manufacturing production held up through September and October 2008 (Figure 7.3). Notable exceptions were electronic parts and devices as well as transportation equipment, the production of which had shown earlier signs of softening. In November, however, manufacturing production collapsed precipitously in all major sectors (from 100 in October to 93, seasonally adjusted). Overall manufacturing production continued to fall and reached 70 in February 2009 before recovering somewhat. The collapse was even more spectacular for transportation equipment (52 in February 2009 compared with 110 in September 2008) and general machinery (59 compared with 99). The production of general machinery remained depressed even after production began to pick up in other sectors from the spring of 2009.

The downward movement of industrial production closely followed the downward movement of exports. Although the major factor behind the collapse of Japanese exports was a worldwide shrinkage of demand and trade following the Lehman shock, the sharp appreciation of the yen (caused as a result of an unwinding of the yen carry trade) was an additional blow to Japan's export-oriented firms.[3] The total value of exports, which stood at 7360 billion yen in September 2008, declined moderately to 6915 billion yen in October and collapsed thereafter. Exports in January 2009, at 3480 billion yen, were less than 50 per cent of the previous peak in September 2008. The decline was across the board, but most pronounced in the export of industrial supplies, capital equipment and consumer

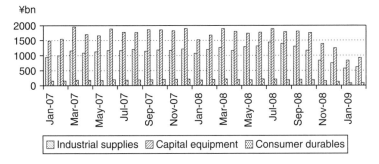

*Source:*    Japan Tariff Association.

*Figure 7.4    Japanese exports to emerging Asia by product category.*

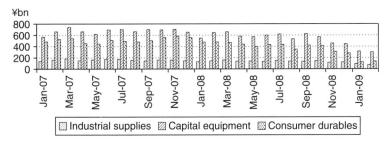

*Source:*    Japan Tariff Association.

*Figure 7.5    Japanese exports to the USA by product category.*

durables, Japan's three main categories of export products (which together account for over 90 per cent of Japan's total exports). The decline was also registered not only for exports to the US and western Europe (which together account for over 40 per cent of Japan's total exports), where the financial crisis originated, but also for exports to emerging and developing Asia, Japan's largest export market, now accounting for over 50 per cent of total exports (Figures 7.4 to 7.6).

Of the decline in exports of 3880 billion yen from September 2008 to January 2009, emerging (and developing) Asia accounted for over 51 per cent, which is roughly the share of emerging Asia in Japan's total exports. This implies that Japanese exports collapsed almost uniformly across destination markets. The composition of export declines, however, differed across regions, reflecting the different content of trade. With emerging Asia, 86 per cent of the decline was in industrial supplies and capital

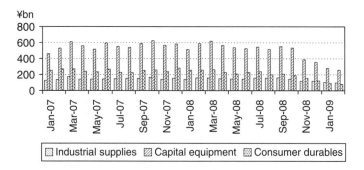

*Source:*    Japan Tariff Association.

*Figure 7.6    Japanese exports to western Europe by product category.*

goods, whereas this share for the US and western Europe was smaller at 60 per cent. On the other hand, only 6 per cent of the export decline for emerging Asia was consumer durables, while the share for the advanced markets was larger at 36 per cent.[4] This is a reflection of the fact that, though emerging Asia is the largest export market, it is not the dominant market for consumer durables; more consumer durables are shipped to the advanced markets of the US and western Europe.

Essentially, the export of industrial supplies and capital goods to emerging Asia was most severely affected as the region's demand for Japanese parts, components and capital goods – all critical inputs for the production of final consumer products – declined steeply. Japan was affected by the shrinkage of 'triangular trade' where Japan and the Asian NIEs (Korea, Singapore and Taiwan) export parts and components to China and other emerging Asian economies, which in turn assemble them to produce final products for the US and European markets. Thus, Japanese exports collapsed because both the export of consumer durables to the advanced markets and the export of industrial supplies and capital goods to emerging Asia fell sharply, as a consequence of the contraction of private consumption and the softening of investment spending in the US and Europe.

## 7.3    WHY IT HAPPENED

There are two aspects to the mechanism whereby Japan's output was so much affected by the collapse of exports in late 2008 and early 2009: Japan's trade structure and its industrial structure. We will examine each of these.

**Japan's Trade Structure**

As noted in the previous section, over 90 per cent of Japanese exports consist of highly income-elastic industrial supplies, capital goods and consumer durables. Hence a collapse of the US and European markets exerted a severe negative influence on Japanese exports. Japan was not alone in this. Sommer (2009) shows that economies with a greater share of advanced manufacturing in GDP tended to experience sharper output declines than others, with Singapore and Taiwan belonging to this group of economies. In Japan, as discussed above, both the export of consumer durables to the advanced markets (accounting for less than 15 per cent of total exports) and the export of industrial supplies and capital goods to emerging Asia (constituting over 40 per cent of total exports) were adversely and severely affected by the financial crisis. In particular, the export of industrial supplies and capital goods declined along with the softening of investment demand throughout the world.

Much has been said about the recent growth of intra-regional trade within Asia (see Kawai and Urata, 2004; Takagi and Kozuru, 2010). For example, within the member countries of the Association of Southeast Asian Nations (ASEAN), China, Japan, and Korea (ASEAN + 3), the share of intra-regional trade rose from around 30 per cent during 1980–90 to over 38 per cent in 2006; with Hong Kong and Taiwan included, the share was almost 55 per cent. Closely related to intra-regional trade is intra-regional foreign direct investment (FDI), which has recently accounted for as much as half of the region's total FDI. Direct investment in plant and equipment has created production networks and supply chains in industries such as electronics, automobiles and other machinery products, which cut across national borders – a flipside of the growing intra-regional trade. Japan has been the center of this increasing intra-regional trade, mainly in parts, components and capital equipment. This explains why Japanese exports to emerging Asia expanded sharply over the last two decades (Figure 7.7), with the share of exports to emerging Asia in total exports rising from 34 per cent in 1990 to 54 per cent in 2008.[5]

**Japan's Industrial Structure**

The industrial structure of Japan has undergone significant changes over the past 20 years. The change it underwent from around 2005 was particularly significant, as the real effective exchange rate of the yen returned to a level more consistent with the long-run average (Figure 7.8). The yen, which had begun to appreciate in real effective terms in early 1985, peaked in 1995 when the level was some 80 per cent higher than in 1980. Then

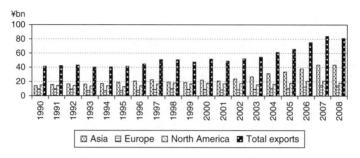

*Source:*   Japan Tariff Association.

*Figure 7.7    Japanese exports by destination.*

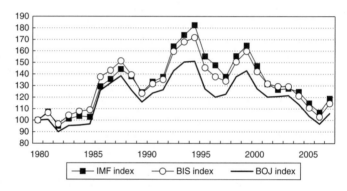

*Source:*   International Monetary Fund; Bank for International Settlements; Bank of Japan.

*Figure 7.8    Alternative measures of the real effective exchange rate of the yen (1980 = 100).*

the yen began to decline as a trend until 2007, except for the brief period 1999–2001 when the value rose temporarily.[6]

During the period of the 'lost decade', the share of the non-tradable goods sector in the Japanese economy expanded, in a way consistent with the real exchange rate level that was higher than the historical average. From theoretical perspectives, a high real value of the yen increases the relative price of non-tradable goods, thus encouraging their production; resources therefore should shift away from the production of tradable goods. This relative price change, moreover, should reduce the price competitiveness of manufacturing firms that produce tradable goods, so that it also encourages them to shift their production activities abroad through foreign direct investment. Indeed, this is what we observed.

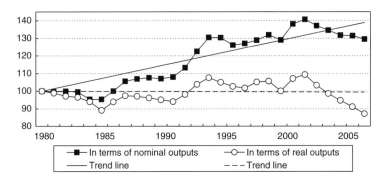

*Source:* Authors' estimates based on Japan Cabinet Office, National Income Accounts.

*Figure 7.9*     *Japanese production of non-tradable goods relative to tradable goods (1980 = 100).*

Figure 7.9 depicts the production of non-tradable goods relative to tradable goods from 1980 to 2007 in terms of both nominal and real outputs; the two straight lines (one solid, one dashed) represent the respective trend lines (for our purposes here the non-tradable goods sectors include construction, electricity, gas, water, wholesale and retail trade, banking and insurance, real estate, transportation, telecommunications and services; the tradable goods sector includes manufacturing). The figure indicates clearly that the share of the non-tradable goods sector rose steadily over this period in terms of nominal value, although the rise in the share of non-tradable goods was not pronounced when measured in terms of real value (reflecting the relatively more rapid growth of non-tradable goods prices). An important point is that, during the period of a strong yen, i.e. 1993–2002, the production of non-tradable goods relative to tradable goods exceeded the trend, regardless of whether it is measured in nominal or in real value.

What is more important to observe for our purpose is that the share of non-tradable goods began to decline from a peak achieved in 2002. When Japan began slowly to emerge out of the prolonged recession, it relied on the export sector as an engine of growth as the yen fell in real effective terms, especially given the limited space for expansionary fiscal policy. As a result, not only did the GDP share of exports increase, but also Japan's overall openness rose from the early 2000s to 2008 when the country was hit by the global financial crisis (Table 7.2). For instance, Japan's exports-to-GDP ratio, which was 11 per cent in 2000, rose to over 17 per cent in 2008. Over the same period, trade openness increased from about 20 per cent of GDP to almost 35 per cent.

Although net exports did not show an upward trend during this period,

*Table 7.2    Japan's exports, imports, net exports and trade openness as percentages of GDP*

|      | Exports | Imports | Net exports | Trade openness[a] |
|------|---------|---------|-------------|-------------------|
| 1995 | 9.1     | 7.7     | 1.4         | 16.8              |
| 1996 | 9.8     | 9.3     | 0.5         | 19.2              |
| 1997 | 10.9    | 9.8     | 1.1         | 20.6              |
| 1998 | 10.9    | 9.0     | 1.9         | 19.9              |
| 1999 | 10.3    | 8.7     | 1.6         | 19.0              |
| 2000 | 11.0    | 9.5     | 1.5         | 20.5              |
| 2001 | 10.6    | 9.9     | 0.6         | 20.5              |
| 2002 | 11.4    | 10.1    | 1.3         | 21.4              |
| 2003 | 12.0    | 10.4    | 1.6         | 22.4              |
| 2004 | 13.3    | 11.4    | 1.9         | 24.7              |
| 2005 | 14.3    | 12.9    | 1.4         | 27.3              |
| 2006 | 16.1    | 14.9    | 1.3         | 31.0              |
| 2007 | 17.6    | 15.9    | 1.7         | 33.5              |
| 2008 | 17.4    | 17.3    | 0.1         | 34.7              |

*Note:*    [a]Defined as (Exports + Imports)/GDP.

*Source:*    Cabinet Office, Government of Japan.

they positively contributed to economic growth when there was a withdrawal of fiscal stimulus from 2003 to 2006 (Table 7.3). Undoubtedly, the export-led recovery and growth was made possible by the expansion of the global economy, particularly that of the US economy that followed the post-IT-bubble recession. The restructuring of the banking sector and the resolution of bank nonperforming loans also likely supported the recovery process in Japan. This export-led growth, however, became increasingly vulnerable to US economic turbulence because the export expansion was being fueled by an unsustainable increase in US personal consumption backed by the housing price bubble, a bubble that eventually burst in the summer of 2006 and led to the subsequent eruption of the global financial crisis.

## 7.4    QUANTIFYING THE NATURE OF THE STRUCTURAL CHANGE

How these changes in Japan's trade and industrial structures may have affected the response of the Japanese economy to global demand shocks can be analyzed by a vector autoregression (VAR) technique. VAR is a standard statistical procedure to investigate how shocks are transmitted

*Table 7.3   Contributions to real GDP growth in annual percentage rates*

| | Real GDP growth | Domestic demand | | Net exports |
|---|---|---|---|---|
| | | Private sector | Public sector | |
| 1995 | 1.5 | 1.5 | 0.6 | −0.6 |
| 1996 | 2.3 | 2.0 | 0.8 | −0.5 |
| 1997 | 1.3 | 0.9 | −0.5 | 1.0 |
| 1998 | −2.1 | −2.3 | −0.1 | 0.3 |
| 1999 | −0.3 | −1.2 | 1.1 | −0.1 |
| 2000 | 2.7 | 2.3 | −0.0 | 0.4 |
| 2001 | 0.2 | 0.7 | 0.3 | −0.8 |
| 2002 | 0.3 | −0.5 | 0.1 | 0.7 |
| 2003 | 1.7 | 1.3 | −0.2 | 0.6 |
| 2004 | 3.1 | 2.4 | −0.1 | 0.8 |
| 2005 | 2.3 | 2.4 | −0.2 | 0.1 |
| 2006 | 1.8 | 1.5 | −0.2 | 0.6 |
| 2007 | 3.5 | 2.2 | 0.1 | 1.2 |

*Source:*   Cabinet Office, Government of Japan.

from one entity to another. Using this statistical technique, we examined the respective impacts of three separate shocks, namely one that originates within Japan (a Japan shock), one from within emerging Asia (an emerging-Asia shock) and one in the rest of the world (a global shock), in order to see how changes in Japan's economic structure over the past decade or so affected the responsiveness of its GDP to supply or demand shocks originating abroad.[7]

For convenience, we used the Asian financial crisis of 1997–98 to divide the sample. We then used two measures of the responsiveness of Japanese GDP to global and Asian shocks. The first measure is the response to a one-standard deviation shock to the global and regional outputs. The second measure is the extent to which the total variance is explained by the variance of respective shocks. In order to quantify the nature of the structural change that may have taken place in Japan over the past decade, we compared these measures obtained from the pre-crisis and post-crisis samples. It should be noted, however, that VAR helps uncover only temporal statistical relationships among several variables but gives no indication of how and why they affect each other.

Consider the following moving average (MA) representation of the VAR model, which consists of three equations representing global, Japanese, and emerging-Asian outputs:

$$X_t = \Sigma \phi_{1j} u_{t-j} + \Sigma \phi_{2j} v_{t-j} + \Sigma \phi_{3j} w_{t-j} \qquad (7.1)$$

$$Y_t = \Sigma \lambda_{1j} u_{t-j} + \Sigma \lambda_{2j} v_{t-j} + \Sigma \lambda_{3j} w_{t-j} \qquad (7.2)$$

$$Z_t = \Sigma \eta_{1j} u_{t-j} + \Sigma \eta_{2j} v_{t-j} + \Sigma \eta_{3j} w_{t-j} \qquad (7.3)$$

where $X_t$ is real GDP in the US and Europe (henceforth referred to as 'global'), $Y_t$ is real GDP in Japan, and $Z_t$ is real GDP in emerging Asia, all expressed as indices in order to remove the influence of nominal exchange rate changes; $u$, $v$ and $w$ are, respectively, a shock to global GDP (a global shock), a shock to Japanese GDP (a Japan shock), and a shock to emerging Asia's GDP (an emerging-Asia shock). We are particularly interested in examining the pattern of response of Japanese GDP ($Y$) to the past global and emerging-Asia shocks, before and after the Asian financial crisis of 1997–98.

The simplified setup of equations (7.1) to (7.3) is dictated by the small number of observations, especially when the data are divided into the pre-Asian crisis and the post-Asian crisis period. Even with this simple setup, various data limitations have restricted the coverage of countries as well as the choice of sample.[8] The results reported below assume that in the long run global GDP affects both Japanese and emerging-Asian GDPs; Japanese GDP affects only emerging-Asian GDP; and emerging Asian GDP affects neither. In the short run, all the GDPs affect each other. We have verified, however, that the substantive results are robust to the choice of ordering. Lag length is determined by the Akaike information criterion (AIC). The pre-crisis period refers to Q1:1988–Q4:1996, while the post-crisis period covers Q1:1999–Q4:2006.

Figure 7.10 shows the responses of Japanese GDP to a one-standard deviation shock to global, Japanese and emerging-Asia GDPs. Before the Asian financial crisis of 1997, Japanese GDP did not respond significantly to a global shock (in each graph, the broken upper and lower curves indicate a confidence interval). In the post-crisis period, however, Japan's output became significantly responsive to a global shock, while the response to its own shock declined significantly. There was little change in the responsiveness to an emerging-Asia shock across the two samples.

Next, Figure 7.11 indicates the variance of Japanese GDP that can be explained by a global shock, a Japan shock and an emerging-Asia shock. Before the Asian financial crisis of 1997–98, virtually 100 per cent of the variance of Japanese GDP was explained by a Japan shock alone. Global and emerging-Asia shocks had no role. In the post-crisis period, however, the portion explainable by a global shock increased significantly (to about 40 per cent after a few quarters), with little change observed for

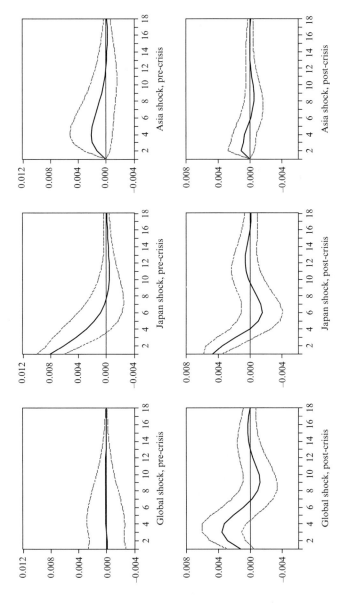

*Figure 7.10 Impulse responses of Japanese GDP: comparing the pre- and post-Asian financial crisis periods.*

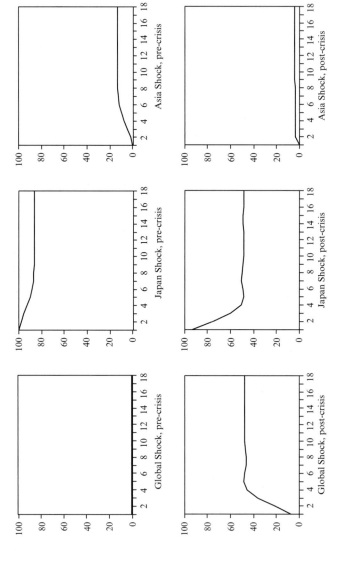

*Figure 7.11  Variance decomposition of Japanese GDP: comparing the pre- and post-Asian financial crisis periods.*

the emerging-Asia shock. Consistently with the impulse response analysis reported above, global GDP shocks have tended to have a much more significant impact on Japanese GDP in recent years. As a result, the variance of Japanese GDP can be explained almost equally by Japan and global shocks.

## 7.5 CONCLUSION

Japan was hit hard by the global financial crisis even though its relatively resilient financial system initially limited the direct impact. The severe collapse of industrial production that followed was no doubt attributable to a confluence of factors, including the stock price declines that eroded the capital base of commercial banks and thus limited their willingness to lend as well as the lagged impact of the sharp rise in oil and other commodity prices in the summer of 2008. This chapter has however highlighted, as a primary cause of the severe recession, the impact that came from the contractionary effect of global deleveraging on the real economy. In this environment, Japan was particularly vulnerable because of the structural changes that had taken place over the past decade in its trade and industrial structures. VAR analysis has confirmed that, as a result of these structural changes, Japanese output became much more responsive to output shocks in the advanced markets of the US and western Europe.

Japan's structural changes had two components. First, over 90 per cent of Japan's exports consisted of highly income-elastic industrial supplies, capital goods and consumer durables. Though emerging Asia is Japan's largest export market, the region's imports from Japan consist largely of industrial supplies and capital goods that are necessary at least in part for the production of final consumer goods destined for the advanced markets of the US and western Europe. Asia's intra-regional trade had expanded rapidly until the outbreak of the global financial crisis, with Japan as the most important supplier of foreign direct investment and technology-intensive products, but much of it had been in the trade of parts, components and capital equipment. With final demand coming from the advanced markets outside the region, the demand contraction in these advanced economies due to global deleveraging had direct and secondary impacts on Japan – and on other similar emerging economies like Korea, Singapore and Taiwan.

Second, Japan's trade dependence had increased since the early 2000s, as evidenced by a rising export-to-GDP ratio and a declining share of the non-tradable sector. This was induced by the return of the real effective exchange rate of the yen to a level more in line with the long-run average, allowing the Japanese economy to finally come out of a decade-long stag-nation. Fundamentally, increasing trade openness can be thought of as a natural part of the process of economic globalization and regional integra-tion that has been advancing throughout the world and especially in Asia. But the manner in which this process played out made Japan particularly vulnerable to a large output shock coming from outside.

In looking to the future, one must make a distinction between the outcome of the natural process of economic globalization and integration, of which Japan has been a part, and the need to manage that process. As Japan continues to integrate with the regional and global economies, as it should, a rise in the ratio of exports to GDP is likely to continue; the share of emerging Asia in Japan's total exports may well continue to increase, especially as the region's income levels rise. What matters is the geographical and product diversification of the likely increases in exports. To make Japan more resilient to external shocks, policymakers could create enabling environments to stimulate the export of finished goods to emerging Asia, for example, through the establishment of a region-wide free trade arrangement. In this context, it is instructive to note the experi-ence of Germany during the current crisis. Although Japan and Germany share similar industrial structures, German industrial production declined less despite the fact that its export dependence was even greater than that of Japan.[9]

Domestically, there is no rational ground where one can advocate a policy of reducing trade openness just to minimize vulnerability to external shocks. Japan, as a relatively large economy, however, cannot rely on external demand alone to sustain its economic growth over the medium term. To the extent that there are impediments that may inhibit the vigorous expansion of domestic demand or the non-tradable goods sector, policy needs to address them. To promote domestic demand, the social sector protection system (for education, health, unemployment and pensions) needs to be substantially reformed so as to reduce households' uncertainty about the future. To promote a better allocation of resources between the more regulated non-tradable goods sector (such as medical, health, and care of the young and old) and the less regulated tradable goods sector, further deregulatory measures are called for. A substantial lifting of restrictions in agriculture, especially the corporatization of agri-cultural production, would be especially helpful. More liberal immigration policy should help invigorate private investment in an aging society. With little available fiscal space, these and other measures will help create a climate in which private investment can flourish, driven by final domestic demand.

# NOTES

1. This is a revised version of the paper presented at the Samuel Hsieh Memorial Conference, hosted by the Chung-Hua Institution for Economic Research, Taipei, 9–10 July 2009. The authors are thankful to Ainslie Smith for her editorial work. The views expressed in the paper are those of the authors and do not necessarily reflect those of the Asian Development Bank or the Asian Development Bank Institute (ADBI). Names of countries or economies mentioned are chosen by the authors, in the exercise of their academic freedom, and the ADBI is in no way responsible for such usage.
2. The Euro Area in 2009 included 16 countries: Austria, Belgium, Cyprus, Finland, France, Germany, Greece, Ireland, Italy, Luxembourg, Malta, the Netherlands, Portugal, Slovakia, Slovenia and Spain.
3. The nominal value of the yen appreciated by 17 per cent against the US dollar and by 27 per cent against the euro, on a monthly average basis, from September 2008 to January 2009.
4. US imports, on a customs basis, declined by more than 30 per cent from July to December 2008; the import of transportation equipment showed an even sharper decline, of about 40 per cent.
5. In contrast, the share of exports to the US and Europe declined precipitously from 55 per cent to 35 per cent over the same period.
6. When the yen began to appreciate sharply following the Plaza Agreement, there was a contraction of manufacturing activity. The Japanese policymakers reacted by expanding both fiscal and monetary policies. Coupled with the favorable terms of trade changes (caused by a fall in energy and commodity prices) at the time, these policy actions allowed economic growth to pick up from the fall of 1987 but subsequently led to the emergence of a bubble economy, with sharp rises in stock, real estate and other asset prices. Monetary policy then was reversed.

   With a bursting of the bubble economy in 1991, the Japanese economy decelerated and, in 1992, entered a prolonged period of stagnation. Annual growth over the next decade averaged less than 1 per cent, compared with over 4 per cent during the previous decade. Growth appeared to pick up in 1995–96, only to fall back. In 1998, in the midst of a systemic banking crisis, severe recession set in and the economy contracted in 1998 and 1999. The stagnation was compounded by sustained deflationary pressure; annual consumer price index (CPI) inflation averaged less than 1 per cent over the 'lost decade.' Although annual economic growth finally exceeded 2 per cent in 2003 and 2004, this moderate recovery did not end the deflation. The corporate goods price level was 13 per cent lower in 2003 than in 1991.

   During the prolonged period of stagnation, the authorities eased both fiscal and monetary policies substantially to support domestic demand and to fend off deflationary pressure. The general government balance, which was in small surpluses in the early 1990s, deteriorated sharply; it has been in deficit every year since 1993 – with deficits exceeding 7 per cent of GDP in virtually every year from 1999 to 2003. As a result, the balance of gross public debt rose from about 70 per cent of GDP in the early 1990s to over 180 per cent in 2005. As to monetary policy, the BOJ lowered the discount rate in several steps from 4.5 per cent in December 1991 to 0.5 per cent in September 1995. With no additional room left to maneuver, in February 1999 it reduced the overnight call rate to virtually zero, a policy it continued to follow until March 2006, except for the brief period of August 2000–March 2001. A new framework of 'quantitative easing' – with the de facto 'zero' policy rate – was adopted in March 2001.
7. Takagi and Kozuru (2010) used the same methodology and data set to analyze the macroeconomic interdependence of Asia.
8. The sample countries include: (1) for Asia, in addition to Japan, China, Hong Kong, India, Indonesia, Korea, Malaysia, the Philippines, Singapore, Taiwan and Thailand; and (2) for the rest of the world, Belgium, France, Germany, Italy, the Netherlands, Spain, the United States and the United Kingdom. Global and regional GDPs are

the weighted averages of the individual country GDPs in the respective regions, with US$2000-GDPs used as the weights. The underlying data were provided by the Asian Development Bank.
9.  German industrial production did not decline noticeably during the last quarter of 2008; even during the first quarter of 2009 the decline was around 20 per cent from a year earlier – significantly less than Japan's decline.

# REFERENCES

Bank for International Settlements (BIS) (2009), 'An Assessment of Financial Sector Rescue Programmes,' BIS Papers no. 48, July.
Bosworth, Barry and Aaron Flaaen (2009), 'America's Financial Crisis: The End of An Era,' paper presented at the Asian Development Bank Institute Conference on Global Financial and Economic Crisis: Impacts, Lessons and Growth Rebalancing, Tokyo, 22–23 April.
International Monetary Fund (IMF) (2009) *Global Financial Stability Report*, Washington, DC, April.
International Monetary Fund (IMF) (2010), *World Economic Outlook*, Washington, DC, April.
Japan Tariff Association, *The Summary Report on Trade of Japan*, monthly issues.
Kawai, Masahiro and Shujiro Urata (2004), 'Trade and Foreign Direct Investment in East Asia,' in Gordon de Brouwer and Masahiro Kawai (eds), *Exchange Rate Regimes in East Asia*, London and New York: Routledge Curzon, pp. 15–102.
Sommer, Martin (2009), 'Why Has Japan Been Hit So Hard by the Global Recession?' IMF Staff Position Note SPN/09/05, Washington, DC, 18 March.
Takagi, Shinji and Issei Kozuru (2010), 'Output and Price Linkages in Asia's Post-Crisis Macroeconomic Interdependence,' *Singapore Economic Review*, **55** (March), 1–23.
Wyplosz, Charles (2009), 'The Euro Area in the Current Crisis,' paper presented at the Asian Development Bank Institute Conference on Global Financial and Economic Crisis: Impacts, Lessons and Growth Rebalancing, Tokyo, 22–23 April.

# 8. China's policy responses to the global financial crisis[1]

## Yongding Yu

Since undertaking reform and opening up its economy, China has experienced an economic miracle. Its average annual GDP growth rate over the past three decades has been 9.8 per cent. This unprecedented growth has vastly improved the living standards of the Chinese people. In the period 2002–07, China registered an average annual growth rate of 10.5 per cent, while the inflation rate was kept under 2 per cent. This period can be said to be the best period over the past three decades as far as macroeconomic performance is concerned.

In 2007, China's GDP growth rate was 13 per cent. In 2008 China's GDP growth fell gradually at first; then, after the Lehman Brothers fiasco, it fell in a dramatic fashion. In the first half of 2008 China was still able to manage an annual growth rate of 10.4 per cent. In the third and fourth quarters, the rate fell to 9 per cent and 6.8 per cent respectively. In the first quarter of 2009, the growth rate fell further to 6.1 per cent.

In hindsight, the turning-point in China's growth happened in September 2008, after the Lehman Brothers bankruptcy. The monthly growth rate of industrial products is a better reflection of the changing fortunes of the Chinese economy. In August and September 2008, the growth rate of industrial products was 14.7 per cent and 11.4 per cent respectively. In October and November 2008 it dropped to 8.2 per cent and 5.4 per cent. In February 2008, China's CPI hit 8.7 per cent, the highest in more than a decade. But the CPI index fell to 2 per cent in November and has remained negative since then, though sequential CPI growth has turned positive recently. The fall of the Producer Price Index after August 2008 was even more dramatic.

There is no doubt whatsoever that – owing to China's extremely high export dependency – the single most important impact of the global financial crisis on the Chinese economy came from the fall in global demand. China's export dependency is the highest among the major world economies. China's exports-to-GDP ratio in 2007 was 35 per cent. In November 2008 exports shrank by 2.2 per cent on the year, compared with a positive growth rate of 25 per cent in September. The fall of exports may have cut GDP growth by 3 percentage points. If its indirect impact is included, it may have shaved more than 5 percentage points off China's 2008 growth rate.

## 8.1   THE FEATURES OF CHINA'S GROWTH PATTERN

China's high export dependency is a result of the country's export promotion policy, which has been in place for decades. However, from the macroeconomic point of view, China's high export dependency is, to a certain extent, attributable to China's overcapacity caused by overinvestment.[2] This has been especially true over the past 5 years or so.

Fixed asset investment (FAI) and exports were the two most important engines of China's growth during the period 2002–07. In this period, the average annual growth rate of exports and FAI were 29 per cent and 24 per cent respectively (Figure 8.1). In 2007, the combined contribution of FAI and net exports to GDP growth was more than 60 per cent. Both China's investment rate and exports-to-GDP ratio are strikingly high. These are the two most important characteristics of China's growth pattern.

FAI has long been the single most important factor contributing to China's economic growth, because of its high growth rate as well as its sizable share in GDP.[3] A noteworthy phenomenon in the past decade or so has been that the growth rate of FAI has been consistently higher than that of GDP and hence the investment rate has been increasing persistently since 2001 (Figure 8.2).

The persistent rise in the investment rate means that the growth of the Chinese economy is in a non-steady state. By definition, a steady state

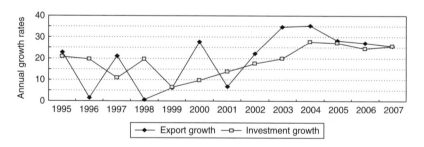

*Source:   Statistical Year Book*, various issues, Statistics Bureau of PRC.

*Figure 8.1   Growth rates of exports and investment (current prices).*

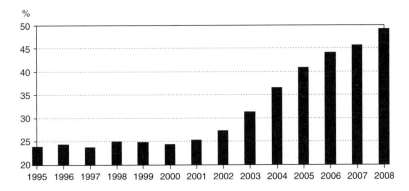

*Source:* Zhongjing Net Data Bank.

*Figure 8.2 China's investment rates.*

means that (1) aggregate demand is equal to aggregate supply (and so are their growth rates); (2) the growth rates of all components of aggregate demand are equal; (3) the shares of all components of aggregate demand are constant; and (4) a growth process in a steady state is sustainable. Our question here is how, in a non-steady state, characterized by a constant rising investment rate, is China's growth drama being played out? Let us set out a framework of analysis first.

1.  If the initial steady state is disturbed by an external shock in the form of a sudden acceleration in the growth rate of FAI, the investment rate of the economy increases.
2.  Starting from the initial steady state and equilibrium, an increase in the growth rate of FAI means aggregate demand is greater than that of supply, and hence overheating occurs.
3.  Provided that there is no change in the capital–output ratio, a higher investment rate means a higher potential growth rate of the economy in the future.
4.  However, in the periods immediately following, if the growth rates of the other components of aggregate demand remain unchanged, the excess demand caused by the initial rise of the growth rate of FAI, which disturbed the initial equilibrium, will persist until the gap of excess demand narrows gradually to zero. However, the new equilibrium is temporary. Because the growth rate of FAI is higher than that of the other components of aggregate demand, the investment rate and hence the potential growth rate will continue to rise. As a result, excess demand (overheating) will shift to overcapacity.

Equilibrium is just a transitional stage between overheating and overcapacity. The specific point in time of the turning-point from overheating to overcapacity depends on initial conditions.[4]

5.   It should be emphasized that equilibrium between aggregate demand and supply does not imply a steady state, because growth rates of different components of aggregate supply are different. In other words, the growth is imbalanced. Here, the growth rate of FAI is higher than those of the other components of aggregate demand.

6.   If the growth rate of the components of aggregate demand other than FAI as a whole fail to rise,[5] overcapacity can be absorbed only by a further rise in the growth rate of FAI. As a result, the investment rate will rise further and so will the potential growth rate.

7.   With both a higher investment rate and a higher potential growth rate, the growth rate of FAI must be increased further and further in subsequent periods so as to absorb overcapacity. Correspondingly, the investment rate will rise further and further and so will the potential growth rate. This implies that although a steady increase in the growth rate of FAI can help the economy achieve temporary equilibrium (aggregate demand = aggregate supply), it will worsen the balance of growth of different components of aggregate demand, with investment occupying an increasingly higher share of GDP, and overcapacity will continue to widen.

8.   Obviously, the growth rate of FAI cannot accelerate forever. Sooner or later the growth rate of FAI will hit a ceiling imposed by social, environmental or other constraints.

9.   Even if the growth rates of all components of aggregate demand, including FAI, become constant, owing to the fact that the growth rate of FAI is higher than those of the other components of aggregate demand, the investment rate will continue to rise and so will overcapacity. This is an unsustainable process. Under the pressure of overcapacity, deflation will set in eventually and the growth process of the economy will break down.

10.   To prevent the breakdown of the growth process, either the growth rate of FAI can be lowered, or the growth rates of the other components of aggregate demand can be raised, so that the balanced growth of all components of aggregate demand is restored.

11.   If the growth rate of FAI is lowered, the immediate result will be the worsening of the overcapacity. However, as a result of the fall of the growth rate of FAI, the investment rate will fall and so will the growth rate of potential GDP. If the growth rate of FAI continues to fall, balance can be restored when the growth rate of FAI is equal to that of the other components of aggregate demand as well as that of GDP.

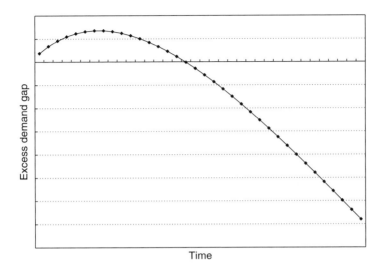

*Source:*     Drawn by Dr Xu Qiyuan.

*Figure 8.3     Overheating and overcapacity in tandem (a numerical
            simulation).*

12.  If the growth rate of the other components of aggregate demand
     is raised, not only will overcapacity be reduced, but the growth of
     all components of aggregate demand will become more balanced.
     The feasibility of this policy of adjustment depends on external con-
     straints on the potential growth rate.
13.  The balance of growth of all components of aggregate demand, or,
     more precisely, the equality of the growth rate of FAI and that of the
     other components of aggregate demand, is a necessary and sufficient
     condition for staying at a steady state and maintaining sustainable
     growth. Government policy should be aimed at pulling the economy
     back to the steady state following one deviation after another, while
     recognizing that the steady state itself can be variable, owing to
     changes in exogenous conditions.

   These dynamics can be simulated by numerical examples (Figure 8.3).
   The vertical axis and horizontal axis represent the excess demand gap
and periods of time, respectively. The positive figures represent a positive
excess-demand-gap-to-GDP ratio, and the negative figures represent overcapacity (negative excess-demand-gap-to-GDP ratio). The shape of the
excess-demand-gap-to-GDP ratio is determined by various assumptions

such as the initial shares of each component of aggregate demand, the initial growth rate, the growth rate of FAI after the initial shock, the government's reaction to overcapacity, enterprises' responses to the existence of the excess demand gap and so on. In Figure 8.3, it is assumed that, initially, all components of GDP grow at a rate of 8 per cent, and the shares of FAI and consumption in GDP are 40 per cent and 60 per cent respectively – hence, there are only two components of aggregate demand. The capital output ratio is assumed to be 5. Provided that, as a result of an external shock, the growth rate of FAI jumps to 10 per cent, then in the next period, despite the increase in supply as a result of the higher investment rate in the preceding period, the increase in aggregate demand as a result of the increase in FAI more than offsets the increase in aggregate supply, and the excess demand gap appears. Assuming that in the following periods the growth rates of FAI and consumption remain unchanged at 10 per cent and 8 per cent respectively, the excess demand gap will increase until the seventh period, when the gap will decrease. After the seventeenth period, overcapacity will appear. If overcapacity is absorbed by increases in FAI in the current period, the overcapacity gap will increase further in the next period.[6] Obviously, this process is not sustainable.

Over the past three decades, overheating and overcapacity have occurred in tandem in China. During this process, the fluctuation of the growth rate of FAI has played a pivotal role. Since the turn of the century, the growth rate of FAI has begun to accelerate and has surpassed that of GDP, owing to the expansionary fiscal and monetary policies implemented since the Asian financial crisis. As a result, the investment rate has risen since 2001 (Figure 8.2) and overheating (excess demand) has surfaced gradually since 2002. As we have mentioned, a sudden acceleration of the growth rate of FAI will create excess demand immediately afterwards for a period of time, and then, after the investment rate reaches a certain level, the economy will shift from overheating to overcapacity.

The turning-point seems to have been 2004, when signs of overcapacity began to surface. The government tried to clamp down on the launch of new investment projects. The clampdown on investment in the steel industry is a case in point. In 2004, China's steel production capacity was about 400 million tons. Worrying about overcapacity, the government started to clamp down on the building of new steel mills. The government used administrative methods to ban the unapproved construction of steel mills. Perpetrators even got jail terms. However, owing to the strong demand for steel, attributable to the real estate development fever and strong export demand, new steel mills were mushrooming exponentially. China's steel production rose to more than 600 million tons in 2007 (Figure 8.4).

Despite the fact that China's investment rate was increasing steadily,

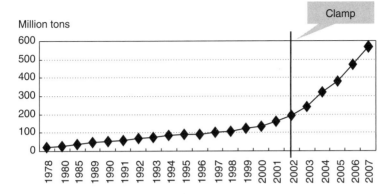

*Source:*     Collected by Dr Zhang Bin.

*Figure 8.4    China's steel production capacity.*

which implies that overcapacity pressure was building up, until the onset of the US financial crisis, the surfacing of overcapacity was postponed by a further rise in the growth rate of FAI and the accelerating growth rate of exports. For example, excess steel products were absorbed by building more steel mills and selling more steel products abroad. Growth was sustained at the expense of a widening imbalance between the growth of investment and exports and, from the middle of 2007, that of consumption. Owing to the investment fever and strong external demand, from the middle of 2007 China's inflation rate worsened rapidly.

Since the turn of the century, the Chinese economy has become more and more reliant on external demand, and the share of the current-account surplus (mainly the trade surplus) in GDP has been rising rapidly. In 2007 the contribution of the trade surplus to GDP growth was almost 10 per cent of GDP (Figure 8.5). The strong external demand delayed the surfacing of overcapacity for many years.

The trouble is that export demand is highly unstable. More importantly, when the Chinese economy was relatively small, increasing exports to absorb excess capacity was not a big deal. However, as a result of the expansion of the Chinese economy, it has become increasingly difficult for the global market to absorb China's excess capacity. Again, the steel industry is a case in point. China has already become the world's number-one steel producer. In 2007, 37 per cent of global crude steel was provided by China. It is easy to see that if external demand collapses, overheating caused by strong investment demand and strong export demand will turn immediately into overcapacity, and inflation into deflation. In the second

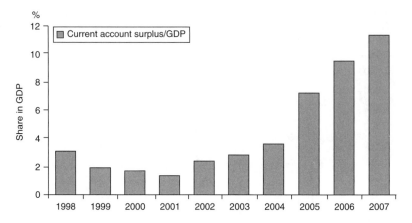

*Sources:*   Estimates of China Ethnic International Economic Cooperation Co. and of
United Bank Switzerland.

*Figure 8.5    Share of China's current account surplus in GDP.*

half of 2008 export demand collapsed owing to the global financial crisis.
Long-postponed overcapacity surfaced suddenly.[7] The rapidity of the shift
from overheating to a sudden loss of speed, and from inflation to deflation, in September to October 2008 was truly stunning.

China's investment-driven and export-led growth pattern is not sustainable. The investment rate cannot increase forever. The growth rate of
China's exports cannot remain persistently higher than that of the global
economy. With or without the global financial crisis, overcapacity will
surface and correction is inevitable. The global economic crisis exposed
the vulnerability of China's growth pattern in a dramatic fashion.

## 8.2   CHINA'S POLICY RESPONSES TO THE GLOBAL ECONOMIC CRISIS

### The Stimulus Package

Faced with the dramatic fall of GDP growth, the Chinese government
took action swiftly. In November 2008, the government introduced a 4
trillion yuan stimulus package for 2009 and 2010. The prescribed dosage
of the stimulus is very large, at 14 per cent of GDP in 2008. In March
2009, the People's Congress approved the government's new budget for

2009. According to this budget, in 2009 total government expenditure (central plus local) would be 7.635 trillion yuan, up 22.1 per cent over the previous year. In 2009, the total government deficit would be 950 billion yuan (US$139 billion), the highest in 6 decades, compared with 111 billion yuan in 2008. The central government deficit will be 750 billion yuan, 570 billion yuan more than last year. The State Council will allow local governments to issue 200 billion yuans' worth of government bonds through the Ministry of Finance. The expected budget-deficit-to-GDP ratio will be about 3 per cent of GDP in 2009. The expansionary fiscal policy has been a great success, and it has played a pivotal role in stabilizing and reviving the economy. However, the success of China's stimulus package is not surprising at all. I have been very confident all along that China will be able to achieve a growth rate as high as 8 per cent. The reason is very simple – China has a very good fiscal position. As long as the government so wishes, China can spend its way out of the slowdown, provided it remains affordable for the country.

China can afford such an expansionary fiscal policy. Over the past decade, China's budget deficit was very low, and in 2007 and 2008 it ran a small budget surplus and a small budget deficit of 0.4 per cent of GDP respectively. As a result, China's debt should be only about 20 per cent of GDP, even after the stimulus. It is easy to see that there is plenty of room for the Chinese government to use expansionary fiscal policy to supplement the lack of demand caused by the fall in export demand and, to a lesser degree, the fall in non-governmental investment demand.

The central government finances one-quarter of the 4 trillion yuan package, in the form of direct grants and interest rate subsidies. In the case of a central-government-sponsored project, with the approval of the National Development and Reform Commission (NDRC), the Ministry of Finance provides all the funding for the registered capital. Bank credit is the second most important source of finance for the stimulus package. Local governments proposed their own stimulus packages of 18 trillion yuan. The central government will issue 200 billion yuan in government bonds on behalf of local governments. Commercial bank credit is expected to be the most important source of finance for the local-government-proposed projects.

**Monetary Expansion**

Since 2009, the People's Bank of China (PBOC) has adopted a very expansionary monetary policy to support the expansionary fiscal policy. In the first half of 2009, bank credit increased by 7.3 trillion yuan, which was above the official target for the full year. Credit growth was surprisingly high, and the same was true of the broad money supply, M2, which grew at a record rate relative to GDP. As a result, the interbank money market has been inundated with liquidity. In contrast, the annual increases in bank credit in 2006 and 2007 were 3.18 trillion yuan and 3.63 trillion yuan, respectively. Previously, corresponding to the rapid increase in liquidity caused by the PBOC's intervention in the exchange market, which was aimed at offsetting the appreciation pressure on the yuan created by the persistent trade surplus (and capital account surplus), the PBOC sold a large amount of central bank bills to mop up the excess liquidity. Since the fourth quarter of 2008, the PBOC has almost stopped selling more bills. As a result, liquidity has inundated the interbank money market, and once even made the interest rates in the interbank market lower than interest rates on deposits with commercial banks with the same terms of maturity. This phenomenon was described in China's banking circles as 'flour being more expensive than bread'.

China's financial conditions were very different from those in the United States and Europe during the global financial crisis. China had just completed overhauls of its banking system by writing off nonperforming loans and injecting a large amount of capital. Its banking system was relatively safe and sound when the Western banking system was on the edge. As a result, there was no liquidity shortage, no credit crunch, and the monetary multiplier in China has not fallen as dramatically as in the United States. Therefore, the dramatic increase in liquidity in the interbank money market has duly translated into a rapid increase in bank credit and broad money.

## 8.3  THE LONG-TERM IMPACT OF THE STIMULUS PACKAGE AND EXPANSIONARY MONETARY POLICY

The very expansionary fiscal and monetary policies have succeeded in arresting a fall in growth. However, the medium- and long-term impacts of the expansionary policies are worrying.

First, the most important feature of China's growth pattern is the high investment rate. China's investment rate has been increasing steadily since 2001. The rate has increased from 25 per cent in 2001 to 50 per cent as a result of the stimulus package centered on FAI. This means that China's overcapacity will become more serious in the future.

Second, China's investment efficiency has been falling as a result of the stimulus package. The government knows very well that the Chinese economy has been suffering from overcapacity. Therefore, government-financed investment in the stimulus package is concentrated in infrastructure, rather than on new factories. However, there are still problems with an infrastructure-centered stimulus package. With an investment rate of 50 per cent and a GDP growth rate of 8 per cent, the incremental capital–output ratio will be 6 or higher. In comparison, Japan's incremental capital-output ratio was about 3. From 1991 to 2003, China's incremental capital–output ratio was 4.1. The fall of investment efficiency will have an important negative bearing on China's long-term growth.

Third, infrastructure investment is long-term investment and will take a long time to create revenue streams. Furthermore, despite the fact that investment in infrastructure has the virtue of avoiding overcapacity, investment in infrastructure without accompanying investment in manufacturing capacity means investment in infrastructure will not bring returns. Where will tolls come from, if there is no traffic in an eight-lane highway? To make things worse, owing to the hasty and undersupervised implementation, waste in infrastructure construction is ubiquitous. All this means not only low efficiency but possibly also a significant increase in nonperforming loans in the future.

Fourth, the overenthusiasm of local governments for local investment may worsen China's fiscal position in the future in an unexpected and dramatic way. On top of the central government's stimulus package, provincial governments were encouraged to raise money to launch their own complementary stimulus packages. The total amount of planned stimulus packages announced by local governments was 18 trillion yuan. The bulk of the local stimulus packages will be financed by commercial loans guaranteed by local governments. A small portion of the finance is raised by selling bonds issued by the central government on behalf of local governments. As a result of the particular institutional arrangements in China, local governments have an insatiable appetite for grandiose investment projects. Investment led by local governments is likely to lead to a suboptimal allocation of resources. More importantly, the central government's contingent liabilities may shoot up in the future.

Finally, as already mentioned, China's monetary policy is too loose. There is no need for China to drop the benchmark interest rate to such a low level. Interest rates are an important screening device in developing countries. The rapid expansion of credit and money supply was, to a certain extent, the result of non-market interferences. There are no sound economic rationales for supporting such a dramatic expansion. If commercial banks had been allowed to make decisions based purely on economic considerations, growth of credit and money supply would not have been so fast. And there would have been less need to worry about the possibilities of a rising nonperforming loan ratio, a worsening of the economic structure and resurging asset bubbles. Actually, anecdotal evidence shows that a large chunk of excess liquidity has entered stock markets and real estate markets. Asset bubbles are returning with a vengeance. The huge gap between the growth rate of M2 and nominal GDP implies very large inflation pressure in the future. With near-zero interest rates, small and middle-sized private and innovative enterprises will be discriminated against vis-à-vis state-owned monopolistic enterprises. The progress made in enterprise reform may be reversed.

## 8.4   THE REBALANCING OF THE CHINESE ECONOMY AND THE SAFETY OF CHINA'S FOREIGN EXCHANGE RESERVES

Before the global financial crisis, the critics of China's imbalances in the form of running twin surpluses concentrated mainly on the double-misallocation of resources. As a developing country, China should use its resources for domestic investment and improving people's living standards. As an FDI-recipient country, China should translate capital inflows into the current-account deficit. After the global financial crisis, more and more attention has shifted to the safety of China's foreign exchange reserves. When Fannie Mae and Freddie Mac were on the brink of bankruptcy, the issue of the safety of China's foreign exchange reserves was brought to the fore.

China is resigned to the fact that in essence it is borrowing with high costs and lending back the money to the United States with low or zero return. More troubling is that now the safety of China's foreign exchange reserves is under threat. And capital losses – let alone obtaining decent returns – seem inevitable. As Paul Krugman warned could happen, China has fallen into a 'dollar trap'. In terms of capital losses, China is facing a triple whammy.

First, the devaluation of the dollar is inevitable, which will lead to capital losses in China's foreign exchange reserves. The bulk of China's 2.3-trillion-dollar foreign reserve holdings are not held for the purpose of self-protection; rather they are savings in the form of US Treasuries. China needs to preserve the value of its savings. There is no question whatsoever that the US dollar will go south, which started in April 2002 and, after a short interval, restarted in March 2009. Unless the US economy is rebalanced, the dollar will fall. And unless the dollar falls, the US rebalance will not be achieved. As a result, capital losses from China's foreign exchange reserves are inevitable.

Second, though inflation may not be an immediate threat, the US inflation rate should be around 4 per cent according to US Federal Reserve officials. This would mean that each year China's purchasing power devalues by 4 per cent. Furthermore, owing to an extremely expansive monetary policy, the dollar has been debased. Unless the Fed implements the exit strategy successfully, which is doubtful, the real value of China's foreign exchange reserves will be eroded. Finally, as a result of Helicopter Ben dropping money from the sky, serious inflation in the future cannot be ruled out.

Third, owing to the huge budget deficit and supply of bonds by the United States, there is no guarantee that there will be enough demand for the US securities. As a result, the price of US government securities will drop, and China's US security holding will suffer losses.

First of all, China should reduce its current and capital account surpluses. If it cannot reduce the twin surpluses, it has to translate the surpluses into assets other than US Treasuries, which include increasing outbound FDI, investing in strategic resources, engaging in mergers and acquisitions and foreign portfolio investment, lending to international organizations, selling panda bonds, engaging in currency swaps and providing aid to developing countries.

With regard to stocks, the US government should offer more Treasury Inflation Protected Securities – like financial instruments. This would allow China to convert some of its holdings of US government securities into similar but safer assets. China should be allowed to convert part of its foreign exchange reserves into special drawing rights (SDR) denominated assets. China should not rule out the possibility of adjusting the composition of its foreign exchange reserves to mimic the composition of SDR. If the US government cannot safeguard the value of China's holdings of US government securities, the US government should compensate China in one way or another.

## 8.5 CONCLUDING REMARKS

All in all, the negative impact of the measures taken as part of the efforts in crisis management by the Chinese government on China's long-run growth can be serious, if the government fails to tackle structural problems head-on. However, it is also worth noting that the Chinese government is well aware of the problems and has begun to take measures to put structural adjustment back high on the agenda. We must hope that the Chinese government will succeed not only in reviving the economy, but also in reversing the worsening of the structural problem, and will lay a solid foundation for China's future economic growth.

# NOTES

1.  Editors' note: This chapter appeared originally as part of the Richard Snape Lecture, 25 November 2010, and has been reprinted here with the permission of the Australian Productivity Commission.
2.  I discussed the reason why China has been running current account and capital account surpluses in detail in 'Global Imbalances and China.' *Australian Economic Review*, **40** (1), 1–21, written on the basis of my presentation at the David Finch Memorial Lecture, delivered at the University of Melbourne, 17 October 2006.
3.  There have been controversies about the FAI real growth rate statistics. However, despite the inaccuracy, it is difficult to deny the fact that the growth rate of FAI in real terms has been consistently higher than that of real GDP.
4.  For example, if the growth of FAI is maintained at the given higher rate after the one-off disturbance, the growth rate of potential GDP will rise gradually in the subsequent periods. At a certain point in time, when the growth of potential GDP has reached a certain rate, which is higher than that of the rest of the components of aggregate demand but lower than that of FAI, the macroeconomic situation will shift from excess demand to overcapacity.
5.  We assume that there is no endogenous mechanism to ensure that the growth rates of these components of aggregate demand increase so as to catch up with FAI growth.
6.  In this analysis, the question of how prices will react to changes in the excess demand gap to GDP ratio has not been discussed.
7.  Contractionary monetary policy aimed at containing investment fever and asset bubbles began to take effect in 2008, which also contributed to the slowdown in the growth of FAI.

# PART III

# Policy constraints

# 9. Fiscal discipline in the recovery from a global financial crisis

**Chih-Chin Ho,[1] Yu-Shan Hsu and Ching-Shin Mao**

## 9.1 INTRODUCTION

How much debt can a country sustain? Government debt is growing faster than GDP in most countries. Figure 9.1 shows the government debt of the United Kingdom and the United States as a percentage of GDP. The Congressional Budget Office of the United States estimate that the debt-to-output ratio will reach 113 per cent by 2026 and 200 per cent in 2038 under their most realistic scenario. The editorial of the *Washington Post* on 29 June 2009 even coined the term 'debt tsunami'. In this chapter, we

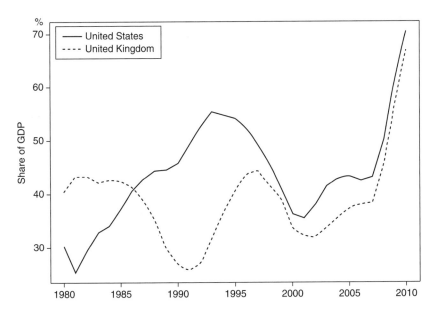

*Figure 9.1   Debt as percentage of GDP.*

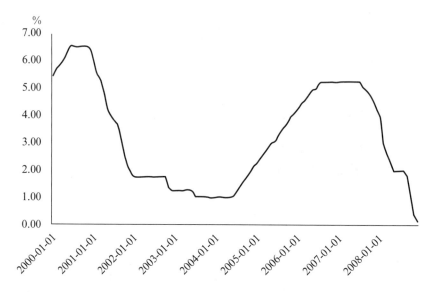

*Figure 9.2     United States federal funds rates.*

want to discuss fiscal discipline in the recovery from crises. It is not that we have to disagree with expansionary fiscal policy to rescue the economy; it just seems that the government never thinks of the exit strategy. (The government always talks about more spending and less taxes. Few heads of government would dare to say 'No more spending, let's increase taxes and save more (for the sake of our next generation) to pay our debt' during their term of office.)

People can easily forget crises, the causes behind them and the lessons we learnt. When the dot-com bubble burst in 2000, the central banks set interest rates at the lowest level ever. They did a nice job. But the rates stayed too low for too long, leading to another bubble, in housing. Figure 9.2 shows the federal funds rate in the United States. Even after the recovery from the bursting of the dot-com bubble, the rate was kept below 2 per cent until the end of the year 2004. And as we can see in Figure 9.3, the housing bubble took a while – until 2007 – to burst. Of course one can blame high-tech finance, bad risk management or anything else, but the cheap money caused by the loose monetary policy was unarguably the major reason for the financial crisis of 2007. Now the US government has turned to fiscal policy, since there is no longer room to lower interest rates. But if the government is not careful with its massive expansionary fiscal policy it could plant the seed of a future bubble, possibly in the bond market.

An expansionary monetary or fiscal policy is the right one to use to escape

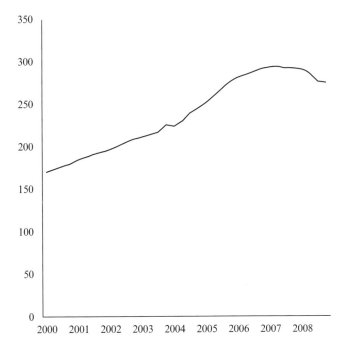

*Figure 9.3   US House Price Index.*

from a crisis, but not the right one when the market is calm. We have been living in boom–bust cycles for the last several decades, and those trillion-dollar deficits make people worry about the risk of inflation, leading to a demand for rising returns from bonds. The 30-year Treasury yield has risen from 2.5 per cent at the start of 2009 to around 5 per cent at time of writing (the 30-year Treasury yield at 5 August 2009 hit 5.25 per cent).

The huge increases in the cost of government borrowing make it even harder to reduce the level of borrowing, which means the debt-to-output ratio is likely to rise to an unmanageable level. And these high interest pay-ments will divert government spending from more productive spending and investment within the economy, limiting the scope of future growth and reducing social welfare. It may get even worse, since all the rates in the markets are linked to the government debt yield curve which can affect borrowing costs throughout the economy very directly, and threaten consumers and businesses before the recovery has gained any significant traction.

As we have emphasized, without fiscal discipline a budget deficit could easily get out of control. To achieve a smooth exit from the crisis means gaining control of fiscal policy. There must be no more mistakes this time; otherwise the next crisis could be on its way. Now must be the time to consider the seriously high debt-to-output ratio. We have to face the fact that the debt must be paid eventually. With people's preference for consumption-smoothing, the boom–bust cycle is not an option. Instead of burdening the country with a huge amount of debt in pursuit of their political interests, reduction in social welfare can be avoided if governments practice some fiscal discipline during their term of office.

In Section 9.2 we develop a general equilibrium model under uncertainty, with its two-state transition probabilities functions of the parameters that capture the debt-to-output ratio of the economy. Section 9.3 shows the simulation results for the benchmarks of three fiscal policy options, and the extensions of two sets of comparisons, including different initial fiscal capacities and different fiscal discipline regimes. Section 9.4 offers policy implications. Section 9.5 reaches a conclusion.

## 9.2   THEORETICAL FRAMEWORK

### Literature Review

There are many studies identifying the circumstances under which fiscal expansions, such as raising spending and cutting tax, will tend to be relatively effective in stimulating economic activities. It is well known that it matters how fiscal policy is financed. Lump-sum finance is widely used in the literature, which includes Aiyagari et al. (1992), Barro (1981, 1987) and Baxter and King (1981). These studies expand the neoclassical growth model with a government sector, and show that increases in government expenditures create negative wealth effects for the household sector, which will reduce consumption and increase labor supply. An increased labor supply induces real wages to decrease and interest rates to increase.

The macroeconomic effects of lump-sum taxation, which does not alter relative prices, have been widely investigated. Distortionary taxation, which drives a wedge between marginal product and its after-tax return, and generates substitution effects, is also analyzed, for example in Abel (1982), Abel and Blanchard (1983) and Judd (1985, 1987). These papers show that cuts in a distortionary tax rate on capital which is financed by increases in government debt will lead to increases in investment and output. However, when studying the effects of the changes in fiscal policies, one of two assumptions is usually made, explicitly or implicitly: either an assumption of perfect foresight, which means agents are perfectly aware of the future fiscal policies, or one of myopic foresight, which means agents believe that no changes will ever occur. Since these two assumptions are extreme and unrealistic, another strand in the literature assumes that fiscal policy changes are generated by some stochastic process, instead of treating them as movements from one deterministic regime to another. This alternative substantially alters the impact of fiscal policy changes on investment and other macroeconomic behavior variables.

Bizer and Judd (1989) introduce a random tax policy in a dynamic general equilibrium model. They find that capital stock will fall when taxes are high and rise when taxes are low if the random tax rates or credits are serially correlated. Moreover, if the random tax rates or credits have independent and identical distributions, this randomness will generate large fluctuations in investment. Following Bizer and Judd (1989), Dotsey (1990) incorporates persistent shocks to the distortionary tax rates by having them follow a discrete-state Markov chain, and then examines how the economy will behave with respect to particular realizations of tax rates. In this case, where tax rates are assumed to follow a two-state Markov process, a greater fraction of output will be invested in the low-tax state because the low-tax state implies a greater likelihood that taxes will be low in the future. This study can be considered as the complement to the previous results. In addition, Braun (1994) and McGrattan (1994) show that introducing stochastic distortionary taxes on labor and capital income in the context of a dynamic recursive stochastic equilibrium model could improve its ability to reproduce features of the US economy, such as the variability of hours worked and the weak correlation between real wages and employment. They suggest that substantial intertemporal substitution effects in the labor supply decision may be the result of changes in distortionary taxes.

Although the effects of stochastic distortionary taxes have been considered, all these studies assume that an increase in government debt resulting from a tax cut will be financed by non-distorting future fiscal policies. Therefore, another study concentrates on the case where distortionary taxes are levied to pay for deficits. Dotsey (1994) shows that under an inelastic labor supply setup, when current government deficits are financed by future distortionary taxation, lower tax rates and higher deficits will lead to reductions in investment and output. The tax rates follow a two-state Markov chain, and the transitional probabilities depend on the debt-to-GDP ratio. Moreover, Dotsey and Mao (1997) include elastic labor supply to investigate whether the debt could affect the economic activities or not. In this chapter, we follow the setup employed by Dotsey and Mao (1997). We allow the government to reduce the deficit through cuts in government expenditures or increases in distortionary taxation in order to study the effect of expansionary fiscal policies on real variables.

## A Debt-Smoothing Model

The firms solve a series of simple one-period problems. By using a constant returns-to-scale technology, $f(k_t, n_t)$, capital and labor inputs are hired to maximize the profit:

$$\max_{\{k_t, n_t\}} d_t = f(k_t, n_t) - r_t k_t - w_t n_t,$$

where $d_t$ denotes the profit obtained by the firm, $r_t$ is the rental rate on capital and $w_t$ is the real wage rate. The rental rate on capital and real wage rate are both taken as given in the competitive market. The first-order conditions equate each factor's marginal product with its rental rate.

The representative agent maximizes the lifetime utility which depends on both consumption and leisure. Agents are endowed with one unit of time each period, which can be allocated towards production or leisure, an initial stock of capital, and make their labor–leisure, consumption, and investment–saving decisions, taking as given wage rates and rental rates. They also purchase one period government debt at a price $p_t$. Each bond promises to pay one unit of consumption in the succeeding period. Further, consumers observe the current state of fiscal policy, which is summarized by beginning-of-period per capita government debt $B_t$, current tax rates, and the current level of government spending. They are also assumed to know current aggregate economic magnitudes such as output, the capital stock, employment, investment and end-of-period debt $B_{t+1}$.

Formally, the individual's problem is written

$$\max_{\{c_t, n_t, b_{t+1}, k_{t+1}\}} U = E_0 \left[ \sum_{t=0}^{\infty} \beta^t u(c_t, 1 - n_t) \right]$$

subject to

$$c_t + i_t + p_t b_{t+1} \le (1 - \tau_t^n) w_t n_t + (1 - \tau_t^k) r_t k_t + b_t + TR_t,$$

$$i_t = k_{t+1} - (1 - \delta) k_t,$$

where $TR_t$ is aggregate per capita transfers (lower-case variables indicate values at the individual level).

Maximization yields the following first-order conditions:

$$u_2(c_t, 1 - n_t) = u_1(c_t, 1 - n_t)(1 - \tau_t^n) w_t, \tag{9.1a}$$

$$u_1(c_t, 1 - n_t) = \beta E_t [u_1(c_{t+1}, 1 - n_{t+1})[(1 - \tau_{t+1}^k) r_{t+1} + (1 - \delta)]], \tag{9.1b}$$

$$p_t u_1(c_t, 1 - n_t) = \beta E_t u_1(c_{t+1}, 1 - n_{t+1}). \tag{9.1c}$$

Equation (9.1a) equates the marginal rate of substitution between consumption and leisure to the after-tax wage rate. In order to smooth consumption, individuals choose consumption today or consumption tomorrow according to an intertemporal Euler equation, as shown in (9.1b). Finally, (9.1c) represents that marginal gain from an extra bond holding must be equal to its marginal cost.

### Government – Fiscal Policy Specification

The government spends resources and finances its spending through taxes and debt. Any shortfall is met by issuing public bonds which will be paid by a competitive market interest rate in the next period. Thus, debt evolves according to

$$p_t B_{t+1} = G_t + B_t - \tau_t^k r_t K_t - \tau_t^n w_t N_t + TR_t, \tag{9.2}$$

where capital letters refer to per capita aggregate quantities, and $B_t$, $G_t$, $\tau_t^k$, $\tau_t^n$ denote public bonds, government spending, capital income tax rate and labor income tax rate, respectively. It is worth noting that many empirical studies suggest that the debt-to-GDP ratio displays mean reversion; that is, that the government will take corrective actions in controlling fiscal deficits, and that the government primary surplus should be an increasing function of the debt-to-GDP ratio. Bohn (1998) examines the existence of a feedback from debt to deficit, and suggests that US fiscal policy does satisfy an intertemporal budget constraint. Hence, if the current debt-to-GDP ratio is high, the government will either cut tax rates or reduce expenditures in the future so that the current deficit can be offset by the sum of expected future discounted primary surplus. While Fève and Hénin (2000) find further support for the sustainability of the fiscal policy within the G7, Uctum et al. (2002) and Uctum et al. (2000) also provide evidence among emerging and industrialized economies. In order to capture this mean-reverting phenomenon, we employ simple two-state transition probabilities for tax and spending as follows:

$$\text{prob}\,(\tau_{t+1} = \tau_l | \tau_t = \tau_l) = \min\,\{\max[(1 - \gamma \tilde{b}_t)^{1/\mu}, 0], 1\}, \tag{9.3a}$$

$$\text{prob}\,(\tau_{t+1} = \tau_h | \tau_t = \tau_h) = \max\{\min\,[\gamma \tilde{b}_t^{1/\mu}, 1], 0\}, \tag{9.3b}$$

$$\text{prob}\,(\tilde{g}_{t+1} = \tilde{g}_l | \tilde{g}_t = \tilde{g}_l) = \max\{\min\,[\gamma \tilde{b}_t^{1/\eta}, 1], 0\}, \tag{9.3c}$$

$$\text{prob}\,(\widetilde{g}_{t+1} = \widetilde{g}_h | \widetilde{g}_t = \widetilde{g}_h) = \min\,\{\max[(1 - \gamma\widetilde{b}_t)^{1/\eta}, 0], 1\}, \quad (9.3\text{d})$$

where the subscripts $l$ and $h$ refer to low and high values respectively, and $\mu, \eta > 0$ are parameters governing the persistence of the process. Given the value of $\widetilde{b}$, if $\mu$ increases, then the probability of staying in the specific tax rate state will also increase; similarly, if $\eta$ increases, then it is more likely to stay in the specific government spending state. These transition probabilities imply that the debt-to-output ratio will be bounded and lie only rarely outside the interval $[0, 1/\gamma]$. The bounding of the debt-to-output ratio occurs because as $\widetilde{b}$ approaches a value of $1/\gamma$, taxes will be high with a probability of 1 and spending will be low with a probability of 1. In other words, the higher values of $\mu$ and $\eta$ imply that the government is more likely to take disciplinary measures in fiscal policy. As long as a combination of high taxes and low spending reduces debt, the debt-to-output ratio will be driven down. Similarly, as $\widetilde{b}$ approaches 0 the economy will be in a low-tax, high-government-spending state and the debt will rise. Thus, there is some tendency for debt to revert toward its mean. Hence, we will hereafter call this policy a 'managed debt policy'. The bounding of debt implies that

$$\lim_{T \to \infty} E_t\!\left[ p_T B_{T+1} / \prod_{s=t}^{T} (1/p_s) \right] = 0, \quad (9.4)$$

for the equilibrium price paths in this model.

**Equilibrium Solutions**

Equilibrium is obtained when quantities and prices solve both the firms' and consumers' maximization problems, do not let either consumers or the government borrow more than can be repaid, and obey the following aggregate equilibrium conditions:

$$C_t + I_t + G_t = f(K_t, N_t), \quad (9.5)$$

$$b_t = B_t, \quad (9.6)$$

$$k_t = K_t, \quad (9.7)$$

$$n_t = N_t. \quad (9.8)$$

While equation (9.5) denotes the market-clearing condition, (9.6) to (9.8) are consistency conditions. Equilibrium is solved for by first using

(9.5) to substitute out consumption. Equation (9.1a) together with the relationship $w_t = f_2(K_t, N_t)$, and equations (9.7) and (9.8), are then used to solve for labor $n_t = n(k_t, \tilde{b}_t, \tau_t^n, \tau_t^k, \tilde{g}_t, k_t + 1) = n(s_t, k_t+1)$ where the state $s_t = (k_t, \tilde{b}_t, \tau_t^n, \tau_t^k, \tilde{g}_t)$. This solution for labor is then substituted into equation (9.1b) to yield

$$u_1[f(k_t, n(s_t, k_{t+1})) + (1 - \delta)k_t - g_t - k_{t+1}, 1 - n(s_t, k_{t+1})]$$

$$= \beta E_t\{u_1[f(k_{t+1}, n(s_{t+1}, k_{t+2})) + (1 - \delta)k_{t+1} - g_{t+1} - k_{t+2},$$

$$1 - n(s_{t+1}, k_{t+2})] \times [(1 - \tau_{t+1}^k)f_1(k_{t+1}, n(s_{t+1}, k_{t+2})) + (1 - \delta)]\}.$$
$$(9.9)$$

Note that equation (9.9) is a nonlinear second-order stochastic difference equation. Given $n(s, k')$, where the prime indicates the next period's value of a variable, we solve for the function $k' = h(s)$, which is the fixed point of (9.9). This equilibrium policy function for $k'$ then yields the equilibrium policy function for labor $n$, since $n$ was a function of arbitrary $k'$.

## 9.3   SIMULATION RESULTS

Owing to complexity, we use some simulation results to look at the effects of fiscal policy changes on real variables, such as output, investment, labor hours, consumption etc. First, we use a standard log-utility function

$$u(c_t, l_t) = \theta \ln c_t + (1 - \theta) \ln l_t,$$

and a Cobb–Douglas production function

$$y_t = k_t^\alpha n_t^{1-\alpha}.$$

To begin with, we choose the discount factor $\beta$ as 0.99, capital share in output $\alpha$ as 0.32, depreciation rate $\delta$ as 0.06 and $\theta$ as 0.244, making labor hours worked in steady state 0.2. Government spending, capital income tax rate and labor income tax rate are bounded between [0.14, 0.22], [0.18, 0.52] and [0.23, 0.31], respectively. All of the parameters are chosen to reproduce some key features representative of the US economy at annual frequencies, which is also standard practice in real business cycle theory literatures. For instance, $\beta$ as 0.99 implies a 1 per cent real interest rate per quarter, matching the fact that the historical average of real interest rates in the US is 4 per cent annually; capital share $\alpha$ as 0.32 or 32 per cent also represents the historical average value in the US data; boundary values of fiscal policy parameters are arranged so that the values are centered around the historical average, for example, government spending ratio ranges between $0.18 - 0.04$ and $0.18 + 0.04$. For more references, one can consult Dotsey and Mao (1997).

**Benchmarks: Three Fiscal Policy Options**

**Case 1: $g$ increases, $\tau^k$ fixed and $\tau^l$ fixed**
In this case, we examine the effects of an increase in government spending, holding tax rates fixed. Since the government spending has neither utility value nor productive value, it is well known that changes in government spending generate wealth effects and crowding-out effects. A higher government spending induces agents to work more and consume less, thereby producing more. Real interest rate also rises with debt. As shown in Figure 9.4, labor hours increase and consumption decreases; meanwhile output rises but by less than government spending. Since tax rates are fixed, debt increases. As debt rises, the future path of government spending is expected to fall. Therefore, labor hours and output decline, and debt crowds out investment. These results are similar to standard Keynesian behaviors with respect to quantities.

Compared with a permanent change in government spending, a temporary policy of government spending induces a smaller wealth effect. Thus, the impact of a temporary change in government spending is much smaller than that of a permanent change.

**Case 2: $g$ fixed, $\tau^k$ fixed and $\tau^l$ decreases**
A deficit-financed labor tax cut induces substitution effects between labor and leisure choices. As shown in Figure 9.5, the lower labor tax rate motivates a substitution away from leisure, thereby increasing output. This lower tax rate also increases the marginal product of capital, which leads to more investment. However, as debt rises, the lower labor tax rate implies that the probability of a high labor tax rate in the next period increases. This means that agents expect that there will be a lower after-tax return on saving, leading to higher consumption. Owing to consumption growth, the real interest rate will be higher than its steady-state value.

**Case 3: $g$ increases, $\tau^k$ decreases and $\tau^l$ decreases**
The response of the economy to an increase in government spending along with deficit-financed tax cuts is depicted by the impulse response function in Figure 9.6. As we mentioned above, while expansionary fiscal policy brings out wealth effects, deficit-financed tax cuts generate substitution effects. When the government decides to increase spending and decrease

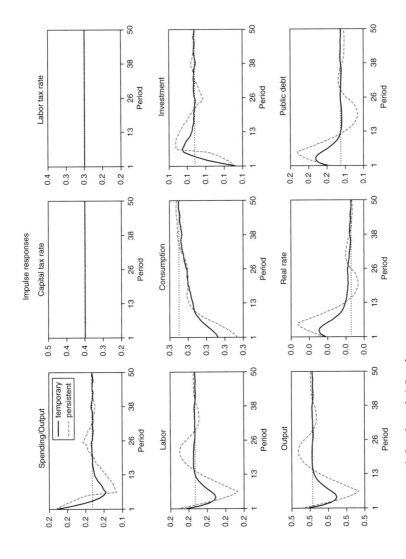

*Figure 9.4   g increases, $\tau^k$ fixed, and $\tau^l$ fixed.*

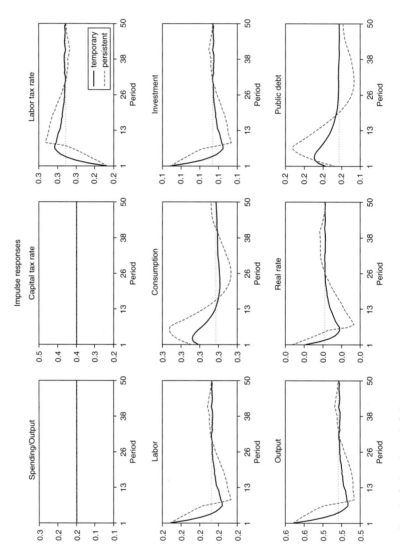

*Figure 9.5  g fixed, $\tau^k$ fixed, and $\tau^l$ decreases.*

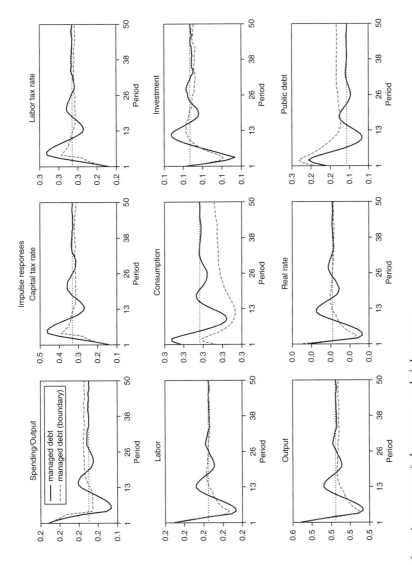

*Figure 9.6* g increases, $\tau^k$ decreases, and $\tau^l$ decreases.

tax rates simultaneously, these two effects will mutually reinforce one another. Hence, labor hours, and thereby output, increase by a large amount so that consumption and investment levels are above their steady-state values.

**Different Initial Fiscal Capacities**

As we have seen, the transition probabilities are endogenously decided by debt-to-GDP ratios. A deficit-financed policy will result in rising debt levels, and increase the probability of switching back to a high-tax-rate state or low-government-spending state. Individuals' responses to a fiscal policy shock will depend on what future tax burden they expect, and these expectations rely upon what kind of fiscal situation they start from; that is the initial debt-to-GDP ratio. In this section, we consider two different fiscal positions – strong and weak, and reexamine the effects of fiscal policies under different initial debt-to-GDP ratios. In this setting, the economy with a strong fiscal position has an initial debt-to-GDP ratio of 0.1, and the other one with a weak fiscal position an initial debt-to-GDP ratio of 0.4.

**Case 1: An increase in government spending alone**
If the government decides to stimulate the economy by raising expenditures, the impulse responses will depend critically on the initial debt-to-GDP ratio (Figure 9.7). Compared with its weak counterpart, an economy with a strong fiscal capacity, with an initial debt-to-GDP ratio of 0.1, will have stronger wealth effects. The fiscally healthier government can smooth its debt slowly, and those stronger wealth effects in turn motivate agents to work harder, thereby producing more and consuming less.

Facing a fiscal policy shock, an economy which inherits heavier liabilities will have weaker wealth effects since the debt-to-GDP ratio hits the upper bound quickly and will revert to its mean. As a result, agents increase consumption and leisure, but reduce investment in response to higher government spending.

**Case 2: A decrease in labor tax rate alone**
The effect of a deficit-financed labor income tax cut also depends on the inferences individuals draw regarding the future tax burden (Figure 9.8). As we have seen, a decrease in labor tax rate induces agents to work more, consume more and invest more. However, in a weak initial fiscal situation the effect of a reduction in labor income tax rate will be less persistent, since a deficit-financed tax cut implies a strong likelihood of a switch to a higher tax rate state in the following period. As a result, the labor supply in a weak initial fiscal situation will drop faster than its counterpart in a

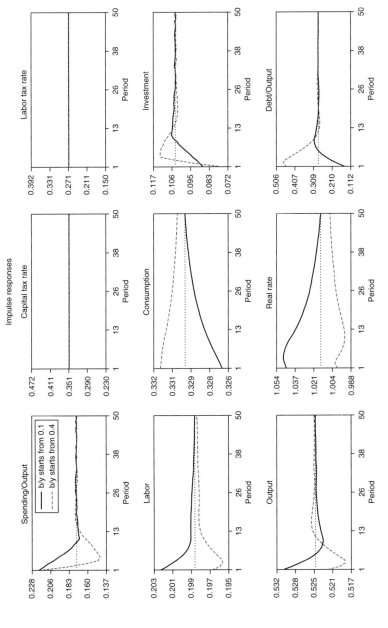

*Figure 9.7   The effects of an increase in g under different initial fiscal capacities.*

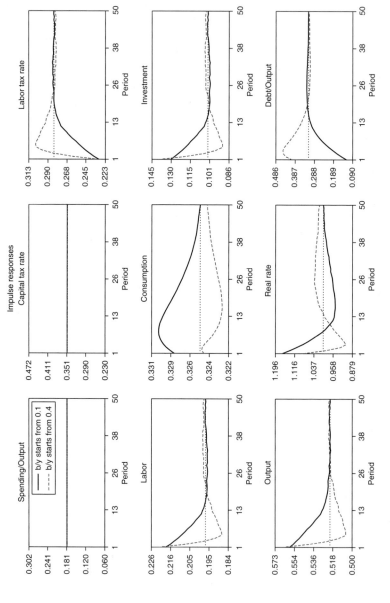

*Figure 9.8  The effects of a decrease in τ^l under different initial fiscal capacities.*

stronger initial fiscal situation in response to a relatively temporary high after-tax wage rate. Therefore, output in a weak fiscal situation will also drop faster than its counterpart, and even fall below its steady-state value.

Moreover, whether the allocation of this tax-cut-induced output will increase towards consumption or investment depends on initial fiscal capacity. If the initial fiscal situation is strong, the additional output will be allocated towards both consumption and investment. However, if the initial fiscal situation is weak, most of the additional output will be allocated towards investment, but away from consumption, since the labor tax rate in the next period is expected to increase with higher probability, which makes investment in this period more attractive.

### Case 3: An increase in government spending and a decrease in both tax rates

When the government simultaneously increases spending and cuts tax rates (Figure 9.9), on impact, labor supply increases, thereby increasing output no matter what initial fiscal position it holds. However, an economy with a weak fiscal capacity will experience more fluctuations in real variables.

### Different Fiscal Discipline Regimes

Consider two different institutional designs for controlling fiscal deficit and national debt – one is more disciplined (conservative), and characterized by a lower ceiling of debt-to-GDP ratio at 0.5; the other is less disciplined (liberal), with a higher ceiling at 1. In this subsection we examine the effects of fiscal policy options under different fiscal discipline regimes.

### Case 1: An increase in government spending alone

Based on our simulation results, if a less fiscally disciplined government increases spending and takes a more liberal attitude towards debt, then in the short run labor supply and output will increase more than they will under its more disciplined counterpart. This is because the government can do more without breaking its ceiling on debt-to-GDP ratio. However, as labor supply starts to decline, output will fall below the steady-state value for a long time, and welfare will be lower than in the disciplined case, since consumption drops and labor supply rises significantly. (See Figure 9.10.)

### Case 2: A decrease in labor tax rate alone

The impulse response of a tax cut on labor income in this case moves in the opposite direction to that in the previous case of increased government spending. Under a less disciplined regime, the economy will be more likely

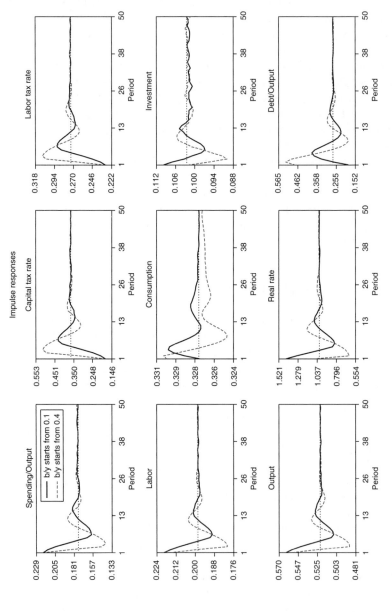

*Figure 9.9   The effects of an increase in g and a decrease in both $\tau^i$ and $\tau^k$ under different initial fiscal capacities.*

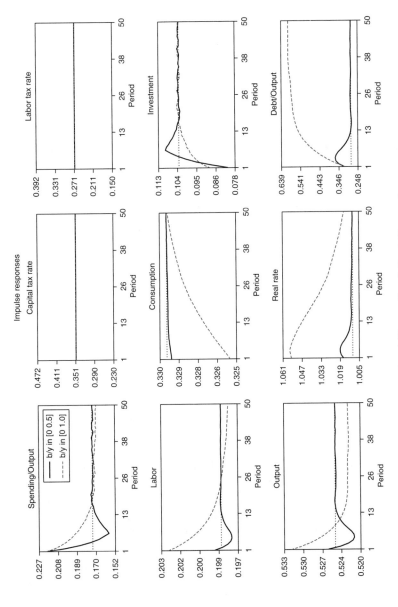

*Figure 9.10 The effects of an increase in g under different fiscal discipline regimes.*

to raise taxes in the future and to motivate people to work than will its more fiscally disciplined counterpart. In the meantime, this less disciplined regime has much more time to smooth its debts, so that the real variables drop less quickly than under its more disciplined counterpart. (See Figure 9.11.)

**Case 3: An increase in government spending and a decrease in both tax rates**
When a government increases its spending and reduces its tax rates (both capital and labor income) at the same time, our simulation shows a hybrid of results. If we evaluate the effects in terms of output, a less disciplined fiscal regime will have a larger labor supply and a higher output in the short run. However, if we evaluate the effects from the perspective of welfare, a less disciplined fiscal regime will have lower consumption in the short run. (See Figure 9.12.)

## 9.4    POLICY IMPLICATIONS

Most countries around the world use fiscal stimulus plans to fight the ongoing global crisis. Basically, these are different combinations of government spending and tax cuts. Most countries choose to boost the economy directly with deficit spending by their governments. But some countries like Hungary have tight budget control; they just cannot afford to finance the deficit spending, and choose to launch billions of dollars' worth of stimulus packages in the form of tax cuts.

**Fiscal Policy Option – Fiscal Stimulus vs. Tax Cut**

Whether government spending and tax cuts policy are used independently or are both implemented together, the results in Section 9.3 have shown us that all kinds of fiscal policy succeed in stimulating output to grow, differing only in how they make their own way back to the steady state. Increases in government spending will drive up market interest rates, since government must raise money to fund the deficit spending. Although output rises temporarily, investments in the country are reduced because of the high cost of borrowing – the classic crowding-out effect. The economy will therefore experience some downturns below the steady state in the future, which is thus consistent with the traditional results. Any government that uses this policy should be aware of this effect. Meanwhile, a tax cuts policy increases output and then brings it quickly back to the steady-state level. Government spending combined with tax cuts policy mixes both effects together.

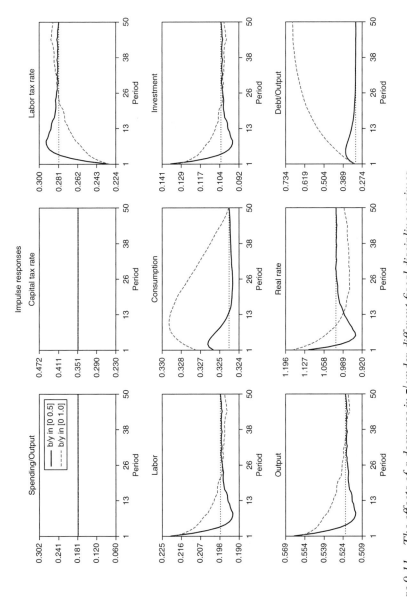

*Figure 9.11   The effects of a decrease in τ′ under different fiscal discipline regimes.*

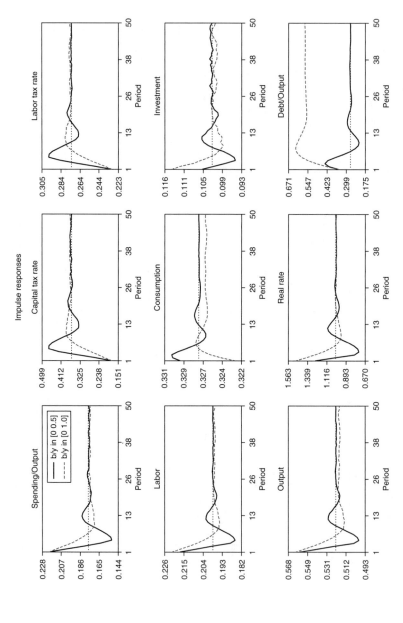

*Figure 9.12   The effects of an increase in g and a decrease in both τ^l and τ^k under different fiscal discipline regimes.*

**Fiscal Initial Capacity – Strong Position vs. Weak Position**

The reduction of output due to the crowding-out effect could be even worse if the initial debt-to-output ratio is higher. Inferior results also occur when government uses tax cuts policy under the circumstances of a high debt-to-output ratio: output falls to below the steady-state level. Compared with a country that starts with a markedly low debt-to-output ratio, both of the fiscal policies could push output up in an endeavor to keep the level above its steady state. These facts should suffice to encourage government to maintain a debt-to-output ratio as low as possible. Just as with monetary policy, where central bankers must not keep interest rates too low when the economy is in good condition, in order to avoid the liquidity trap in a recession, so the debt-to-output ratio should be kept low in order that fiscal policy can be an effective weapon to fight a downturn.

**Fiscal Discipline Regime – More Disciplined vs. Less Disciplined**

In terms of fiscal discipline, an increase in government spending can cause serious damage to the economy under a less-disciplined government. Even though a stimulus package can raise output initially, it will decrease to below the steady-state level. The explosive debt-to-output ratio makes it harder for output to climb back to its steady-state level. The situation is better in the case of a more disciplined government. The strict institutional design of the debt-to-output ratio restricts the debt from growing too much, so that output can move back to the steady-state level after it has decreased for a while. The results are somewhat different when governments adopt tax reduction policies. The less disciplined government seems to enjoy rising output longer than does the more disciplined one. Perhaps the reason for this is that the less disciplined government could be capable of raising its debt more aggressively. After all, the outputs of both countries still reduce to the steady-state level.

## 9.5   CONCLUSIONS

Almost every country in the world has used fiscal policy to save the economy in the late-2000s global recession. We must be concerned about the recent wildly rising long-term yields in the bond market, which show expectations of future higher inflation. We should be mindful of the debt tsunami and think of the exit strategy. In this chapter, we have compared the effects of an expansionary stimulus package under both high and low debt-to-output ratio conditions and more or less fiscally disciplined regimes.

We analyze fiscal policy under dynamic general equilibrium with uncertainty. The transitional probabilities associated with it make sure that the debt-to-output ratio will be bounded. As debt approaches the upper bound, taxes will be high and government spending low, with probability 1. Hence, the combination of high taxes and low spending reduces the debt, and the debt-to-output ratio will be driven down. The debts in this model are mean-reverting. We do not include the possibility of debt crises in the model. In other words, no explosion in the debt-to-output ratio is allowed, so that the existence of the equilibrium solution is guaranteed.

The debt inherited from a previous government is something that cannot be changed. Stimulus packages in a strong initial position of debt are certainly more effective than in a weak one. But fiscal discipline is also important. Even if government starts with the strong position, social welfare could be reduced if there is no fiscal discipline. In a weak position of debt, government may improve the social welfare of the economy after some tough times if fiscal discipline is enacted.

## NOTE

1.   Address for correspondence: Chih-Chin Ho, College of Social Sciences, National Cheng Kung University, No. 1 University Rd, 70101 Tainan, Taiwan. Phone: (886-6) 275-7575, ext. 56001; email: henryho@mail.ncku.edu.tw

## REFERENCES

Abel, Andrew B. (1982), 'Dynamic Effects of Permanent and Temporary Tax Policies in a *q* Model of Investment,' *Journal of Monetary Economics*, **9**, 353–73.
Abel, Andrew B. and Olivier J. Blanchard (1983), 'An Intertemporal Model of Saving and Investment,' *Econometrica*, **51**, 675–92.
Aiyagari, Rao S., Lawrence J. Christiano and Martin Eichenbaum (1992), 'The Output, Employment and Interest Rate Effects of Government Consumption,' *Journal of Monetary Economics*, **30**, 73–86.
Barro, Robert J. (1981), 'Output Effects of Government Purchases,' *Journal of Political Economy*, **89**, 1086–21.
Barro, Robert J. (1987), 'Government Spending, Interest Rates, Prices, and Budget Deficits in the United Kingdom, 1701–1918,' *Journal of Monetary Economics*, **20**, 221–47.
Baxter, Marianne and Robert G. King (1981), 'Fiscal Policy in General Equilibrium,' *American Economic Review*, **83**, 315–34.

Bizer, David S. and Kenneth L. Judd (1989), 'Taxation and Uncertainty,' *American Economic Review*, **79**, 331–6.

Bohn, Henning (1998), 'The Behavior of U.S. Public Debt and Deficits,' *Quarterly Journal of Economics*, **113**, 949–63.

Braun, Anton R. (1994), 'Tax Disturbances and Real Economic Activity in the Postwar United States,' *Journal of Monetary Economics*, **33**, 441–62.

Dotsey, Michael (1990), 'The Economic Effects of Production Taxes in a Stochastic Growth Model,' *American Economic Review*, **80**, 1168–82.

Dotsey, Michael (1994), 'Some Unpleasant Supply Side Arithmetic,' *Journal of Monetary Economics*, **33**, 507–24.

Dotsey, Michael and Ching-Sheng Mao (1997), 'The Effects of Fiscal Policy in a Neoclassical Growth Model,' Federal Reserve Bank of Richmond Working Paper 97–08.

Fève, P. and P. Hénin, (2000). 'Assessing Effective Sustainability of Fiscal Policy within the G-7,' *Oxford Bulletin of Economic Research*, **62** (2), 175–95.

Judd, Kenneth L. (1985), 'Short-Run Analysis of Fiscal Policy in a Simple Perfect Foresight Model,' *Journal of Political Economy*, **93**, 298–319.

Judd, Kenneth L. (1987), 'Debt and Distortionary Taxation in a Simple Perfect Foresight Model,' *Journal of Monetary Economics*, **20**, 51–72.

McGrattan, Ellen R. (1994), 'The Macroeconomic Effects of Distortionary Taxation,' *Journal of Monetary Economics*, **33**, 573–601.

Uctum, Merih and Michael Wickens (2000), 'Debt and Deficit Ceilings, and Sustainability of Fiscal Policies: An Intertemporal Analysis,' *Oxford Bulletin of Economics and Statistics*, **62** (2), 197–222.

Uctum, Merih, Thom Thurston and Remzi Uctum (2006), 'Public Debt, the Unit Root Hypothesis and Structural Breaks: A Multi-Country Analysis,' *Economica*, **73** (289), 129–56.

# 10. A challenge to sustainable development: the dual crisis of energy and the economy

## Daigee Shaw and Pi Chen

The year 2008 witnessed two global crises of a severity unprecedented in over half a century: oil prices shot up to historical peaks, and a financial turmoil started in the United States that touched off a global economic meltdown. The energy crisis, caused by a rapid increase in demand for energy that outstripped the very limited ability of supply augmentation, created a supply shock to the world economy in early 2008. The financial crisis, initially a severe credit crunch, was turned into an economic epidemic characterized by universally falling consumption, reduced investment, rising unemployment, and deflation. Not only was the impact of these crises felt worldwide, but so also was their timing adjacent to one another.

The spatial overlap and temporal adjacency displayed by the energy crisis and the global financial crisis did not occur by mere chance. The two crises had several features in common, and derived from similar causes. The energy crisis, actually, was itself one of the causes of the economic meltdown and the eventual bursting of the financial bubble.

The near-collapse of the financial sector and the resulting downturn in the wider economy had led to a dramatic fall in demand for energy, and it may seem that the energy crisis was over. This, however, would probably not have been the case. Once the global economy starts to revive again, energy prices may very well start to rise again too. In fact, oil prices have regained their momentum and bounced back since the second quarter of 2009, as the world economy seemed to start pulling itself out from a colossal muddle. Looking ahead at the next 20 years at least, it is likely that energy production may fail to keep pace with rising demand.

Rapidly increasing energy consumption has contributed to yet another global crisis – the threat posed by climate change. Fossil fuels such as petroleum, coal and natural gas currently constitute the world's most important primary energy source, with petroleum alone accounting for 34 per cent of the total in the year 2007. Fossil fuel consumption inevitably generated greenhouse gas emissions so that, in 2006 for instance, 82.3 per cent of global greenhouse gas emissions derived from the burning of fossil fuels. Greenhouse gases, being a major cause of global warming, could in turn inflict dramatic environmental change. This is another problem whose effects would be felt over a long period. Although the Kyoto Protocol stipulated that the developed countries (the 'Annex I countries') must reduce their greenhouse gas emissions to at least 5 per cent lower than their 1990 levels by 2008–12, the vast majority of developed countries, however, were as of 2007 continuing to increase their greenhouse gas emissions.

While economic growth has led to increased energy consumption, high energy consumption and over-exploitation of environmental resources may, in turn, restrict the potential for future economic growth. The sky-rocketing oil prices of the first half of 2008 and the subsequent economic crisis were a warning, pointing up the way in which energy use and economic growth each affect the other, and can constrain one another.

Below we begin by presenting an examination of the causes of the energy crisis, before going on in Section 10.2 to reason how the energy crisis and the global economic crisis were related. Section 10.3 discusses the implications of the energy crisis on the prospects for energy depletion and global economic growth. The final section proposes strategies to cope with the energy and the long-term economic challenges.

## 10.1   ROOT CAUSES OF THE ENERGY CRISIS

### Supply and Demand vs. Speculative Trading

Fossil energy seemed to be abundant for quite a long time. Oil prices, except during the 1991 Gulf War, never exceeded 40 dollars per barrel (in constant 2008 dollars) from the mid 1980s to 2003. Things have never been the same, however, since 2004. Oil prices started soaring, reaching historical peaks in July 2008, with the spot price of West Texas Intermediate crude oil hitting 145.31 dollars a barrel. The oil price tripled within just 5 years (Figure 10.1).

Why were oil prices soaring? The conventional wisdom in political circles and on the news media is that the runaway of oil prices was, to a great extent, an outcome of speculative trading. Similar views were also voiced by some academic economists (e.g. Calvo, 2008). 'Reasonable' oil prices in the long term should not be above 80 dollars, many of them asserted.

Is the speculative-trading hypothesis a better explanation than simple supply and demand? Although bubbles emerged from time to time in

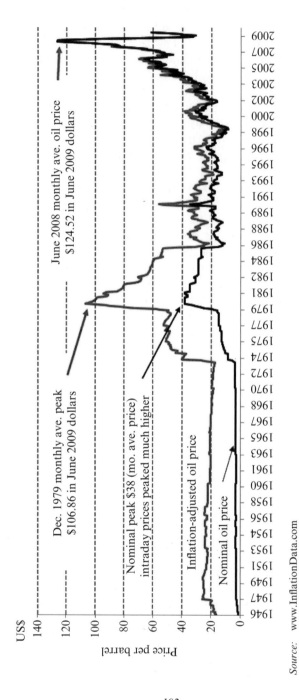

*Source:* www.InflationData.com

*Figure 10.1 Monthly crude oil prices in June 2009 US dollars, January 1946–June 2009.*

the futures market, IEA (2008a, 2008b), Hamilton (2009a, 2009b), and Krugman (2008a, 2008b), all pointed to two key fundamental economic factors that sustained rocketing oil prices over the past several years. (1) On the demand side, the emerging economies had been growing substantially for years, and hence oil demand in the spot market kept expanding before the first half of 2008. The short-term price elasticity of oil demand, meanwhile, was fairly small. (2) On the supply side, the production of many of the largest oil fields had already peaked out. Expansion of new capacity, meanwhile, required a long lead time, making it difficult to augment the production capacity mightily in the near term. Moreover, these messages from economic fundamentals, Hamilton (2009a, 2009b) argued, might well have persuaded oil-producing countries that oil prices would continue to rise, and that they would profit from delaying drilling.

Are these arguments warranted? What do they imply from the perspective of energy? We address these questions below.

## Oil Depletion

The short-term fluctuation in oil prices, like those in the prices of other assets, was, to be sure, not always simply the result of changes in economic fundamentals. Hot money must have flowed in and out frequently, looking for chances of arbitrage.

Oil prices, however, had been escalating for 5 years since 2004 before their dramatic plunge during the fourth quarter of 2008 and the first quarter of 2009. Excess supply must have appeared and noticeable inventories of oil must have accumulated if, over such a long span of time, the skyrocketing prices resulted mostly from financial speculations. To the contrary, one can find hardly any obvious ballooning in global oil stocks in recent years, and the oil inventory of the United States (excluding strategic reserves) in the first half of 2008 was actually even less than that in the same period of 2007. If there were indeed a large sum of inventories, the only way to store them was to hoard them underground. To have oil producers deliberately slow down the pace of oil production, one had to convince them that oil prices would be unswervingly high.

The oil producers' expectation of future petroleum values was determined by their conjectures about future oil demand and supply. Prices in the futures markets were one indicator. Information also came from outside the futures market. On the supply side, as mentioned, most of the largest oil fields had already passed their production peaks, while it would take several years' lead time to build up new facilities. Global oil production was 85 million barrels per day in 2005, at 55 dollars per barrel, but expanded only to 85.5 million barrels, hardly more than that of 2005, when the oil price hit 142 dollars per barrel in the first half of 2008. The production capacity of oil was anything but able to grow significantly.

Such incapability of expansion in production could, at least partly, be attributed to the energy policies, especially the price regulation, of many countries in the last two decades or so. Many emerging economies, including Taiwan, capped energy prices, thus implicitly subsidizing energy consumption. Some goods and services complementary to fuel consumption, such as roadside parking or parking on publicly owned land, besides, also received public subsidies or were freely provided. Energy-pricing mechanisms were subjected to long-term, ongoing distortion.

In addition, apart from some western and northern European countries, most countries lacked an 'effective' energy tax, their energy pricing having failed to take into account such externalities of energy consumption as greenhouse gas emissions.

Years of low energy prices have led many countries to consume fossil energy in an extravagant fashion. From the mid 1980s onwards, there had been little improvement in energy efficiency in most countries (Figure 10.2). Oil, as expected, depleted rapidly in the face of a gush of income-induced demand that will now be discussed.

## Income Effect

Energy consumption has usually increased with income, even if an advance in energy technology has occurred. Empirical researches indicate that income elasticities of oil demand in developing countries are in general over 1, while long-term data for the United States also show that oil consumption growth varies closely with economic growth (Hamilton, 2009a). Over the past 10 years, oil consumption in emerging economies has grown enormously. China's oil consumption grew by 7.25 per cent per annum during 1991–2006, for example, making its consumption growth between 2003 and 2006 account for 33 per cent of the total growth of world consumption (EIA, 2008). The driving force behind this was clearly the high-speed income growth of emerging economies.

The impressive growth in the global economy over the period 2003–07 derived, to be sure, not only from advances in productivity but also from a 'pseudo wealth effect' backed up by inflated asset prices. The global boom in energy demand, as well as general consumption in the US and other developed countries, therefore also benefited from bubbles in asset markets.

In view of the income-induced consumption and the incapability of production expansion, to what extent could the physical supply and demand of oil explain an oil price swing, from, say, 55 dollars per barrel in 2005

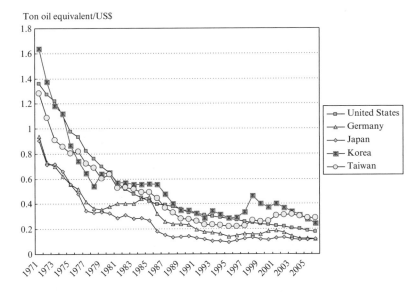

Ton oil equivalent/US$

*Note:* GDP is measured in current prices when calculating the energy intensity.

*Source:* IEA (2006), *Energy Balances of OECD Countries, Energy Balances of Non-OECD Countries*; Energy Bureau, Ministry of Economic Affairs, Taiwan, ROC; Directorate-General of Budget, Accounting, and Statistics, Executive Yuan, Taiwan, ROC.

*Figure 10.2   Energy intensities of selected countries, 1971–2006.*

to 142 dollars per barrel in the first half of 2008? Hamilton (2009b) illustrated how the price turmoil could be accounted for simply by the forces of supply and demand. Assuming that the income elasticity of global oil demand between 2006 and 2007 was 0.6, a number approximately equal to the global income elasticity between 2004 and 2005, and that the short-term price elasticity of oil demand was 0.06, a very small number consistent with some of the most recent evidence (Hughes et al., 2008), then, Hamilton demonstrated, the oil price, in order to balance supply and demand, had to rise from 55 dollars per barrel in 2005 to 142 dollars in the first half of 2008!

Furthermore, the oil price had to drop, in a free-fall fashion, from 142 dollars per barrel in the first half of 2008 to 40 dollars at the end of 2008 – a time of worldwide economic downturn – in order to balance supply and demand if, Hamilton asserted, the price elasticity, after oil prices had been surging for so long a time, began to respond and increased to, say, 0.1.

**The Hotelling Rent**

To summarize, pronounced growth in energy demand due to income growth and the asset bubbles had, since 2003 or thereabouts, been outstripping the increase in global energy supply. If the oil-producing countries had been deliberately refraining from drilling much right now, this just demonstrated that they had been aware of a possible 'depletion' of oil in the years ahead, and thus were sanguine about future oil prices.

If economic fundamentals can, to a large extent, justify the oil price turbulence, a paradox seems to arise: Because cheap oil, brought about partly by price subsidies and by government failure to correct the market failure arising from $CO_2$ emissions from fuel burning, caused the fast depletion of oil, then the runaway inflation of oil prices was actually, with assistance from positive demand shocks, a result of the previous artificially low price! This, however, is actually not a paradox, but simply an implication from the well-known 'Hotelling rule', which proposes that, when free of perturbation by supply or demand shocks, the price in a market economy of an exhaustible resource will increase over time as the scarcity rent gets higher. While the historical trend of oil prices in the last century was indeed shaken by both supply shocks and demand shocks, and thus did not fully vindicate this rule, the rule implies that price subsidies and the failure to cope with negative externalities from oil consumption will make oil prices initially too low, only to rise sharply later on when the oil is running out and its scarcity rent becomes visible (Hotelling, 1931).

The fast escalation of oil prices, and the slow pace in production augmentation by oil-producing countries, therefore very probably signaled the market's recognition of a potential 'depletion' of oil in the coming years and the emerging scarcity rent from oil.

## 10.2 COMMON TRAITS OF, AND INTERPLAYS BETWEEN, THE ENERGY CRISIS AND THE GLOBAL ECONOMIC CRISIS

**Shared Characteristics and Similar Causes**

The energy crisis and the global financial and economic crisis had several things in common, and interacted on one another in a circular fashion. Both crises spread worldwide, and both incurred the consequence of profits being privatized and losses being socialized. The two crises also shared three common causes: price distortion, market failure and government failure.

Governments in the developing world, as mentioned above, have often distorted the market mechanism by subsidizing energy consumption through setting ceilings on energy prices, and have also failed to correct, with an 'effective' energy tax, the side-effect of energy consumption. Market distortion and the government's inability to correct market failure have both vindicated government failure.

Similar distortions and failures were seen in the financial markets. Following the bursting of the dot-com bubble in 2001, central banks in the US and around the world implemented a series of cuts in their target interest rates; the ready availability of funding encouraged investors to accept more risk. Governments of many developing countries, meanwhile, sought trade surpluses by providing export subsidies, setting import barriers and manipulating exchange rates, thus forcing their citizens to build up excessively high levels of savings and, as Bernanke (2005) pointed out, to fund American popular consumption. After the global financial crisis unfolded, governments' bailout of the financial markets, combined with the existing market failure in the financial markets, created a situation where some private enterprises appropriated the benefits but the taxpayer bore the burden.

## Interplays Between the Energy Crisis and the Global Financial and Economic Crises

Not only energy consumption was enhanced by the asset bubbles; a surge of energy consumption, conversely, also helped sustain economic bubbles, thus creating a vicious circle of mutual reinforcement. This circular loop, best summarized by the journalist Thomas Friedman, took the following form:

> [Inflated asset prices fostered by low interest rates and slack money supply produced a pseudo wealth effect in wealthy countries, which] built more and more houses and bought more and more stuff, which was made in more and more Chinese factories powered by more and more coal that earned more and more dollars to buy more and more US T-bills that got recycled back to America in the form of cheap credit to build more and more houses and to buy more and more stuff that gave rise to more and more Chinese factories . . . (Friedman, 2009)

Another link between the energy crisis and the global financial crisis is that the energy crisis was probably one of the main reasons for the bursting of the bubble economy. While income growth helped to lift energy consumption, without the availability of easy money the energy prices would have had to anchor somewhere and would not have been able to create an across-the-board inflationary pressure. This inflationary pressure prompted the Fed and other central banks to rapidly raise target interest rates, and then the bubble popped. To put it another way, the energy crisis was due in no small part to the development of the bubble economy, and the bursting of the bubble economy was at least partly attributable to the energy crisis.

Finally, the oil shock surely had great impacts on the real economy. Without the oil crisis, Hamilton (2009b) argued, the US would not have sunk into a year of recession as early in 2008.

## 10.3   LONG-TERM OUTLOOK

### The Post-Financial Crisis Challenge

The stunning skyrocketing of oil prices from 2005 to early 2008, as well as their dramatic collapse in late 2008, we argued above, could well have been due to an imbalance between physical supply and demand. If this was so, we may wonder if oil supply will be able to catch up with oil demand in the future. To what extent will oil production be able to expand in the next 20 years or so? Will the world be experiencing another series of energy shortages?

For one thing, huge emerging economies such as China, India, Brazil, Mexico, the ASEAN countries etc. may yet have another 20 years or more of high growth to look forward to, as long as they are not yoked to the availability of energy. In 2006, for example, China had only 3.3 cars per hundred people, while the United States had 77. Each person in China, on average, consumed only 2 barrels of crude oil in the same year, and each Mexican 6.6 barrels, compared with the fact that each US citizen consumed 25 barrels (Hamilton, 2009a). Thus, while 'peak demand' in oil is now evident in the OECD countries, oil consumption in China and other emerging economies, whether in the per capita sense or in total amount, is still relatively small. The pressing needs for more energy, induced by income growth after the economy recovers from the slump, will likely come back again.

The world, on the other hand, will still depend largely on fossil fuels, at least until 2030, to meet its primary energy needs; renewable energy will not have replaced fossil fuels within this timeframe. The IEA (2009) expected that petroleum alone would occupy more than 30 per cent of total energy supply in 2030, and fossil fuels as a whole at least more than 67 per cent. The US geologist M. King Hubbert forecast, in 1956, that global oil production would peak in 2000 (Deffeyes, 2005), but in 2008 annual global production of crude oil was still increasing. Cambridge Energy Research Associates (CERA), an energy research firm well known for its stance that the production capacity of oil fields depends to a large extent on technological advances and future oil demand, and that oil production will not peak in the near term, predicted in 2006 that the apex of conventional oil production will not happen until 2040 (Jackson, 2006).

However, in a field-by-field assessment for the production capability between 2008 and 2030 of 798 oil fields, which cover three-quarters of initial proven and probable global reserves, the IEA (2008b) depicted a gloomy landscape for oil supply: 580 of the world's largest fields in this data set have passed their production peaks, and the inferred average decline rate of production for worldwide post-peak fields is 6.7 per cent per annum, which may well deteriorate to 8.6 per cent by 2030. While the IEA did not expect global oil production to peak before 2030, in its latest outlook for energy it did warn that conventional oil would 'level off' *sometime before 2030* (IEA, 2009: 103).

The US Energy Information Administration (EIA), coincidentally, trimmed down its forecast for the global production of conventional oil in 2030, from 102.9 million barrels per day projected in 2008, to year 2009's meager forecast of 93.1 million (EIA, 2009).[1] The EIA and the IEA, both historically optimistic about oil supply, concurrently conceived of an alarming 'post-peak' or 'post-plateau' scenario in the coming two decades or so. Human beings, if lacking economic alternatives, would have to count on the still environmentally destructive and carbon-intensive non-conventional oil, such as Canada's tar sands, to offset the shriveling up of conventional oil production. Even CERA now toned down its stance by saying that 'post-2030 supply may well struggle to meet demand', although, CERA argued, 'an undulating plateau rather than a dramatic peak will likely unfold' after 2030 (CERA, 2009).

The tendency for the oil supply not to be able to keep pace with a surging oil demand, thus causing an 'oil crunch', might linger around in the next 20 years. Failing to overcome this potential energy squeeze would jeopardize not only the recovery of the world economy but also the world's long-term economic growth.

**The New Malthusian Constraint**

While the global financial and economic crisis has certainly been very serious, and may have a pronounced impact on the restructuring of the financial market, eventually the crisis will come to an end. The current crisis is basically a short-term economic dislocation; it will not in and of itself limit long-term economic growth.

Economic growth will be constrained not by any financial crisis, but rather by scarcity of energy and natural resources. Oil production will someday peak and start to decline anyway. The threat that global warming, mostly due to the $CO_2$ emissions from fuel burning, poses to the global environment is another potential Malthusian constraint that owes much to consumption of fossil energy. The prerequisite for sustained economic growth is therefore that humanity continues to discover new energy sources in time to replace old ones. The key factor in succeeding in finding new, cheap sources of energy is the advance in technology that makes it possible to exploit energy resources that could not previously be utilized.

Over the course of human history, new energy sources have replaced existing energy sources on numerous occasions, and there has seldom been an across-the-board shortage of energy that caused human civilization to regress. Of those civilizations that did go into decline because of resources shortage or deterioration in the environment, Easter Island is an outstanding case.

Easter Island, an island situated in the South Pacific just over 3200 km from the coast of Chile and inhabited by Polynesians whose ancestors arrived there around the fifth century AD, was once blessed with a bountiful supply of natural resources. With these, the islanders were able to maintain a high level of food production, and gradually grew more and more prosperous. By the twelfth to fifteenth centuries they were wealthy enough to support a class of full-time artisans, who carved the large human figures made of stone for which Easter Island is so famous. As the rate at which trees were being felled exceeded the rate at which the forest could regenerate itself, however, the palm trees that had covered the island gradually disappeared, leading to soil erosion. The islanders lost the material with which they had built their boats and houses, and were finally reduced to subsisting on chickens and rats, so that the population fell dramatically.

The history of Easter Island represents an embodiment of how over-exploitation of natural resources in the face of limited technological progress can constrain economic growth and human civilization. The restrictions imposed by the availability of resources in a situation where technological progress is not rapid enough to find new, substitute resources to compensate for depletion of old resources are, as we all know, the 'Malthusian constraint'.

Will the potential 'oil crunch' pose a new Malthusian constraint to humanity? What could we do when facing the prospects of a rapid expansion of oil demand, a shortage of production capacity, and high oil prices? If the oil-producing countries did indeed deliberately slow down their production pace in recent years, and if this was just a manifestation of the market mechanism in the Hotelling rule's fashion, should we rely on this market function? Should government intervene? What are the guidelines for government regulation? What strategies should we adopt to elicit sufficient technological innovation to help overcome this constraint? We address these questions below.

## 10.4  STRATEGIES FOR COPING WITH THE ENERGY AND ENVIRONMENTAL CRISIS

In reality, it is very difficult to forecast what new technologies will be developed, or how quickly. The two main factors behind the current energy and environmental crisis, however, as emphasized, were market distortion and market failure. So the key is to reverse the course of distorted measures that encourage consumption of fossil energy, and to create incentives for competing in finding new energy. Any serious effort to solve the world's energy and environmental problems will therefore need to focus on these issues.

Many countries around the world have, since the two oil crises of the 1970s, used various tools at various times to achieve energy conservation or the development of alternative energies, although different countries have tended to focus on different measures. These include: (1) fuel-economy standards, (2) subsidizing energy technology R&D, (3) subsidizing the sale of new energy (price subsidies), (4) deregulating gasoline prices, abolishing price caps, (5) a more effective energy tax or carbon tax, (6) promoting mass transportation, (7) coercive energy management standards for the public and private institutions (Japan being an outstanding case), and (8) cap and trade schemes for $CO_2$ emissions.

The effectiveness of some of these policy instruments in terms of energy conservation, carbon dioxide emissions reduction, and stimulating the R&D of alternative energy may be very limited, and some may even be counterproductive because many of them have neglected the incentives needed to correct market failure. People tend to economize most when they know that they will have to foot the bill. If they expect that they can get a free lunch, they will tend to do a lot of things they wouldn't have done had they had to pay the whole bill.

The key strategy to providing incentives for finding and developing new energy is that they should reflect the scarcity of energy and the fragility of the environment, so that the signals can be transmitted effectively. We advocate four tactics in materializing this key strategy as follows:

1.  Remove the caps on energy prices, so that a shortage of energy is sig-
    naled by price, making people adjust their consumption in line with
    the price they have to pay. (This is an application of the Hotelling
    rule.) This has been accomplished in most developed countries, but
    stubbornly neglected in many developing countries, including Taiwan.
2.  An effective energy tax, or a carbon tax, to reflect the externalities of
    energy consumption, is essential. The combination of price liberaliza-
    tion and energy tax will provide incentives for people to save energy,
    look for alternative sources of energy, and reduce greenhouse gas
    emissions, thus bringing about adjustments in economic structure
    and in the transportation system. The revenue generated from energy
    taxes, in addition, will enable the government to lower income tax
    rates, providing a stronger incentive for work and investment.
3.  Do not subsidize the use of energy, old or new! (Again, this is an appli-
    cation of the Hotelling rule.) Some people believe that subsidizing the
    new energies is an effective, direct means of stimulating alternative
    energy development. By directing its tax revenues to promoting the
    sales of particular firms, however, price subsidies effectively mean
    that the government decides on behalf of the market which firms and
    which forms of energy will survive the contest of substitute energies.
    While it is unknown *ex ante* whether the types of energy that the gov-
    ernment selects are really the best forms of alternative energy, subsi-
    dizing the sales of particular firms will squeeze the resources available
    to other firms, artificially weakening their competitiveness in develop-
    ing new energies. The government's, rather than the market's, picking
    the 'winners' a priori also diminishes the incentive to undertake R&D,
    both for the subsidized firms and for their competitors. At the same
    time, the provision of extensive subsidies will make it more difficult for
    the government to lower income tax rates.
4.  Revenues generated from taxes should be used (only) for investment
    and in areas where market failure has emerged. In particular, govern-
    ment funding support should be directed towards basic research and
    the development of new energy technologies as the public-goods traits
    of R&D make the market-determined amount of R&D lower than
    its efficient level. Hartwick (1977) proposed that if each generation
    invests the 'scarcity rent' earned from mining exhaustible resources so
    that the accumulation of reproducible capital exactly offsets the (effi-
    cient) decline of natural capital, then it is possible for each generation
    to enjoy a constant stream of consumption by living on the proceeds
    from the capital. This Hartwick rule could be used as a normative
    guide to how revenues from taxation should be allocated for a goal of
    sustainable consumption.

As stressed above, price distortion through energy subsidies and the market's failure to count externalities from energy consumption led to the result where the benefits of private consumption accrued to private individuals, while part of the opportunity cost of this consumption was borne by society as a whole, present or future. Efficient environmental regulatory measures such as energy tax, as Porter (1991) pointed out, can lead to win–win situations, in which social welfare as well as the private net benefits of firms operating under such regulation can both be increased. The adoption of energy taxes and R&D subsidies alone may not necessarily, to be sure, be enough to stimulate sufficient technological innovations to help overcome the Malthusian constraint in terms of energy and the environment. These measures will however encourage people to find new energies and to reduce carbon dioxide emissions, and will stimulate the competition needed to bring about alternative energy sources with real potential, thus assisting us not only to recover from a short-run economic recession but also to cope with the long-term energy and economic challenges.

## NOTE

1. Both the EIA and the IEA's definitions for 'conventional' oil include condensate and natural gas liquids, but CERA's does not.

## REFERENCES

Bernanke, Ben (2005), 'The Global Saving Glut and the U.S. Current Account Deficit,' at: http://www.federalreserve.gov/boarddocs/speeches/2005/200503102/

Calvo, Guillermo (2008), 'Exploding Commodity Prices, Lax Monetary Policy, and Sovereign Wealth Funds,' at: http://www.voxeu.org/index.php?q=node/1244

Cambridge Energy Research Associates (CERA) (2009), *The Future of Global Oil Supply*, Cambridge, UK.

Deffeyes, Kenneth S. (2005), *Beyond Oil: The View from Hubbert's Peak*, New York: Hill and Wang.

Energy Information Administration (EIA) (2008), *World Petroleum Consumption, Most Recent Annual Estimates, 1980–2007*, Washington, DC.

Energy Information Administration (EIA) (2009), *International Energy Outlook 2009*, Washington, DC.

Friedman, Thomas (2009), 'The Price Is Not Right,' *New York Times*, 31 March.

Hamilton, James (2009a), 'Understanding Crude Oil Prices,' *Energy Journal*, **30** (2), 179–206.

Hamilton, James (2009b), 'Causes and Consequences of the Oil Shock of 2007–08,' National Bureau of Economic Research, Working Paper no. 15002, Cambridge, MA.

Hartwick, John M. (1977), 'Intergenerational Equity and the Investing of Rents from Exhaustible Resources,' *American Economic Review*, **67** (5), 972–4.

Hotelling, Harold (1931), 'The Economics of Exhaustible Resources,' *Journal of Political Economy*, **39** (2), 137–75.

Hughes, Jonathan E., Christopher R. Knittel and Daniel Sperling (2008), 'Evidence of a Shift in the Short-Run Price Elasticity of Gasoline Demand,' *Energy Journal*, **29** (1), 93–114.

International Energy Agency (IEA) (2008a), *Mid-Term Oil Market Report*, Paris.

International Energy Agency (IEA) (2008b), *World Energy Outlook 2008*, Paris.

International Energy Agency (IEA) (2009), *World Energy Outlook 2009*, Paris.

Jackson, Peter M. (2006), *Why the Peak Oil Theory Falls Down: Myths, Legends, and the Future of Oil Resources*, Cambridge, UK: Cambridge Energy Research Associates.

Krugman, Paul (2008a), 'The Oil Non-Bubble,' *New York Times*, 12 May.

Krugman, Paul (2008b), 'Calvo on Commodities,' at: http://krugman.blogs. nytimes.com/2008/06/21/calvo-on-commodities/, 21 June.

Porter, Michael (1991), 'America's Green Strategy,' *Scientific American*, **264** (4), 168.

# Index